Jemima Gibbons

Monkeys With Typewriters

Myths and realities of social media at work

Published in this first edition in 2009 by:
Triarchy Press
Station Offices
Axminster
Devon. EX13 5PF
United Kingdom

+44 (0)1297 631456
info@triarchypress.com
www.triarchypress.com

A catalogue record for this book is available from the British Library.

Cover artwork by Heather Fallows –
www.whitespacegallery.org.uk

ISBN: 978-0-9562631-4-8

To Dad, who always 'got' it

Contents

DIY and customisation: why structure matters; the explosion in mass creativity that is being enabled by standardisation, remixability and modularity

Social networking: play-time and the compulsive attraction of social tools

Knowledge sharing & data exposition: the user-friendly power of wikis, tagging and bookmarking; the semantic web; why data will soon be 'thinking' for you

Confessional profiling: blogs, microblogging and the new corporate transparency

Long-tail visibility: how important insights and ideas can be reached through peer-to-peer and many-to-many communications

Collaborative innovation: how to make open source, crowdsourcing and creative commons work

Practical tips for making your workplace more happy and productive

List of Interviewees

Name	Role	See Chapter/s
Andy Bell	Creative Director, Mint Digital www.mintdigital.com/blog/	2. Passion/ 6. Generosity
Stowe Boyd	Consultant, The /Messengers www.stoweboyd.com/	2. Passion
James Boyle	William Neal Reynolds Professor of Law, Duke University School of Law www.ft.com/comment/columnists/ technologyforum/	6. Generosity
Lee Bryant	Co-founder/Director, Headshift www.headshift.com/blog/	3. Learning
Dominic Campbell	Managing Director, FutureGov www.futuregovconsultancy.com/	4. Openness
Suw Charman-Anderson	Freelance Social Software Consultant strange.corante.com/	6. Generosity
Tom Coates	Social Software Consultant, Yahoo! www.plasticbag.org/	3. Learning/ 4. Openness
Lloyd Davis	Founder, Tuttle Club perfectpath.co.uk/	1. Co-creation
Arie de Geus	Former Head of Strategic Planning, Royal Dutch Shell www.ariedegeus.com/	Introduction/ 2. Passion/ 5. Listening
Benjamin Ellis	Managing Director, RedCatCo redcatco.com/blog/	3. Learning
Jason Fried	Founder, 37signals 37signals.com/svn/	2. Passion
Matt Glotzbach	Product Management Director, Google googleblog.blogspot.com/	3. Learning
James Governor	Co-founder, RedMonk www.monkchips.com/	6. Generosity

Name	Role	See Chapter/s
Roland Harwood	Director of Open Innovation, NESTA blogs.nesta.org.uk/connect/	1. Co-creation/ 6. Generosity
John Horniblow	Head of Social Media and Digital Marketing, LABEL Group blog.label.ch/	6. Generosity
David Jennings	Consultant, DJ Alchemi alchemi.co.uk/	2. Passion
Pat Kane	Consultant, The Play Ethic www.theplayethic.com/	2. Passion/ 6. Generosity
Ramsey Khoury	Managing Director, Head blog.headlondon.com/	Introduction
Tariq Krim	Founder, Netvibes www.tariqkrim.com/	5. Listening
Steve Lawson	Musician & consultant, Freelance www.stevelawson.net/wordpress/	2. Passion
Stewart Mader	Consultant, Future Changes www.ikiw.org/	Introduction/ 3. Learning
Ross Mayfield	Chairman, President & Co-founder, SocialText ross.typepad.com/	3. Learning
Alistair Mitchell	Founder & CEO, Huddle blog.huddle.net/	1. Co-creation
Scott Monty	Head of Social Media, Ford Motor Company www.scottmonty.com/	4. Openness
Steve Moore	Founder, 2gether www.policyunplugged.org/	1. Co-creation
Ziv Navoth	VP Marketing & Business Development, *Bebo* nanotales.net/	2. Passion

Name	Role	See Chapter/s
Craig Newmark	Founder, craigslist cnewmark.com/	5. Listening
Tim O'Reilly	Founder, O'Reilly Media radar.oreilly.com/	3. Learning
Christian Payne	Social Technologist, Our Man Inside ourmaninside.com/	4. Openness
Emma Persky	Organiser, London BarCamp6 blog.emmapersky.com/	1. Co-creation
Gina Poole	Vice President, Social Software Programs & Enablement, IBM www.ibm.com/	3. Learning
Nic Price	Former Corporate Intranet Manager, BBC www.beatnic.co.uk/	4. Openness
M. T. Rainey	Founder & CEO, Horsesmouth www.horsesmouth.co.uk/	2. Passion
J. P. Rangaswami	Managing Director, BT Design confusedofcalcutta.com/	3. Learning
Arseniy Rastourguev	Social Media Consultant, MMD catscrossing.livejournal.com/	4. Openness
Karin Robinson	Regional Field Director, Americans Abroad for Obama www.obamalondon.blogspot.com/	5. Listening
Mark Rock	CEO, BestBefore Media blog.audioboo.fm/	6. Generosity
Richard Sambrook	Director, BBC Global News sambrook.typepad.com/	4. Openness
Natasha Saxberg	Partner, Webcom ApS natasha.saxberg.dk/	Conclusion
Otto Scharmer	Senior Lecturer, Massachusetts Institute of Technology www.blog.ottoscharmer.com/	1. Co-creation
Euan Semple	Freelance Consultant www.euansemple.com/	4. Openness

Name	Role	See Chapter/s
David Sims	Head of Management, Cass Business School www.cass.city.ac.uk/	Introduction
Maria Sipka	Founder & CEO, Linqia blog.linqia.com/	2. Passion/ 4. Openness
Luis Suarez	Social Computing Evangelist, IBM www.elsua.net/	2. Passion/ 3. Learning/ 5. Listening
Chris Thorpe	Developer Platform Evangelist, MySpace blog.jaggeree.com/	2. Passion
David Weinberger	Co-author, *The Cluetrain Manifesto* www.hyperorg.com/blogger/	Introduction
David Wilcox	Freelance Social Reporter socialreporter.com/	4. Openness
Duncan Wilson	Associate Director, Arup arupforesight.ning.com/	6. Generosity

Foreword

by Luis Suarez

Monkeys with Typewriters is one of many books published in recent months on Social Computing and its emerging impact on corporates, not-for-profits and other social enterprises.

It stands out as a stunning novelistic approach to Social Computing, based on interviews with thought leaders in the field, vignettes and success stories (as well as examples of where things can go wrong!). These elements are complemented by highly practical advice on how to guide the uptake of *Social Networking* within an enterprise.

Indeed, this book will prove to be an indispensable resource for those who are only just beginning to explore the opportunities Social Software has to offer for changing the way a company operates, both internally and externally. Equally, the author's use of brilliantly written stories of successes (and some exemplary failures) provides plenty of food for thought for established practitioners of the so-called 'Enterprise 2.0' movement. I find her description of the *Tuttle* Club inspirational, as an example of a new way of working together that is much more flexible, dynamic, un-structured, self-regulated, and conversation based. I'm inspired by the idea that the next generation of leaders will emerge from Social Computing through the communities and Social Networks they mingle with, rather than being imposed by the system or organisation that they work for.

Monkeys with Typewriters paves new ground in laying out the various challenges for Enterprise 2.0 within organisations, and Jemima does a beautiful job in showing not only where these challenges come from, but also how to overcome them, using sound advice that everyone can relate to. The author's natural skill as a storyteller reveals things that stop people from embracing these new social tools in the workplace. Her insightful approach shows that it may not be as difficult as it may first appear to get benefits from using them.

Jemima identifies many benefits for enterprise within this new way of working, and here are two, as a taster: One benefit is that you can trust your employees to do a better job with less structure and micro-management. Another is that socialising business makes it feel like it used to be, when we were all working in the same offices and buildings, nurturing our face-to-face relationships and connections. But this time it is in a virtual environment: a globally distributed organisation.

Readers may wonder how this is possible, particularly given the reluctance many companies are currently showing towards embracing *social networking* tools in an open and transparent manner. Jemima addresses this in an inspiring and forward thinking way, showing that the key to success is to focus on people and the tasks that the technology enables them to do together, rather than starting from the technology itself.

Through her delightful interviews with, and quotes from, Enterprise 2.0 leaders, Jemima successfully sets a powerful agenda for the adoption of Social Computing in the business world. She goes one step further, by suggesting that this new wave of doing business is here to stay, and by revealing how it augments trends that have been developing over decades.

The first thing she highlights is the need for a new kind of leadership. A new kind of manager is needed, who is willing to do much more than manage; who wants to let go of command and control, forget about micro-management and over structuring and, instead, nurture a new world of Social Business in which relationships, connections and knowledge are key assets.

The author nicely illustrates a vision of a new workplace; one that is truly open, collaborative, and more transparent, and one in which both customers and vendors actively cooperate in co-creating the products that are exchanged. So it all becomes a conversation within a community that's evolving. The challenge is to create a conversation that benefits all parties. Jemima's responses to that challenge permeate this book.

Jemima identifies the re-emergence of passion as the driving force behind those communities of interest and their leaders. Passion is the key factor behind the adoption of Social Software in businesses.

These communities with their native social responsibility, having these social tools at their fingertips, are part of a major trend from which there is no going back: a humanisation of the corporate world, which provides the perfect background for the emergence of a new wave of 21st century leaders, some of whom are interviewed here by Jemima, such as J P Rangaswami (British Telecom, formerly Dresdner Kleinwort), Lee Bryant (Headshift) and Craig Newman (*craigslist*).

Jemima's conclusion, '30 ways of getting social', is an amazing piece, which I recommend to everyone who wants to be active in using Social Software for Social Business. Whether you are just getting started with *Social Networking*, or you are a maven who has been embracing Social Software for a long time, there is something in this book for you. I hope you will read this book with the same tremendous enjoyment that I did. As summed up nicely by Jemima:

> 'Social media is not about technology. It's about people, relationships and conversations. The web is the enabler.'

I couldn't have said it better myself...

Luis Suarez
November 2009

Editor's Note

Editing *Monkeys with Typewriters* has been both a pleasure and a challenge. It has been a pleasure to see Jemima's ideas and writing developing from blog to book and to explore the issues her research has raised. It also challenged my own attitudes to social media and how we use it at work.

This book addresses myths and prejudices about social media and thoroughly debunks the idea that social networking is an amateurish distraction from real business. For instance, one myth is that email is the best way to share knowledge. Surely there is no arguing with that? Jemima shows that, on the contrary, using social tools such as **Twitter**, **Facebook** and **Huddle** (if you take care to tag your content appropriately!) can increase both productivity and the value of the knowledge in your organisation.

As part of the editing process, we tried and discarded some tools – for example, **GoogleDocs** was not reliable enough to use for complex texts. Later on, we found ourselves with invites to the **Google Wave** preview and so began another collaborative adventure replete with novel interfaces, unexplored possibilities, bugs and crashes. As Jemima advises, beware of using software in beta! However, though the wave lacks crucial features such as offline access or even printing, I don't regret exploring it. After the initial steep learning curve, it proved to be remarkably well suited to the editing process. It is possible to go back and forth many times in discussion while keeping a clean record of what has been decided. So we learned a lot about new collaborative possibilities, and when **Google Wave** is available to all, we'll be well placed to make full use of it.

Triarchy Press publishes works on organisational transformation that have immediate practical application as well as being based on solid thinking. So I'm happy to report that Monkeys with Typewriters amply satisfies both requirements: not only has it taught us much about using social media, we've already applied it to our own workplace. I hope the reader will find it as useful and thought-provoking as we have.

At the end of this book you will find a substantial glossary of ***social networking*** terms; these appear in ***bold italic*** font throughout. The glossary will be especially useful for newcomers to social media and also provides valuable reference material for the more experienced.

Matthew Fairtlough
November 2009

Introduction

'In order to create something original and great, the most important thing is to be prepared and in the right place at the right time. The observation about monkeys and typewriters illustrates this position... there is much to suggest that the success of the Internet and its various protocols derives from a communications technology accident.'

Ute & Jeanette Hofmann, 2001[1]

'In today's cult of the amateur, the monkeys are running the show. With their infinite typewriters, they are authoring the future. And we may not like how it reads.'

Andrew Keen, 2007[2]

The infinite monkey theorem, often seen as a theory of 'accidental' excellence, is a staple of our popular culture. Monkeys with typewriters inadvertently producing works of brilliance appear in literary classics like *Zen And The Art of Motorcycle Maintenance* (Robert Pirsig, 1974) and *The Hitchhikers' Guide to The Galaxy* (Douglas Adams, 1979); they have featured on the cover of *Esquire* magazine (June 1980), in the *Dilbert* Comic Strip (1989) and even in an episode of *The Simpsons* (1993).[3]

The theorem in its modern form was first used by French mathematician, Émile Borel, in 1913. Borel asked his readers to imagine that a million monkeys typing for ten hours a day could produce exact replicas of all the books in the world's greatest libraries; a violation of the laws of statistical mechanics would be even more improbable, he said.[4] Two decades later, the Argentine author Jorge Luis Borges traced the theorem's origins as far back as the Greek philosopher Aristotle (384-322 BC) who argued that the world is made up of different combinations of uniform atoms. Although Aristotle didn't develop his idea and later went on to reject it, Borges suggested that his principle of differing atomic combinations formed the backbone to this illustration of (im)probability that has persisted in various shapes and forms through mathematics, science and literature over the centuries.[5]

The monkeys get keyboards

Given the constant evolution of the monkeys with typewriters theorem, maybe it's no surprise that the industrious apes now pop up frequently online. More often than not, the metaphor is purely humorous: monkeys with typewriters (or keyboards) feature in numerous cartoons and anecdotes and appear in self-deferential **blog** titles and sub-heads. They make great fodder for April Fools jokes – in 2009 one website announced its entire staff would be replaced by monkeys due to cost cuts.[6]

German academics Ute and Jeanette Hofmann saw the image as a positive one: a great metaphor for the haphazard nature in which the internet was created. They argued it was a happy accident that 'infinite monkeys' (rather, a huge, largely self-selected group of people working extremely hard) had managed to produce something which is now so crucial to our daily lives.

The monkey metaphor is also used disparagingly; most notably in the work of Andrew Keen, a British entrepreneur and author based in Silicon Valley. In *The Cult of The Amateur* (2007), Keen argued that **social media** – an intrinsic part of what we call **Web 2.0** – is destroying culture and wreaking havoc with economies because its emphasis on participation means that individual self-expression (from the general public or 'monkeys') is prioritised while professional content suffers.[7]

Keen's argument resonates because we all, instinctively, fear a loss of control. And most of us find it hard to truly embrace change. It's common for people to worry about the break down of traditional institutions or feel they are witnessing a 'dumbing down' of contemporary culture (even if we don't fear these things, the popular press does its best to alarm us). Keen's message successfully hits a nerve with that perennial concern of humankind – the end of civilisation as we know it.

But, whether or not you believe the dystopian vision painted by Keen, he inadvertently makes three good points about **social media** – and these are the golden rules:

(1) It's simple (because monkeys can do it)
(2) It's fun (why else would monkeys bother?)
(3) It's ubiquitous (everywhere you look, there's another goddamn monkey with a typewriter)

The **social media** genie is too far out of its bottle to be squeezed back in.[8] If we apply modern, neoevolutionary[9] principles to our current situation, rather than 19th century, deterministic ones, we'll appreciate that accidents and free will have an important part to play in social evolution; it's best not to judge the other monkeys, or worry too much about what they're saying – time to roll up your sleeves, grab your own keyboard and start typing!

Survival of the fittest

Of course, the internet is anything but perfect. There is plenty of juvenile, irreverent, unpleasant and downright illegal content. There are spammers and **trolls**, cyber-bullies and stalkers and all sorts of nasty types. There are serious issues regarding the violation of personal privacy and justifiable (and not so justifiable) concerns about digital piracy.

On the positive side (which this book largely attempts to illustrate), anyone who cares to look properly will notice a tremendous amount of love, commitment and enthusiasm being expressed through **social networks**. This vast emotional outpouring and connecting is quite new – and incredibly powerful.

What do you think would happen if you could channel just a fraction of this passion through your business? The great thing is, it's not difficult to do and the issues are largely surmountable. In fact, the very simplicity of **social media** is one of the attributes that make its influence so profound.

In writing this book, I wanted to know about the true impact of **social media** on the workplace: what new concepts and values are being introduced? How are attitudes and expectations changing? What new ways of organising are emerging? How is employee behaviour affected?

I was interested in changes to business strategy: how are management decisions being affected by wider cultural changes? Why do so many companies ban **social networks**? Can **social tools**, far from being seen as an 'enemy', actually be used to improve working practices?

Above all, I was curious as to what – and who – makes the best business leader in this new, more porous, environment: how do managers cope with the erosion of executive power? What role is there, if any, for traditional heroic leadership? What new leadership skills and styles are emerging?[10]

The monkeys with typewriters metaphor seemed useful because, for one thing, it conjured up the hopelessness a manager might feel when faced with the prospect of an army of unfettered employees able to do more or less what it pleased. I also liked the industrious image the monkeys projected – they reminded me of a swarm of bees or colony of worker ants: each individual with a role to play. Not only do the infinite monkeys have a history of association with the internet, their enduring appeal makes them viral – and this is a powerful metaphor for the way in which social content can work. Finally, the very idea of these dedicated monkeys should raise a smile – and a happy, open mindset is what you need if you want to get the most from these new technologies.

Ways of seeing

It's November 2008 and I'm sitting with Arie de Geus in the dining room of The Royal Thames Yacht Club in London. It's just after midday and the room is bathed in watery sunlight. We look out over a bright Hyde Park, where people are riding horses, sedately, along Rotten Row, and frost still sparkles on the grass: a scene that hasn't changed much in the last 100 years.

De Geus cuts a careful line down the middle of his Dover Sole, and gently pushes the fish off the bone. After two thoughtful mouthfuls, he takes a sip of Viognier from his glass, and starts telling me about Francisco Varela.

Varela (1946-2001) was a Chilean biologist and neuroscientist who proposed a 'theory of cognitive objects'. Varela argued that we need to 'recognise' something neurologically before we can process it properly; if we have no previous experience of an object (or idea), then we don't pick up on it.[11]

De Geus believes that the main problems faced by businesses today stem from the fact that we fail to see things we don't understand. In addition, we often reject something we do see because the object triggers a recollection of something painful or unpleasant – something we would rather forget. Because of this, we keep riding the same old horses down the same old paths – we hold onto systems and practices that should have been rendered obsolete years ago, simply because they are familiar and habitual.

As a senior executive at Shell in the 1970s and 80s, Arie de Geus' ideas and methods helped set the standard for corporate strategists worldwide, particularly in terms of scenario planning. He is believed to have initiated the concept of the 'learning organisation' and, in 1997, his bible for business innovation, *The Living Company*, became a global bestseller.[12] This book defined an organisation's people as 'the carriers of knowledge and therefore the source of competitive advantage'.[13] It encouraged managers to stop worrying about short-term profits and instead focus on making their employees happy and productive.

A few weeks before our meeting, I had emailed de Geus to introduce myself. I explained that I was writing a book about the impact of the web on business, and that I thought the changes would be profound: I believed that *social technologies* were enabling people to work in innovative, highly collaborative new ways – I was convinced the 'living' company he envisaged all those years ago was finally being realised.

Some days after our lunch, I interviewed de Geus over the phone, and he explained why he'd wanted to meet in person:

> 'The need to have face to face contact and people being together is paramount... language includes body language, especially when it comes to underlying trust. The technology is additional; you cannot substitute... the Internet only works if there is face to face understanding between individuals.'

I tried to get de Geus excited about the potential of online collaboration, but he refused to believe that this could work outside of pre-established relationships. And as for any deeper possibilities, well, de Geus politely made it clear that all that was pretty much nonsense.

Even visionaries, it seems, can have their blind spots. But De Geus' wariness of the web is far from unique. James Boyle, William Neal Reynolds Professor of Law at Duke Law School and co-founder of the **Creative Commons** movement, believes that many of us suffer from a type of 'cultural agoraphobia' – a type of cognitive bias against open systems.

Cognitive theories help explain why, despite years of experts putting the case for enabling, enlightened leadership, we tend to revert to primitive, command and control-type methods when it suits us. And nowhere are these outdated methods more destructive and, potentially, more dangerous than in the online world – a world which, for better or worse, we all now inhabit.

Managers behaving badly

A Chartered Management Institute survey of UK managers found that the most commonly experienced management styles were bureaucratic (as experienced by 40 per cent of respondents), reactive (37 per cent) and authoritarian (30 per cent). In contrast, less than a fifth of the 1,500 managers polled felt their line management was innovative, while even fewer found it to be trusting.[14]

At the time the report was published, The CMI's Jo Causon said: 'The effect of management styles on performance can be marked and has a direct bearing on the levels of health, motivation and commitment linking employers and staff. Of course, improving the sense of well-being, determination and productivity is no easy task but one that cannot be ignored. Left alone, it will only serve to reduce morale and lower the quality of working life.'[15]

If un-engaged management has a negative effect on productivity, why do we continue to manage in ways that are abrasive, coercive or indifferent? Why do we persist with business structures that might be seen to enable or even encourage these approaches? In assessing the impact of the latest, 'social' technologies, I set out to find what new lessons – if any – were being learned.

The end of the (production) line

When manufacturing formed the backbone of Western economies, cost efficiencies and economies of scale were paramount. Methods pioneered in the early 20th century, such as **Taylorism** – breaking down working processes into precise, replicable tasks – were perfectly suited to the then innovative assembly lines.

Henry Ford, the father of modern day factory techniques, was obsessed with streamlining every possible part of the production process. 'Any colour...so long as it's black!' he famously said, apparently after discovering that black paint took less time to dry than any other.

Each shiny Model T to roll out of Henry Ford's new factory in 1908 was indiscernible from the one that preceded it. Ford's manufacturing process – which ensured the ability to replicate, speedily and with minimum error – was a fantastic achievement for the time. This was the dawn of mass production, mass communication and mass marketing. Ford's vision included the creation of a huge publicity machine that aimed to ensure that everyone in America was aware of his invention. By 1918, half of all the cars in the United States were Model Ts. In 1927, when the line was finally discontinued, The Ford Motor Company had sold more than 15 million of these legendary vehicles.

Today, few of us wish to drive the same car as everyone else, but many of our workplace practices date back to an age when this desire was the norm. Rigid hierarchies, bureaucracy, micro-management, coercion, stick and carrot techniques are all characteristic of that age.

Since September 2008, we have witnessed the bankruptcy of some of the world's best-known companies, including Lehman Brothers, WorldCom and General Motors – but there are few signs that these firms' industries (finance, telecommunications and motor, respectively) are seriously pursuing alternative ways of doing business. For example, despite much talk of ending the bonus culture in banking after the Lehman Brothers collapse, million pound bonuses in the City of London returned with a vengeance in 2009.

In the UK, the public sector has been particularly inspired by Ford's factory model. The sector relies on centrally set targets and managers are charged with ensuring compliance. Rigid standards are set and complex IT processes defined to enforce them. Our education, social services, local government and tax offices are virtually choking on rules and regulations, but the only solution seems to be to add more layers.[16]

Many now accept that **Fordism**, **Taylorism** and other related systems are, ultimately, dehumanising. We know that a highly compartmentalised working environment is damaging to personal self-esteem and skills development. But sometimes it's as if, like Varela observed, we are caught in a kind of blind spot: unable to see the best way forward, indifferent to the opportunities that many believe are there for the taking.

The dream work environment

Wouldn't it be great to have a system where people worked together constructively without the need for micro-management? Where people were passionate about what they did? Where there was a common understanding of objectives and protocols? Where people knew who to ask if they wanted advice or where to go if they needed feedback on something? Where there were numerous experts on hand to give advice for free? Where people co-operated and shared stuff without arguing, and got rewarded for doing so? Where people were valued and appreciated by their peers? An overwhelmingly creative environment, where ideas and materials were frequently re-used, re-purposed and mashed together in order to form new, eminently desirable products and services – desirable because it was the consumers themselves who had shaped them?

This system exists. It's called the World Wide Web. And, while of course it is still a project in development, the repercussions of the lessons we learn from the web every day are spreading way beyond the confines of the internet. The web throws up tools and concepts that are fundamentally altering the way we communicate with each other and, by extension, the way the world is organised.

No more heroes

We live in a society that loves to worship charismatic, larger-than-life leaders. Seldom a day goes by when millionaire entrepreneurs such as

Rupert Murdoch, Richard Branson, Steve Jobs or Simon Cowell don't feature in the media. These public figures have made their names through their confrontational or flamboyant style; they all have reputations for 'telling it like it is'. But for all the column inches they gather, it seems that these men aren't necessarily the best at business.

Since the early 1990s, management theory has been moving in favour of a type of 'distributed' or 'dispersed' leadership[17] – where leadership is seen as a process rather than trait, its qualities embedded in the very structure of an organisation rather that a specific individual: each stakeholder in a business is seen as an expert in his/her own right and everyone is responsible and accountable for decisions within their own area. This trend inspires a leadership style that is very networked, and evocative of the social web.

Peter Senge's *The Fifth Discipline* (1990) and Arie de Geus' *The Living Company* (1997) are seminal texts in the field of distributed leadership. Both books place the emphasis on businesses as living, learning, inter-related organisms. The ideal CEO is depicted as a 'steward' who plays a nurturing, protective role. The prime motivation of such guardian-CEOs is to pass on the company to a successor in a healthier, happier state than that in which it was inherited.

Management consultant Jim Collins reached a similar conclusion. For five years in the late 1990s, he and his team worked from a laboratory in Boulder, Colorado, studying the performance of 1,435 Fortune 500 companies. Collins' research, published in *Good To Great*[18], showed that the companies that consistently put in the best stock market returns were run by leaders he saw as surprisingly 'unheroic':

> 'Compared to high-profile leaders with big personalities who make headlines and become celebrities, the good-to-great leaders seem to have come from Mars. Self-effacing, quiet, reserved, even shy – these leaders are a paradoxical blend of personal humility and professional will. They are more like Lincoln and Socrates than Patton or Caesar.'[19]

In the old industrial era, the leaders who thrived were men and women of conviction: driven, domineering, and committed to excellence. As businesses grew and profits quadrupled, the people that rose to the top frequently took on some kind of mythical quality – defined by academics as charismatic or heroic. From Henry Ford, to newspaper magnate William Randolph Hearst and General Electric's Jack Welch, to the modern day celebrities above, the hero CEO has been with us throughout the 20th century.

But the late 1990s and 2000s witnessed a subtle change. In recent years, we've seen more diversity in the workplace and, in tandem with this (although not necessarily because of it), the ascendancy of leaders who excel in the 'softer' management skills. Examples include Terry Hill (Arup), Craig Newmark (*craigslist*), Eric Schmidt (Google), Terri Kelly (Gore), Samuel Palmisano (IBM) and Barack Obama during his presidential campaign.

These are people who display high 'emotional intelligence' (or 'EQ' – as defined by the American psychologist, Daniel Goleman, in 1995) and tend to display humility as much as ego. They have been identified variously as 'Enabling' leaders (Robert Kaplan 1996), 'Level 5' leaders (Jim Collins, 2001), 'Quiet' leaders (David Rock, 2006) and, even, '*Maslovian*' leaders (Chip Conley, 2007).

Unlike the heroic managers who thrived in command-and-control environments, the ideal leader for the 21st century appears to be quieter and more considered. Because of their reticence, and possibly our lack of interest, we don't get to hear so much about them. These men and women are not necessarily 'grey' personalities – they often have oodles of charm; it's just that charisma isn't their dominant (or only) quality.

Free-falling into the Net

While we may have a natural obsession with heroes, and show an innate preference for the hierarchical systems that promote them, the world around us is changing fast. Today, our idols will topple almost as quickly as we can elevate them. Public scrutiny is intense. Yes, everyone can be famous for 15 minutes, but we are all – therefore – expendable. In this brave new world, where celebrities are ten a penny, being 'bold' or 'reckless' is not so crucial. Integrity and honesty are of the essence.

The success of PageRank, the Google algorithm that gives a numerical weighting to web documents based on the relationship between hyperlinks, is one example of how 'bottom up', peer-evaluated positioning is increasingly important. Meanwhile, the sheer speed and ease of global communication is crushing information asymmetries (i.e. the advantage that one party holds over another by possessing privileged information).

Knowledge and data is no longer stored physically in silos, with gatekeepers. On the web, information flows freely, quickly and easily, and can travel from Newcastle to New Zealand in the click of a mouse. In this sense, a key element of the traditional managerial role has vanished. Employees no longer rely on their bosses to spoon feed information to them – if any of us want to find something out, more often than not we can do that online. Furthermore, if our means of research (news websites, **social networks** etcetera) are censored in any way, we might be – rightly – indignant. This expectation and desire to be connected to many 'nodes' simultaneously – and not just the one node (our boss) – marks a sea-change in workplace culture.

In 1999, Rick Levine, Christopher Locke, Doc Searls, and David Weinberger published a text that soon became legendary, in **social media** circles at least. Its name was *The Cluetrain Manifesto*. Unlike Senge's *Fifth Discipline* and de Geus' *Living Company*, *Cluetrain* didn't immediately become a set text for business schools around the world, but it should have done.

The argument put forward by Levine et al was that the web was going to change not only the way companies did business with the 'outside world', but also the way in which they operated internally. Furthermore, the web was going to pull down the 'Berlin Wall' that traditionally stood between customers and employees.[20]

> 'In both internetworked markets and among **intranet**worked employees, people are speaking to each other in a powerful new way[...] These networked conversations are enabling powerful new forms of social organisation and knowledge exchange to emerge.'[21]

The authority of the authoritarian manager was not only being questioned – he or she appeared to risk being bypassed altogether. And in the same year, *Cluetrain*'s message was reinforced when *Fast Company* magazine, the bible of high-tech start-ups, ran a 'Leadership 2.0' issue with an editorial declaring that:

> 'The old-economy model of leadership is obsolete [...] Equally obsolete are the old images of the charismatic leader, that jut-jawed hero on a white horse, or of the know-it-all leader, that genius at the top of a corporate pyramid who is always the smartest person in the room – any room. Work is changing. Organizations are changing. Careers are changing. Competition is changing. Leaders have to change.'[22]

The idea that the web could have a profound impact on the way we run business was a new one, and might have gained momentum immediately had it not been for the worldwide market crash in technology stocks of March 2000. The dotcom boom went bust and, for a short while, 'web' and 'internet' became dirty words – certainly terms to be avoided in a business plan.

But the new, emergent philosophy did not fade away, instead it spread out horizontally – and put down roots. The internet pioneers who'd lost their jobs in the crash took time out to pursue the things they were really passionate about – and developed their ideas online. Before long, a new layer of the web had emerged, stronger and more resilient.

The birth of 'Everything 2.0'

In 2004, Dale Dougherty, a senior executive at the San Francisco-based technology publisher, O'Reilly Media, used the term '**Web 2.0**' to describe the energy that was again sweeping Silicon Valley. His boss, Tim O'Reilly, wrote on the company **blog**:

> 'Dougherty...noted that far from having "crashed", the web was more important than ever, with exciting new applications and sites popping up with surprising regularity. What's more, the companies that had survived the collapse seemed to have some things in common.'[23]

O'Reilly pointed out that, typical of a disruptive technology, the web had become over-blown and over-hyped first time round. Now it had bounced back. And this time it had a strong, confident identity, which clearly marked a break with the past. '**Web 2.0**' came to define the new generation: participative, networked, iterative, social.

In Autumn 2004, I was re-reading Senge and De Geus while preparing to teach a course on leadership to MBA students at Cass Business School. The bottom up revolution that was taking place on the web seemed to be a perfect metaphor for the type of distributed leadership that was being mooted by organisational psychologists and management consultants. It made sense to draw parallels between the two.

Although Fast Company's mention of 'Leadership 2.0' pre-dated O'Reilly by five years, the '2.0' meme spread like wildfire in the years following the success of O'Reilly Media's first '**Web 2.0** conference' in October 2004.

In April 2006, Andrew P. McAfee, associate professor with the Technology and Operations Management Unit at Harvard Business School, coined the phrase 'Enterprise 2.0' to cover 'those platforms that companies can buy or build in order to make visible the practices and outputs of their knowledge workers'.[24] The term was quickly picked up and popularised through the **blogs** of software gurus like Dion Hinchcliffe,[25] Thomas Otter[26] and Ross Mayfield.[27]

At the time of writing, a veritable army of consultants, commentators and **bloggers** are using 'leadership 2.0' and 'organisation 2.0' as a type of shorthand for the changes they feel businesses have to make.[28] Never one to miss a trend, the business guru Gary Hamel pens his Harvard Business and Wall Street Journal **blogs** under the title 'Management 2.0'.

A new catchy **tag** will come along soon (if it is not already with us). In the meantime, it's worth noting that the idea of 'leadership 2.0' was instrumental in writing this book – just through mentioning it, interviewees and collaborators had an instant feel for the issues I wanted to address. It seemed to conjure up a positive image of what working with the new web was all about, typing monkeys and all.

The social workplace

Only someone who'd been living in in a nuclear bunker since 1980 could dispute that the World Wide Web has arrived. Today, 93 per cent of UK businesses are online.[29] The majority of employees carry out their work in front of a computer terminal or laptop with some kind of connection to the internet. Even the smallest company is likely to have its own website. Email and online search engines are used frequently every day. Web-hosted **blogs** and **wikis** are commonplace.

Within the enterprise, IT is a lucrative business: the global market in corporate software alone is estimated to be worth £140 billion in 2010.[30] Typically, this market has been dominated by a handful of players offering big, proprietary solutions but recently there has been a shift to more open, collaborative, online services. The market leaders, SAP, Oracle and Microsoft, are being challenged by innovations from companies like Salesforce and Google.

With the onset of **software as a service** (**SaaS**) and **Cloud computing**, businesses are effectively being asked to lower their firewalls as documents, messaging and corporate communications move en masse onto the internet (rather than be hosted on in-house servers). Clearly there are concerns, not least security issues, but the cost efficiencies and huge capacity that the **Cloud** (information storage and computing over the internet) offers are proving attractive.

Much of what we call 'enterprise **social media**' takes place in this space. **Social media** tends to be created by consumers rather than professionals, and **social tools** – platforms and software applications – are specifically designed to enable this type of user interaction. Enterprise platforms such as **SocialText** and **Lotus Connections** give people the ability to build profiles, connect with colleagues and share information in the workplace in much the same way that **social networks** like **Facebook** and **MySpace** do in the public domain.

And businesses use this mainstream **social media** as well. Today, it's common for companies to have pages or groups on **LinkedIn** and **Facebook**, and share photos on **Flickr**. Many have **Twitter** or Yammer streams, and communicate internally using **Skype**. Meanwhile, corporate **blogs** are being built on **Blogger** and **Wordpress**, and discussions take place through group pages on Google or Yahoo! (which takes its name from the ape-like beings in Jonathan Swift's 'Gulliver's Travels' and should be approved as a particularly 'monkey-friendly' network).

As the web matures, we cherry-pick the tools and solutions that are right for us. There is less demarcation between business-to-consumer and business-to-business markets. The tools we use are becoming lighter, simpler and more agile. And employees and managers of all ages are becoming increasingly familiar with using them, both inside and outside the workplace. As the means of communication proliferate, the problem is not, so much, our ability to understand and learn from each other, but our risk of being overwhelmed by the sheer diversity and number of technologies on offer.

How the web has won

This huge and apparently unlimited choice is only the beginning. Even in the global economic crisis, which began in 2008, the web was one area earmarked for growth. Whereas the 2000-1 downturn saw new media projects put on hold and the sector starved of investment, this time around, digital and web-based businesses appeared to be Teflon-coated.

One factor is advertising – European online advertising spend was forecast to rise ten per cent in 2009, despite the recession, with the UK taking the lion's share.[31] Another key driver is online retail which, in the UK alone, was predicted to increase by 13.3 per cent in 2009, despite a shrinkage in overall retail growth.[32] At the time of writing, the UK digital sector is estimated to account for nearly 10 per cent of gross domestic product.[33]

The web is evolving in spite of the global economic crisis. Possibly, even, because of it. As financial systems collapse, political structures are tested and business empires crumble, there is a general feeling in **social media** circles that now is the time: web evangelists feel a massive shift in perception is not only necessary but possible. In 2000, the web pioneers moved out of the corporate workplace. Now, in many ways, they seem to be underpinning it.

> 'The world is going to go digital and all players who don't play by the new rules are going to get destroyed,' says Tariq Krim, the founder of **Netvibes** (a popular **RSS reader**). 'There's going to be an adjustment and it'll be painful. In 2000 people said [the internet] is a joke – now it's a reality check.'

Advocates of the social web love to point to 'Metcalfe's law': the heuristic that the more people use a network, the more valuable it becomes. The economics of '**network effects**' were first propounded by Theodore Vail, the early 20th Century US industrialist who fought (and won) a monopoly on telephone services for Bell Telephone, the precursor to AT&T. The concept was popularised by Robert Metcalfe, founder of Ethernet, in the 1980s.

Metcalfe argued that Ethernet uptake needed to be above a certain critical mass if customers were to benefit fully from the network. This rule may sound simple but its impact becomes powerful if you appreciate that, today, **social networking** is now at that tipping point, with savvy businesses poised to benefit from a massive explosion in inter-connectedness.

'Senior management is largely changing right now,' says **wiki** consultant Stewart Mader, who works with Fortune 500 companies in the US. 'The embracing of tools is there. The question is not "Should we use these?" but "How can we optimise these?" '.

The web provides a structural model to emulate as well as an entity from which to extract value. Commentators such as Ori Brafman and Rod A Beckstrom (*The Starfish And The Spider*) and Jeff Jarvis (*What Would Google Do?*) have pointed to the role of the network in offering an alternative to traditional, top-down business hierarchies. Internet guru Stowe Boyd has started talking about the hybrid, 'horizontal' organisation in his research[34] while economist Umair Haque believes that the web has a key role in 'changing our business DNA':

> 'Markets, networks and communities can organize resources more efficiently than firms. These models are popping up in weird spaces...large multinationals like Wal-Mart, Starbucks and Google.'[35]

Indeed, company size is not an inhibitor: from something as simple as Procter & Gamble's 'Digital Night' initiative (see Chapter 2, 'People Power', p. 53) to IBM's re-positioning as a global consulting brand with **social media** at its core (see Chapter 3, 'Inverting the Pyramid, p. 88), some of the best innovations in recent years have come from the world's largest companies. Once a business fully embraces the new principles, a new 'social' culture is inevitable: the viral nature of participative media means that change spreads through the corporate structure as quickly and easily as an electric current. Once you get going, it's easy.

A quiet revolution

Our online experience resonates with wider social change. The contemporary perception is that we are seeing an end to the age of deference. Authorities and institutions are being challenged, and hierarchies flattened, as middlemen and mediators are removed. But is this a substantive change, or merely an apparition? Is this all a passing storm, a tale (as Shakespeare's Macbeth would have it) 'full of sound and fury, signifying nothing'? Human nature has probably changed very little (back to the problem identified by Varela), but the way in which we are communicating has changed a thousand fold. We can only imagine what our Victorian ancestors might have made of *YouTube*, *Twitter* and the other *social tools* that feature so prominently in many of our daily lives.

In writing this book, I interviewed more than 50 people across various sectors. My subjects included leading executives at technology giants like Google, Yahoo and Salesforce; developers at *MySpace* and Microsoft and web pioneers such as Tim O'Reilly, Craig Newmark and Stowe Boyd. I spoke to CEOs of small, savvy, technology outfits like *Netvibes*, 37Signals and *Huddle*, as well as senior staff from large, established multinationals such as British Telecom, Ford, IBM and Shell.

Time and time again, my interviewees referred to certain behaviours that seemed to be underpinned by six drivers – or trends. The book's six chapters describe these behaviours/ trends and give examples of where they resonate with current business practice. I believe that these six can be used as a framework, which, if applied, will create happier, more productive organisations. The conclusion is a practical section, with an outline of the main ideas from each chapter, and a list of calls to action.

Getting down to business

To the reader of *Monkeys with Typewriters* – welcome. I imagine that you are a CEO or manager at some level within an organisation, but you might be an entrepreneur with a new idea to take forward. Maybe you are studying (or have studied) management or communications; perhaps you are a consultant, interested in the future of work. It could be that you are already a big fan of *social media*, curious from an anthropological viewpoint. Or maybe you have a deep mistrust of the social web and are yet to be convinced it offers anything substantial.

Whatever your reasons for reading, I hope *Monkeys with Typewriters* will give you a better understanding of the workplace revolution that we're in the midst of. I hope you'll appreciate the amazing potential for communication and collaboration. I hope you will be encouraged to experiment, challenged to see things differently and, above all, confident to pursue what you're really passionate about. If you're a cynic, I hope you'll be persuaded to give some of this new stuff a try. More than anything, I hope you'll know when it's time to let go: as hinted earlier, sometimes it's okay to sit back and let the other monkeys get on with it!

Notes

1. Ute & Jeanette Hofmann (2001), 'Monkeys, Typewriters and Networks', Wissenschaftszentrum Berlin für Sozialforschung gGmbH (WZB), pp. 4-5.
2. Andrew Keen (2007), *The Cult of The Amateur*. Nicholas Brealey, p. 9.
3. All these examples (apart from The Simpsons) were taken from a comprehensive list by Jim Reeds from AT&T, made in November 2000 and reproduced at www. angelfire.com/in/hypnosonic/Parable_of_the_Monkeys.html; The Simpsons example came via *Wikipedia*: en.wikipedia.org/wiki/Infinite_ monkey theorem
4. Émile Borel (1913), 'Mécanique Statistique et Irréversibilité'. *J. Phys. 5e série 3*: pp. 189-196 (via Wikipedia, page cited above); both Reeds and Wikipedia assert that Borel was the first person to use the image of monkeys with typewriters.
5. See Jorge Luis Borges, 'La bilioteca total' (The Total Library), Sur No. 59, August 1939, translated by Eliot Weinberger (ed), in *Selected Non-Fictions* (Penguin, 1999).
6. www.tech65.org/2009/03/31/management-reshuffle
7. Keen refers to monkeys with typewriters on pages 2-4 and 9 of *The Cult of the Amateur*; for an ongoing development of his ideas visit his *blog*: andrewkeen. typepad.com/the_great_seduction
8. Many commentators have made this observation: the most oft-quoted example comes from Robert Scoble and Shel Israel in *Naked Conversations* (John Wiley & Sons, 2006), p. 24: 'The genie is out of the bottle, and there is no going back'; others to have used this analogy include Yann Ropars, Jim Turner and Johnnie Moore (who was interviewed for this book).
9. Neoevolutionism seeks to explain the cultural evolution of different societies by using a multilineal rather than unilineal approach – it is based on Darwin's theory of evolution and founded on the belief that different societies evolve in separate and distinctive ways; no one way superior to the other.
10. I agree with the American academic Henry Minzberg in that it's not good to separate leadership from management ('The separation of mangement from leadership is dangerous' – from J. Gosling and H. Mintzberg, 'The Five Minds of a Manager', *Harvard Business Review*, Nov 2003). Leadership may have had the spotlight in recent years, but good management is also essential. People who are seen to be great leaders are often excellent managers – and vice versa.

11. This theory is outlined in F. Varela (1992), 'Whence perceptual meaning?; A cartography of current ideas', In F. Varela and J-P Dupuy (eds), *Understanding Origins, Boston studies in the philosophy of science*, v. 130.
12. Arie De Geus (1997), *The Living Company.* Longview Publishing Ltd.
13. *ibid*, p. 25.
14. Chartered Management Institute, *The Quality of Working Life*, October 2007.
15. CMI press release, 11 December 2007: `www.managers.org.uk/listing_media_1.aspx?id=10:347&id=10:138&id=10:11&doc=10:4540`
16. For potential solutions to endemic problems in the UK public sector see John Seddon (2008), *Systems Thinking in the Public Sector*. Triarchy Press Ltd.
17. For a comprehensive list of papers/publications, see Nigel Bennett, Christine Wise, Philip A. Woods and Janet A. Harvey (2003), 'Distributed Leadership: a review of literature', National College for School Leadership, The Open University.
18. Jim Collins (2001), *Good To Great*. Random House.
19. *ibid*, pp. 12-13.
20. Thesis 93, *The Cluetrain Manifesto*, Rick Levine et al, 1999, p. xxviii.
21. Theses 8 and 9, *The Cluetrain Manifesto,* pp. xxii-xxiii.
22. 'A Letter from the Founding Editors', *Fast Company Magazine*, Issue 25, May 1999.
23. Tim O'Reilly, 'What is Web 2.0?', 30 September 2005: `www.oreillynet.com/pub/a/oreilly/tim/news/2005/09/30/what-is-web-20.html`
24. `sloanreview.mit.edu/the-magazine/articles/2006/spring/47306/enterprise-the-dawn-of-emergent-collaboration`
25. `blogs.zdnet.com/Hinchcliffe/?p=62`
26. `theotherthomasotter.wordpress.com/2006/08/18/wikipedia-nicholas-carr-andrew-mcafee-and-enterprise-20-nuked`
27. `ross.typepad.com/blog/2006/08/enterprise_20_t.html`
28. In February 2007, the Dutch developer and entrepreneur, Jurriaan Mous, wrote: 'The network of people led by leadership 2.0 is more fluid and future proof. If the leadership works it creates more solid groups and more passionate users. Organization 2.0 is more difficult to bring down.' (`jurmo.us/2007/02/24/leadership-2dot0`). In November 2007, *social media* consultant Steve Bridger, in an online interview, said he was worried explicitly about 'a lack of Leadership 2.0' in organisations that were trying to effect social change. (`www.livingstonbuzz.com/2007/11/16/the-buzz-director`). In a *blog* post tagged 'leadership 2.0' in March 2008, the organisational psychologist Sally Bibb argued that: '*Generation Y*'s different values and attitudes are causing tensions in the corporate world...*Gen Y*s are natural networkers, they do not respond well to command and control styles of leadership. This actually poses a huge opportunity to those organisations who see the benefit in collaborative working.' (Sally Bibb, 'Gen Y and Leadership', 25 March 2008: `www.talentsmoothie.com/blog/category/leadership-20`). In May 2009, in a Harvard Business *blog* post entitled 'Leadership 2.0, and How Not to Achieve it', economist Umair Haque argued: 'meaning, democracy, participation, collaboration – these are what power leadership' (`blogs.harvardbusiness.org/haque/2009/05/leadership.html`). These are just a few examples.
29. Netview UK, May 2009 (via Google Internet Stats: `www.google.co.uk/intl/en/landing/internetstats`)
30. 'Businesses' here refers to companies with more than 10 employees; figure from Eurostat 'ICT Usage by Enterprises 2008', ICT Statistics, December 2008.
31. Nate Elliott, *Return to the Behavioral Bandwagon* (Forrester Research Report, 31 March 2009).
32. *UK e-retail 2009* (Verdict Research Report, 2009).
33. *Digital Britain – Final Report* (DCMS, June 2009) p. 8.
34. 'The "Horizontical" Organization – a term I am using in the Open Enterprise 2009 Study findings!' Stowe Boyd in a *tweet* to Jemima Gibbons, 19 June 2009.
35. These two quotes come from presentation by Umair Haque at 2gether08, London, July 2008.

1. Co-creation

Myth: 'We're going to need a process for this...'

Reality: 'Just do it!'

In his 1990 book, *The Fifth Discipline*, the American academic Peter Senge uses the Greek term '*metanoia*' to describe the elevated level of innovation and creativity that is possible in a highly charged, well-functioning business environment. The word means, literally, higher-mindedness, or shift of mind. For Senge, '*metanoia*' signifies truly great teamwork, indicating the presence of that which he refers to as 'generative learning, learning that enhances our capacity to create.'[1]

The new *social tools* arriving in the workplace are increasingly cheaper, lighter and easier to use. These technologies really do have the potential to improve working practices and bring companies one step closer to '*metanoia*': they have the potential to enable a genuine shift in the way companies think. But first, a step change in culture is needed.

It's no coincidence that many consultancies offering 'social' solutions bear names that indicate some kind of mental transformation, knowledge creation or cerebral evolution: examples include Head, Headshift, The /Messengers, ThoughtWorks and 37signals.

> 'We're looking for something that encapsulates what we call the "headshift moment"', says Lee Bryant, Director at Headshift. 'That kind of moment of empowerment or connection or understanding that we've all experienced at different times using online tools and in particular online *social networks*. We wanted to get back in touch with that joy, if you like.'

Jason Fried, Founder of 37signals, argues that if you want to create an innovative environment, simplicity is the key:

> 'Fundamentally, everything is really easy, we just [choose to] make things difficult. We add hierarchies and levels of management and policies and requirements and all this stuff... If something happens to go wrong, then address it, but don't assume that everything is going to go wrong. Don't worry about that.'

No going back

Overcoming fear and re-connecting with joy is a key theme of this book. Like Senge, de Geus and others, I wanted to look at ways of dispelling restrictive 'mental models' and explore methods of opening up hearts and minds to the possibilities that exist. The web can be a great facilitator and enabler. The trouble is that all of us – both managers and employees – tend to get stuck in a quagmire of 'what ifs?', 'yes, buts' and 'why nows?' when our time might be better spent focusing on positive outcomes.

Technology in itself doesn't always inspire creativity. And the number of tools available can overwhelm even the most dedicated technologist. If **social media** doesn't seem immediately relevant to your workplace – and this is true for the majority of organisations – then it can be hard to know where to start, let alone how to overcome the very real problems that face you: concerns around security, privacy, cost, relevance and time-wasting.

The fact that **social media** has always been, well, social, is a key sticking point. These technologies and platforms don't look or feel like the enterprise systems we've been used to. They are easy to use, for one thing, and the discussions that take place on them are informal and conversational; their prime focus is enabling communication between friends and like-minded people. They've got be just a superficial distraction – right?

The co-creationists

In 2000, two academic entrepreneurs, C.K.Prahalad and Venkat Ramaswamy, published a seminal paper on a phenomenon they described as 'co-creation'.[2] The concept was originally focused on enabling customers to contribute to the development of products and services, but it was picked up by the business community and soon grew to encompass the role played by consumers in shaping the whole customer experience. Over the years, co-creation has evolved to become something much bigger, as Ramaswamy observed in 2009:

> 'The key learning, from thousands of executives the world over who had begun to explore value co-creation was this: Every organization [needs] a systematic approach to engage not only its customers, but also employees, partners and other stakeholders at large, to both unlock value co-creation opportunities and execute them.'[3]

Ramaswamy and his business partner, Francis Gouillart now focus on what is seen as the 'third stage' of co-creation: transforming traditional organisational practices into co-creative exchanges.[4] Their work comes at a time when enterprise *social tools* are enabling individuals to self-organise in whole new ways.

Into the mix

'I think the most interesting aspects of *Web 2.0* are new tools that... are endowed with a certain flexibility and *modularity* which enables *collaborative remixability*,' wrote journalist Barb Dybwad back in 2005. '[This is] a transformative process in which the information and media we've organized and shared can be recombined and built on to create new forms, concepts, ideas, *mashups* and services.'

Since the web's inception in 1989, dozens of technical standards have been developed, agreed and applied (a fundamental web standard is *HTML*, the hypertext markup language in which most pages are written). Over the years, increased standardisation has led to improved interoperability, accessibility and usability between websites. More recently, the development of *API*s means that third parties are now collaborating with the more popular sites, and building additional features.

Meanwhile, the web itself has become more modular and portable. Today, syndication tools such as *RSS*, *widgets* and badges mean that whole chunks of content can be accessed and experienced independently of their originating website.

Tim Berners-Lee called it the 'Read/Write Web', Dion Hinchcliff called it the '*DIY* phenomenon' while for Tim O'Reilly, this was all part of '*Web 2.0*'. Whichever terminology you prefer, the architecture of today's web is one that lends itself to mass *customisation*. On an individual level, this can mean taking a publishing application like *WordPress* and creating your own personalised *blog* with news *feeds* and clips ('widgets') drawing in your own favourite bits of content. In terms of consumer websites, we're seeing different tools being mixed together: examples of such 'co-creation' include *Digg* (a news *aggregator* controlled by users), MapMyEvent (a mix of Google Maps with *Upcoming*, *Eventful*, *Zvents* and *Yelp*) and AudioBooth (a blend of *AudioBoo*, *Twitter*, Google and *Soundcloud*).

All this marks the dawn of a new way of working, which lends itself to co-creation: individuals participating on an equal footing with those around them. If you're involved in any type of collaborative activity online, then you're a part of the trend towards self-organisation, self-moderation and self-expression; developing your skills and potential by connecting with like-minded others.[5]

Take the business network *LinkedIn*: when it launched in May 2003, the site was little more than a place to post your online CV and be pursued by over-eager online recruiters; today the user experience is a lot more fluid so, for example, you might post a question or start a special interest group (self-organisation), share travel plans, reading preferences or *blog* posts (self-moderation) and experiment with status updates (self-expression).

As part of the 'bottom up' phenomenon, it's increasingly common for people to meet online through mutual interests and then find some way to meet in person. Of course, this has been happening for years in the dating/friendship/gaming worlds – it has only recently become a norm in business. One development has been the growth of highly connected and collaborative meet-ups that approach the very structure of work in a fresh way: the community as starting point.

Do these 'real life' developments mimic changes already taking place online, or are technological innovations driving a whole new approach to workplace problem solving? It's impossible to tell. As online and offline activity increasingly merge, maybe the question is less relevant.[6]

The workplace gets a makeover

> 'In the future, organisations aren't going to be the same. This is about different ways of organising. In fact, it's not the "organisation" we're talking about any more, it's the "collaboration".'[7]

So says Lloyd Davis, consultant, ukulele player and all-round good egg. It's August 2008 and we've met up in London's Covent Garden to talk about his new baby, the Tuttle Club.

Tuttle is part of a wave of loose gatherings which began to proliferate in the UK towards the end of 2007, informal events where people who were already connecting online could get together in person to swap news and ideas, to work and collaborate. These meet-ups bypass corporate structure but seem to plug a gap in the creative process, acting as 'innovation incubators' by bringing disparate people together.

> 'This time last year,' remembers Davis, 'a few people were starting up coffee mornings, where everyone would meet in a café somewhere and

chat. The mornings were popular, but it was all very ad hoc. I felt there was a need for something more permanent, outside of an organisation, where people working in *social media* could meet and talk on a regular basis, and hopefully go on to actually create projects and maybe even work together.'

Inspired by Terry Gilliam's 1985 film, Brazil, in which an engineer, Harry Tuttle (played by Robert de Niro), single-handedly challenges bureaucracy, Davis decided to call his meetings, 'Tuttle Club'. He delights in the random nature of the group that's been created:

'We get such a diverse mix of people and backgrounds – geeky start-up types, *social media* consultants, advertising/digital agency people, classic media people (by that I mean BBC, Channel 4 etcetera), creative people – musicians and filmmakers, mobile geeks...it shifts. We get different dominant cliques from one week to the next. One week a whole load of musicians turned up, the next there was a load of film scripts being passed around. Anything can happen. People come with different perspectives and come up with creative solutions. I want to encourage that.'

There is no marketing for Tuttle: news of meetings spreads virally online and by word of mouth. The friendly, open model has proved popular and 'Tuttles' are now springing up across the UK.[8] As the network grows there have been calls for a more organised approach, but Davis is adamant that this type of gathering can only thrive if the framework is loose.

In organising Tuttle, he has two simple rules:

(1) Let go of control
(2) Minimise structure

'I have to work very hard to stop it becoming more structured,' he admits. 'There is some structure, there is a ritual: every Friday, 10am, Coach and Horses. Step across the bar. That's it.'

You won't see Davis proselytising at a Tuttle meeting. You won't hear him barking instructions or ever feel that he's trying to guide the discussion in a certain way. If you're a regular, it's unlikely that you'll see much of Davis at all. He spends most his time focusing on the new faces, ensuring they feel welcome.

'The Tuttle Club is not about competing with Starbucks or [private members clubs] One Alfred Place or The Hospital. It's about the people you'll meet there. It's about talking, innovating, chatting, sharing. And the people who say "I can't come because I'm at work" are missing the point – this is work, just in a different way.'

A few months after our chat, Davis wrote a line on his **blog** that seemed to encapsulate his approach:

'I treat the whole thing as an exercise in service – when I do that and focus on what I can give, I find that I get an awful lot more back.'[9]

The art of giving

When I went to the first Tuttle back in November 2007, it felt a bit like an AA meeting. It took place one morning in a sparsely furnished, echoing church hall. We sat in a circle and explained, one by one, why we were there ('My name's Jemima and I'm a **Twitter** addict' and so on). Since then, London's **social media** scene has evolved – and Tuttle has grown up with it.

Tuttle is the reason why, a few weeks after my meeting with Davis, I'm standing at the entrance to The Coach & Horses in Greek Street, Soho – the heart of London's West End. This pub reached notoriety years ago as the preferred watering hole of Jeffrey Bernard, Francis Bacon and Dylan Thomas, among others. Now Tuttle takes place in the first floor restaurant. It's 11am on a Friday and a handful of worn-looking regulars are already at the bar downstairs, greeting the day with a pint. I nod politely, say hi to the staff and step quickly past the rows of optics to the narrow staircase behind.

It may be overcast and chilly outside but in here, upstairs, the atmosphere is warm and welcoming. At Tuttle, they serve freshly brewed coffee and a proper (sticky) Danish. Best of all, the crowd is enthusiastic and diverse, just as Davis promised.

Tuttle's regulars include James Whatley from **SpinVox** who sits in the corner tapping away at his laptop, happily offering mobile phone surgery to anyone who asks. There's photographer Christian Payne who, in typical **web 2.0** fashion, now makes more money out of **social media** wizardry than he probably ever will taking brilliant pictures. There's singer Lobelia Lawson and her partner (in life and work), Steve, who came all the way up here on the Number 159 bus from Herne Hill (South London) and will go all the way down again, just for the 'vibe'. Last but not least, there's Davis himself, shunning limelight, smiling sheepishly, and asking for the occasional fiver here and there.

As always, there's a sprinkling of newcomers. Today I meet Laura, who caught the train up from Devon, where she runs a design consultancy; Arseniy, who works for a Moscow-based PR firm; Mala, who flew in from Bangalore and Sofia, who is studying in London but comes from Caracas. In true **social media** style, this is a glocal – a global, local – club.[10]

Everyone is positive, friendly and chatty. They're all interested to hear more about my book; many offer themselves up for interview, or suggest another person I should meet. Some offer writing tips. Others promise they'll buy the book when it's published.

As soon as I get home, I run 'Tuttle' through Google's search engine for some ready-made quotes.

Steve Lawson, a regular contributor to the Creative Choices **blog**, thinks Tuttle has been great for work projects:

> 'The number of work referrals going on Friday mornings is amazing. I was invited to contribute to this **blog** as a result of a Tuttle-related group of contacts. So many great things have come out of [Tuttle] and not once has anyone refused me information because I hadn't paid them, or asked what I was going to do in return. It all comes about via friendships that build up through shared interests and mutually beneficial work opportunities.'[11]

At Tuttle, no one asks for your CV – a relationship built on common interests is enough. In this respect, Tuttle operates much like an online **social network** – people moving quickly through a fluid space where the conversation is the starting point and this conversation often begins at random. There may be something childish about the almost naive openness, the deliberately short attention spans, the excitement, but there is also a maturity about the desire to connect and build relationships.

Christian Payne, writing at www.ourmaninside.com, sees Tuttle as part of a wider trend:

> 'These are the new generation of networking meets. No [more] staring bleary-eyed into a cold egg as a cushion cover embroiderer tries to sell to you over the dawn chorus. No costly subscriptions and suits are most certainly optional. This is truly a meeting of minds where creativity and innovation is [drenched] in coffee as the future of media is forged from white hot ideas...exciting times.'[12]

Where next for Tuttle? Some months after my visit, Davis launches the 'The Tuttle Team' – a flexible consulting group that aims to 'help larger organisations to understand strategic problems more clearly, untangle some bureaucratic knots and work out what to do to make things better'.[13] Davis sends out an open invitation[14] to join and, within weeks of the launch, a handful of consulting opportunities start filtering through to those of us who've expressed an interest.

Tuttle is a free-form organisation that within a year or so has become a viable business unit – in the loosest sense of the term. The profits may not be huge, but Tuttle is sustainable – because there is virtually no structure and the overheads are next to nothing.

Next stop: breakthrough

There's a buzz in the air, an ethereal something, a sense of surreal occasion. The organisers call it a festival and with the Glastonbury weekend only just gone, there's an overspill from Somerset to Shoreditch of certain carnival-esque possibilities: serendipity, revelation, maybe even transformation – if we're lucky.

The crazy weather helps: sudden downpours cut through bright blue sky and brilliant sunshine. No one's brought wellies, but there are sideshows, music, tents and a garden shed. During one sunny spell, there's a baby crawling around on the grass, in rompers. On the first afternoon, as if by magic, someone starts selling chocolate ice cream. Later, random crates of ginger beer appear.

We're in the grounds of The Rochelle School, a refurbished Victorian school in London's East End – for two days of talks, workshops, brainstorming and networking. The idea behind the 'festival', 2gether08, is to explore how digital media can solve big, global, problems. Sponsors include Channel 4, NESTA, The RSA and Unltd (the UK's foundation for social entrepreneurs). Delegates are a mix of creatives, technologists and workers from the public and not-for-profit sectors.

At the heart of the new media love-in is Steve Moore, standing head and shoulders above everyone else, grinning like a Cheshire cat, booming out directions in his clipped, rhotic Belfast accent.

Like Davis, Moore is a convener – he is great at bringing people together and injecting just enough enthusiasm and ideas to stimulate everyone into purposeful action. He is what Ori Brafman and Rod Beckstrom would call a catalyst, someone who 'makes it work because he empowers people and [then] gets out of the way'.[15] Moore's events are famous for their interactivity: typically, delegates are asked to suggest topics for discussion and then lead breakout groups around those themes. Moore calls these occasions 'social conferences' – 'self organising conferences where the participants decide the content and format of the event'.[16]

Here at 2gether, the keynote presentations and panel debates are complemented by 'open space' and pitching sessions where anyone can step up and participate. 2gether's subject matter covers everything from the biggest challenges facing us in the 21st century, to how online technology can reduce gun and knife crime or help disabled people be independent, to how *social tools* have been used to chronicle one man's solo trek across Antarctica[17] or to persuade Coca-cola to save lives in Africa.[18]

There are practical, hands-on workshops too: you can take part in an improvisation group, sing along to '*Web 2.0* – The Musical', pitch your idea for one of two 'Awards ceremonies' or contribute to a short film on youth culture. Presenters/facilitators are invited to run their session anywhere and in any format they wish. The ice cream, it turns out, is part of a marketing experiment, and the garden shed is a 'clinic' where your ideas can be developed (or, rather, 'speed prototyped').

There's a genuine desire to listen and learn, talk and collaborate. Maybe it's nice for the media types not to be discussing demographics, ratings and eyeballs for once. And those from the public and charity sectors seem heartened to find new, receptive ears for their ideas. 2gether08 really feels like a zeitgeist moment: the general sentiment is that the conversations, enthusiasm and sentiments will continue way beyond the festival boundaries.

A few weeks later, I catch up with Moore over lunch. He tells me that the essence of 2gether came from what he sees as three significant trends:

(1) The maturity of *social tools* and platforms
(2) The revival of activism (anxiety about climate change, for example)
(3) A loss of confidence in traditional structures of government

In 2gether08, Moore successfully convened two very different communities: media professionals and charity workers/campaigners. For him, this seemed a natural progression. Like Davis, he's noticed that people are beginning to bond around issues rather than a specific discipline or demographic.

'We've never had more events. People love having events,' says Moore. '[There is] a blossoming of all kinds of things. The ease at which we can bring together large groups of people on issues of common importance [using *social media*] has been grasped...I was interested in [how] you could begin to aggregate this and begin to connect that which wasn't connected already.'

In *Here Comes Everybody*, the American academic Clay Shirky observed how *social media* has become a rallying tool for anyone who is passionate about a particular cause. Today, the 'net enables collaboration on a previously impossible scale. And the ability to self-organise is coming together with that emergent desire to self-actualise.

The building blocks of progress

NESTA's shiny glass and chrome offices on the edge of the City of London are rather swanky. It's a bit like finding yourself in an über-stylish wedding, one of Anouska Hempel's boutique hotels or, possibly, an episode of the cult sci-fi TV series, Battlestar Galactica.

Black Arne Jacobsen chairs are set off by white walls, white drapes and white orchids. Plush grey carpets muffle your feet (hardly needed as everyone seems to be wearing trainers). You can almost hear the doors swish as you step out of the lifts. There are little round rooms for brainstorming which have up-lit walls and are known, locally, as 'pods'.

It seems an appropriate environment for an organisation whose very raison d'être is innovation. NESTA (The National Endowment for Science, Technology and the Arts) was formed by a UK Act of Parliament in 1998 with a mission to 'transform the UK's capacity for innovation by investing in early stage companies, informing innovation policy and encouraging a culture that helps innovation to flourish'.[19]

Since 2007, former physicist Roland Harwood has been running NESTA Connect, a programme to support collaborative innovation. I've come to meet Harwood because so many projects I've seen in my research, including 2gether and RSA Networks (a project to transform the 250 year old Royal Society of the Arts), have received funding from his department.

One major output has been *Social Innovation* Camp: a series of loosely organised weekends, where people interested in solving social problems (for example, reducing unemployment, improving health or regenerating run-down areas), meet up with technologists to chat, do team exercises – playful as well as practical – and, hopefully, develop viable solutions.

As we settle down in one of the 'pods', I ask Harwood what evidence he's seen that the social web is having an impact on our ways of working.

> 'A lot of this behaviour – **barcamps**, **unconference**s and the like – has come out of technological behaviour. What's interesting to me is that if you can take some of those practices that originate online and replicate them in the real world, you can create extremely innovative environments.
>
> 'What's great about digital technology is that you can rapidly develop an idea in 48 hours. This is what we do at **Social Innovation** Camp. That mentality: here's a problem, let's see if we can solve it – is really quite revolutionary and very empowering.'

For Harwood, the ease of uploading data, combined with **realtime**, two way communication, means that the web finally has the potential to be a real disruptor in the workplace. I'm intrigued by Harwood's enthusiasm for **Social Innovation** Camp and am keen to know more about the **barcamp** style format. Luckily, it's March 2009, and arrangements for the sixth London **BarCamp** are under way.

The Earth is flat

The glass-topped coffee table is strewn with empty beer cans, crisp packets, half eaten pots of guacamole and salsa, orange peel and empty blister packs. A bottle of vodka is being passed around; some people complain they 'feel a bit weird'.

But this isn't a student flat at six in the morning, or even a Tracey Emin art installation, it's the plush offices of The Guardian Newspaper in London's King's Cross, and this is a scheduled session at 5pm on day one of **BarCamp** London 6.

Dutch java programmer and internet entrepreneur Reinier Zwitserloot has brought along some 'Mysterious Fruit' tablets from Taiwan to share. The aspirin sized pink pills, which dissolve in a couple of minutes on our tongues, alter the chemical balance of our taste buds almost immediately.

Everything becomes unbelievably sweet. Guacamole and salsa taste like some sort of strawberry jam, lemons seem as if they've had sugar sprinkled liberally on them, and the vodka becomes a sickly – and lethal – alcopop.

'As soon as I discovered these tablets,' says Zwitserloot, a mischievous glint in his eye: 'I thought: gotta do a session at *BarCamp*.'

Zwitserloot's 'Taste Testing Party' takes place alongside more high-level talks such as 'Experiments in data portability' and 'Faster front-end development with Textmate'. Some sessions have provocative titles ('Making kickass video navigation' or 'Reading everyone's deleted *Tweets*'). And some are clearly just there for fun: a geek version of 'Just A Minute', a musical pub quiz, even an 'action theatre' (drama) workshop.

Later this evening, after the unofficial schedule draws to a close at 8.30pm, there'll be rounds of Werewolf and Semantopoly (traditional *BarCamp* games – the latter is a techie version of Monopoly with web urls instead of street names) and snacks, beer and conversation deep into the night. Most people have brought a sleeping bag so they can camp out on sofas and under desks. Tomorrow morning, bright and early, everyone will be up for a hearty breakfast and another whole day of informative (and irreverent) lectures, discussions and workshops. And then it's back to work – for most – on Monday.

BarCamps generally take place over a weekend. And might be considered a strange way for people to volunteer to spend their free time. But barcamping has become a bit of a cultural phenomenon. Since the first *BarCamp* was run in the offices' of Palo Alto-based *SocialText*, in the summer of 2005, and the format was made open and available to everyone via *SocialText*'s *wiki*[20], the concept has spread like wildfire, not only among the geek and internet community, but out into the wider business world.

The first *BarCamp* was set up as an alternative to Foo Camp, an annual invite-only event hosted by Silicon Valley publisher, Tim O'Reilly. Both events take their names from the programmer term, foobar, which is used in computing to denote an unknown value: entirely appropriate for a conference that starts off with no agenda, topic list or designated speakers. Both FooCamp and *BarCamp* are based on a simplified version of Open Space Technology, developed by Harrison Owen in 1985.[21]

The number one rule of a *BarCamp* is that it should be 'user-generated' – the delegates aren't only the speakers, they can opt to be organisers and staffers as well. Anyone who wants to set up a *BarCamp* can do it: events are typically pulled together by volunteers with the food, venue and wifi supplied by sponsors. Attendance is free and usually decided by some type of lottery with enthusiasts waiting online to snap up tickets as soon as they're released.

The driving force behind *BarCamp* London 6 is Emma Persky, a third year computing undergraduate at Imperial College. She's been hooked on the *BarCamp* experience since attending Web2open in Berlin in 2007:

> 'I became a complete and utter *BarCamp* junkie. So far I've been to 15, including Berlin, Copenhagen, Austin and Cork...it's great, you don't have to make any preparations. You can just rock up in a country and see what happens. You send messages out on *Twitter* and your friends tell you what to do. We're all really similar-minded, we're all friendly and nice and fun and we're all interesting people, all trusting. So it works!'

Persky's attitude is probably typical of her (millennial) generation: she's used to traveling on a whim and comfortable with having friends across the globe – many of whom have been met online. This cultural consumerism (wow – that looks good, I'll do it!) is a crucial part of *Web 2.0*'s pic'n'mix dynamic.

Persky's enthusiasm for the serendipitous *BarCamp* culture meant that when she decided to run one, she wanted to stay true to the format's roots: *BarCamp*s are traditionally organised on a *wiki*, with open planning and open meetings in the run up to the event. Previous *BarCamp*s in London had been organised by people working at large companies so full disclosure of details hadn't been possible. Persky took a different approach: she put a notice up on the *BarCamp wiki* and enlisted the help of 'completely random' people.

But while *BarCamps* started out on a small scale with participants bringing everything, from white boards to food and drink, Persky knew that the popularity of the London event would mean that some kind of commercial sponsorship was necessary – hence help from *The Guardian*, Yahoo! and BBC Backstage: 'In many ways we've organised this like a proper big conference,' she admits. 'The one thing that stays the same is the Grid.'

Ah yes, the Grid. In the morning of the first day of every *BarCamp* the blank schedule or Grid is declared open (i.e. stuck up or drawn on a wall somewhere) and anyone who wants to run a session writes their topic on a post-it note and sticks it up. The sessions can be on any subject and in any style. This means that traditional concepts of hierarchy and deference are dispensed of – everyone's voice can be heard, and everyone gets the chance to be talked about.

The idea is that fun, work and learning are not mutually exclusive. And sharing is compulsory: Once the event gets underway, coverage is extensive, with participants expected to record, *blog*, *tweet* and transmit the minutiae of their **BarCamp** experience to the outside world.

Geek affirmation

At **BarCamp** London 6, the atmosphere is one of earnest frivolity. But beneath the silliness and irreverence, there is plenty of serious debate.

After Zwitserloot's session I wander into one of the lounge areas, looking for someone to interview.

In the open plan space, the bright yellow and red chairs are filled with delegates tapping away on their laptops, or chatting earnestly to people around them. Luckily, at a **BarCamp**, it's entirely appropriate to walk up to random people and ask if they fancy helping with your latest project, so I politely ask the person nearest to me if he's got a moment to talk.

Mark Norman Francis is a freelance developer who used to be based at Yahoo's London offices – where the first London **BarCamp** was held. He's been to six **BarCamps** in total, all in the UK. Why does he keep on coming back?

> 'If you go to a typical conference, it's usually very expensive. You assume high relevance and good quality speakers, but that's not always the case. Being very technical and working for Yahoo, I'm surrounded by some of the techie-est people in the world. I often sit in the audience and think, "why am I paying to hear this?"'

Simon Willison, software architect for *The Guardian*, chips in:

> 'At conventional conferences you have this big difference between the attendees and the speakers. The speakers all network with each other in a different place to the attendees. With **BarCamps**, you don't have that.'

Ryan Alexander, a programmer at **YouDevise**, says he's been working with Persky in organising this **BarCamp**. He feels that while a certain pecking order is inevitable, it doesn't matter too much:

> 'There is a hierarchy, but there's also equitability of spirit. You come here to get ideas from other people. I feel really energised when I go back into work. It gives me a sense of security – nerd security! You have animated, passionate discussions with people. It's an interest meritocracy rather than a knowledge meritocracy.'

BarCamp's simple yet dynamic structure may be the reason why the format has been replicated not only globally – *BarCamps* now take place in at least 68 countries – but also across industries. As well as many variations on the theme within the tech community itself, there are also *BarCamps* in banking (BarCampBank), government (Gov2.0Camp), medicine (HealthCamp) and education (EduCamp), in addition to NESTA's event for social entrepreneurs, *Social Innovation* Camp.

These self-moderated events act as innovation incubators and informal job markets specific to the sectors they serve. And, nine times out of ten, they're organised by non-affiliated volunteers like Persky and Alexander who genuinely want the chance to be creative and productive away from the confines of a typical 'office' environment.

BarCamp, 2gether and Tuttle are all variations on the *'unconference'* – a popular geek term which signifies a gathering that generates energy, ideas and projects while avoiding high admission fees and sales-orientated presentations. At *'unconferences'* there's no specific big idea or detailed agenda, just clever people brought together by a common passion, looking to flex their brain cells.

Co-workers of the world unite!

For freelancers, micro-businesses and corporate employees working from home, a more structured approach to collaboration and problem-solving has emerged in the form of co-working. This form of working is a sort of half-way house between home office and corporate cubicle and takes place in a specially-designed space shared with like-minded people, all paying a monthly subscription.

The first co-working space opened in San Francisco at the start of 2006 and there were more than 70 spaces worldwide by the end of 2008. Examples include The Hat Factory and CitizenSpace in San Francisco, Indoor Playground in Toronto, The Hub in London, UK, and Silicon Beach House in Perth, Australia.

The Hub opened its doors in Islington, London, in 2007 and the organisation now has a presence in 12 cities across four continents (locations include Sao Paulo, Cairo and Mumbai). Membership is open to anyone interested in social enterprise, and starts at £10 per month for five hours of desk time – the package includes wifi, a weekly newsletter and admission to events and workshops.

'The Hub brings together a really interesting, diverse group of people,' says consultant Dominic Campbell, a member of The Hub Islington. 'I've made some fantastic contacts – we give each other feedback and swap advice. It's a great place which is designed to encourage interaction and a sense of community – you wouldn't find this type of atmosphere in a normal office: it's driven by the ad-hoc, drop-in, relaxed nature of the space.'

Like barcamping, co-working has been inspired by the '*open source*' approach of today's online development communities: knowledge is seen as something to be shared and built upon, the idea is that collaboration – even with potential competitors – trumps a silo approach. A zero sum mentality is replaced by a philosophy of win-win.

'People who operate within co-working spaces often refer to their way of work as a "movement",' wrote reporter Brad Reed in Network World. 'Although co-working spaces have significant differences in both service and culture, co-working as a whole is generally defined by four major values: collaboration, openness, community and sustainability.'

Consultants Drew Jones and Todd Sunsted, authors of *I'm Outta Here: How Coworking is making the office obsolete* estimated there are around 10 million professionals co-working on a daily basis.[22] In their definition, co-working took place not only in designated spaces like The Hub, but also on an informal basis in coffee shops and other public spaces. Jones and Sunsted were particularly impressed by a loosely structured organisation called Jelly – akin to London's Tuttle Club – which met in a different location every fortnight:

'What is evolving at Jelly is a deep well of potential creativity – in design, HR, strategy, film, advertising, database management, consumer insight analysis, marketing strategy, etc. If today's senior managers really want their firms to be more innovative, as most of them claim, then there are many smart and creative people out there (co)working on tomorrow's agenda. If they have the courage/guts/balls to let their own employees join these post-modern creatives at their local Jelly gathering or co-working club, then the cross-pollination can begin. Not only will they save money in terms of their real estate costs, etc., they will get a more energized community of employees, a community that is out in the world engaged in the creative churn.'[23]

While I disagree that co-working marks the death-knell for the traditional corporate office, Jones and Sunsted's idea of cross-pollination seems really useful. As I'll discuss in more detail in Chapter 6, trusting and letting go (that is: allowing your employees to self-organise where possible) are key to the new management culture. It's not so much about 'having the balls' to let employees do what they like, it's about appreciating that this type of approach creates a competitive edge.

'I'll give you 120 per cent!'

This is a promise often made by over-enthusiastic potential employees. In fact, today, many leading companies are falling over themselves to give time back to their staff. The 20 percent rule, or similar – where employees spend a proportion of their time working on pet projects – is a proven way of establishing free-form, free-flow working space within the corporate environment.

Among the companies to apply such rules, the most famous practitioner is Google:

> 'We offer our engineers "20-percent time" so that they're free to work on what they're really passionate about,' boasts Google's website. '**Google Suggest**, **AdSense** for Content and **Orkut** are among the many products of this perk.'[24]

If, like Google, you have passionate, committed employees – the type who really do give 120 per cent – it all balances out, as journalist Fred Vogelstein found out when he interviewed Google CEO, Eric Schmidt, for Fortune magazine:[25]

> Fred Vogelstein: How do people actually do 20 percent time? How do people actually figure out a way to actually get 20 percent of their time for that without working on weekends?
>
> Schmidt: They work on weekends.

So, that's the secret...but what if your employees don't have the dedication of, say, a typical Google staffer? A discussion on the **blogger** community website, **MetaFilter**, showed that '20 percent' approaches can attract plenty of cynicism:

> 'Google has a uniquely over-powered workforce,' writes MattD (aka Matthew Dundon). 'Your mileage is likely to vary if you don't have the luxury to recruit people who are once intensely ambitious, intensely creative, and very adaptable to hierarchy and benchmarks (as shown by their SATs and Ivy/Stanford/Berkeley credentials).'[26]

'My company used to have a 20 percent time thing,' writes Breath (aka Mattimeo Orezscu), who doesn't name his employer. 'But we migrated away from it because it didn't really work for us. We're a very collaborative company, and the 20 percent time thing was encouraging people to go off and work on their projects on their lonesome, and that basically resulted in a ton of half-assed projects that never really got completed...the divisiveness was not positive.'[27]

The 20 percent concept is nothing new: it is a variation on the idea of 'permitted bootlegging' – a practice that was established in firms such as 3M and Hewlett-Packard in the 1970s, enabling technical staff to spend 10 to 15 percent of working time on their own projects.

The term 'bootlegging' was first applied to business by Austin-based academic Kenneth E. Knight.[28] It has been described, in this context, as 'a bottom-up, non-programmed activity.' It is this self-actualised 'bottom-up' ness that has lead to brilliant innovations outside of any corporate R&D 'box'. The Post-it note, launched by 3M in 1977, was the result of one such personal assignment. Apple's graphing calculator, NuCalc, was also a bootleg project.[29]

If 20 percent rules are successfully applied, everyone can benefit: the challenge lies in setting the right expectations. In 2003, the tiny Glasgow-based creative consultancy, 55degrees, introduced a '5th Day' policy where all nine staff were allowed to do what they wanted on Fridays, using the office resources.

'[We'd] had our heads down since the company started,' said Russell Henderson, 55degrees' Director, interviewed in The Scotsman. '[We'd] been working constantly and that must lead to tired workers. In our business we're paid to be clever for our clients and tired workers are not clever workers.

'We have to remember that all the staff have an artistic background. They're keen to work on their own projects as well as creating great things for clients. They can take great pride and joy in their work but would like time to create their own work. Doing a five-day week means you can't do that and have a weekend break.'[30]

Henderson's policy is still going strong. It has not only garnered some great publicity for his company – and been a fantastic recruitment aid – it has also produced a clutch of short films, music videos, games, software and art installations. The 55degrees team plan to showcase all these on the website – as soon as they get the free time, that is.

Who's afraid of the Big Idea?

The bottom-up, **DIY** approach typified in '**unconferences**', co-working and bootlegging works in this community because outcomes are undecided and schedules are thrown open. These endeavours may all start out half-baked (at best), but because there's no hierarchy of ideas, everyone's voice can be heard. The good stuff will rise to the surface for further development. Meanwhile, structure and staff costs are minimal so risk is reduced.

This lack of deference for 'the big idea' is something close to advertiser Russell Davies' heart. He's been talking about it for some time: our fear of being thought stupid stifles creativity, so why not create an environment where irreverent, often silly ideas are positively encouraged?

In 2007, Davies set up a conference series entitled, simply, 'Interesting'. The idea behind this series was that people should stand up on stage and talk not about their work (a type of presentation which all too often degenerates into a sales pitch) but about something random (and occasionally ridiculous) which they were knowledgeable about. As a result, 'Interesting' is stuffed full of nuggets of fascinating stuff which attendees can then take away, digest and re-purpose in any way they see fit. These conferences are informal, fun, and surprisingly inspiring.

At the opening session on day two of Steve Moore's 2gether, Davies, talked animatedly about the need for change:

> 'Don't spend time and energy worrying about the next "big idea". It may never happen! Be happy to be a contributor, there's no need for any big, "engaged" effort...we don't have to separate strategy and execution any more – we can combine them.'

Davies' point about combining strategy and execution is excellent: if we separate strategy too much from the bread and butter work-flow of a business, we risk allowing it to become too cerebral. Organic, iterative 'suck it and see' processes are best.

James Boyle, co-founder of the **Creative Commons** movement, likes to use the examples of the World Wide Web and **Wikipedia** in the talks he gives around the world. He asks: 'what right-minded business strategist would have backed these rather loopy ideas?'[31]

Luckily, Tim Berners-Lee and Jimmy Wales didn't wait around for someone to approve their visions, they just went ahead with their projects regardless, building them collaboratively from the grassroots up.

Twitter is a similar example: when, back in 2006, San Francisco workmates Jack Dorsey, Biz Stowe and Evan Williams thought it might be fun to have a website where people could post messages in answer to the question 'What are you doing right now?', no-one could have imagined that the platform would evolve to the point where, three years on, its political importance would require the US government to request it not be taken offline for 'maintenance' in the tense period following the contested result of the 2009 Iranian elections.

The web plays host to dozens of similar success stories: *Craigslist* started as an events newsletter for Craig Newmark and his friends in San Francisco; *YouTube* was a simple platform to help a group of work colleagues share their video clips. Neither had ambitions to be disruptive technologies which would rock two established industries (newspapers and film & television production) to the core.

Now that we have the web, it's as easy to build something as it is to talk about it. Easier, in fact. Because in prototyping your idea you actually uncover all sorts of issues that would never have reared their ugly heads at the concept stage – and once these issues materialise, you can address them.

Baby steps are great.

Giant leaps are so 1969.

Iteration, that's the name of the game

Twitter, *craigslist* and *YouTube* all started out small and became huge. The feedback and support from their respective communities turned them into the billion dollar entities they are today.

Of course, most day-to-day problem-solving, decision-making and R&D doesn't require direct online exposure. But 21st century businesses do need to learn to collaborate effectively beyond the corporate firewall. Increasingly, projects involve outside contractors, partners and freelancers. Good communication with customers and suppliers is more crucial than ever. And branches, subsidiaries or franchise-holders always need to discuss plans and targets with the head office or parent company.

If projects or strategies are rigidly set in stone before they leave the starting block, they're destined to fail. As with today's websites, portability and **modularity** is key. Projects need to be broken down into manageable chunks and bite-sized pieces in order to be assessed, reworked and built upon. We need 'iterative' spaces where this work can be done.

There are plenty of **open source** collaboration tools available, some of which are very well-developed: for example, the **Drupal** platform (www.drupal. org), or **Moodle** (www.moodle.org), which is used by The Open University, among others. A commercial tool such as **Huddle** (www.huddle.net) has more functionality, but might be considered expensive (although the basic version is free) when you consider the wealth of free collaboration tools out there.

After decades of promise, the web is finally bringing us the tools we need to communicate extensively. But are we really ready to collaborate? In the UK in particular, we are naturally rather reserved. Are there any signs that we could be open to behaving differently?

If we build it, they will come

Otto Scharmer is a senior lecturer in management at the Massachusetts Institute of Technology in Boston, USA. His extensive private client list includes national governments, international institutions and multinational companies like Daimler, PricewaterhouseCoopers, Fujitsu and Google. Since 1999, Scharmer has been running workshops on 'Presencing' and '**Theory U**' – concepts he has developed as a tool kit to promote evolution and change in business leadership.[32]

It's June 2009 and Scharmer is in Munich, Germany, for a week. But he's found half an hour in his schedule to chat to me on **Skype**. It's half past three in the afternoon, Scharmer has just flown in from the US, and I imagine he's pretty tired, but all that comes across in the call is positivity and enthusiasm.

Scharmer tells me that the time is ripe for change. Like 2gether's Steve Moore, he believes that concerns about the environment and the failure of established institutions, as well as fears around the dissolution of individual careers and livelihoods, are causing us to question the status quo. Furthermore, on an internal level, Scharmer has witnessed what he describes as a 'deeper longing' in his workshops, particularly among younger participants – a desire for 'engaging with each other in different relationships and engaging with oneself in a different relationship'. He believes that people aspire to 'wake up to another level of awareness, of consciousness, as an individual – but also as a community.'

Scharmer sounds optimistic about humankind, but his mood grows darker when I ask him about the web – and **social media** in particular. His view is that our current technologies have great potential, but we need to be wary:

> '[The web] has a great promise but [positive changes] won't happen automatically. It will be a very co-creative process and I think, in our age, the new media, the new technologies, the new web technologies, need to be complemented with a new **social technology**. And it's the **social technology** that allows us as groups, as collective entities across organisational boundaries, to shift our quality of attention from downloading, which is just doing more of the same, to co-creating together, which is really kind of accessing the collective creativity that we could utilise. The web can be a great enabler for that.'

It is up to us to make the change: technology cannot create the breakthrough for us. We need to make sure we build something worthwhile. Leaders need to take the initiative – and, as marketing expert, Seth Godin, pointed out in *Tribes*,[33] the right leaders for this new environment will come from all levels and all backgrounds: they won't necessarily be those with the appropriate job title.

Rebooting growth

To get to the next stage, we've got to find out how to let go. There's a tension, a disconnect between what we, as a society, might want to achieve, and our instinctive lack of trust for one another, especially when it comes to business. Both Lloyd Davis (Tuttle) and Alastair Mitchell (who founded **Huddle**) referred to an idea of 'loose leadership' when interviewed for this book. They're right: we need to become more flexible, we need to cede control.

This might just be beginning to happen. Recently, world leaders have taken up a new language – of sharing, of collaboration, of moving forward together. But it will be interesting to see how much of this is lip-service. Are presidents, prime ministers and heads of state really prepared to be divested of some of their power for the sake of the common good? This is something that remains to be seen.

During the Davos conference in January 2009, the economist Umair Haque *blogged* a 'Smart Growth Manifesto' that was generally received favourably by delegates, mainly because his words seemed to sum up the quandary that the leaders of the world were facing:

> 'Reigniting growth requires rethinking growth. The question [most leaders] are asking is: where will tomorrow's growth come from? Will it result from oil, cleantech, bailouts, China, or Obama? The answer is: none of the above. Tomorrow's growth won't come from a person, place, or technology – but from understanding why yesterday's growth has failed. The same growth models applied to new people, places, and technologies will simply result in the same crises, over and over again. We have to reboot growth: the problem is not what is growing versus what is not, but how we grow.'[34]

Smart economists like Haque, along with the growing army of *social innovators* such as Steve Moore and Roland Harwood, believe the big money for private business in coming years lies in building savvy revenue models around environmental and social concerns. As Haque has succinctly put it: 'Managing the world's energy, hunger, thirst, health, education, finance and freedom – these will be the growth industries of the next ten years.'

Our traditional sources of growth may be drying up, and social values may be changing. One way to deal with the unpredictable external environment is to prepare for constant change internally. It makes sense to adopt simple, agile communications tools. But for the big corporates, that's easier said than done. Large organisations, by definition, aren't particularly fast moving. It's a problem noted by Alan Cane, technology correspondent at the Financial Times:

> 'If only we could start again from scratch. Every chief information officer would like to start with a clean sheet of paper on which to design a system in which every element worked seamlessly with every other. But enterprise IT systems today – the "back office" – are hostages to their history.'[35]

CIOs aren't the only ones to suffer from 'legacy' issues. If you're the founding CEO of a large company, there are no doubt times when you dream of going back to the halcyon early days. About returning to the time when the business was a close-knit family, a handful of people driven to succeed through sheer enthusiasm, who didn't mind working late nights and the occasional weekend because they cared about their workmates and understood the values which united them. Most of all, that time when decisions could be made over a drink in the pub and enacted the very next day.

Young companies like Headshift and 37signals, and self-organising outfits like Tuttle and 2gether, as well as the social entrepreneurs that Roland Harwood inspires, find it natural to adopt the flexible working practices that are synonymous with the best of the socially-driven, **web 2.0** world. But how do you take an organisation that is ten, twenty, one hundred or even two hundred years old and drag it (kicking and screaming) into the 21st century?

Re-wiring the RSA

'We're at A, we'd like to be at C.'

Laura Bunt, Networks Coordinator at the RSA, is standing in front of a large projection of a diagram illustrating three different networks: the first, marked 'A', shows a number of lines radiating from a single point; the second, 'B', shows a handful of smaller clusters, simplified versions of 'A'; the third, 'C' is a block of diamond shapes – a fishnet of connected nodes.

The RSA or, to give it its proper title, The Royal Society for the Encouragement of Arts, Manufactures and Commerce, is one of the UK's oldest and most respected membership organisations. The Society has a global 'Fellowship' of around 27,000 and a civic remit 'to develop and promote new ways of thinking about human fulfilment and social progress'.

The RSA was founded in a Covent Garden coffee shop in 1754 by William Shipley, an artist and teacher. Shipley's co-founders included the leading progressive thinkers of the time: Benjamin Franklin, Samuel Johnson and William Hogarth. The aim of the Society they set up was to award premiums to innovative liberal arts and science projects, and 'to stimulate enterprise for the common good'.

This afternoon, we're in a meeting room at The University of Westminster for an open workshop intended to explore the practicalities of creating a brand new model for the RSA. Twenty-five people, some of us RSA members (or Fellows), are sitting around four tables. We know we're expected to come up with 'innovative' solutions because, in the middle of each table, there's a pile of cling-wrapped Plasticine and a few bags of Lego.

Since November 2007, the RSA Networks project (backed by NESTA) has been looking at new ways to engage and empower Fellows. The ambition of the RSA Fellowship team, says Bunt, is to build a strong, distributed, network. The Society's internal office team of ten is there to support and be fully integrated with this network. The idea that a distributed network was needed and that this network might even 'become' the RSA was not present at the start of the project.

Another Laura, Laura Billings, who's the RSA's Senior Fellowship Researcher, talks about practical developments. Two clear ideas have come out of the Networks project so far: first, to create a Fellows Charter which will define expectations and responsibilities and be written and ratified by the Fellows; secondly, to develop a **taxonomy** (a '**tagging**' system), which will be set up and written by Fellows.

These sound like sensible steps – but there's a lot of anger in the room. The Fellows are restless. The first to speak is Paul Springer, who argues that the lack of accessibility at the RSA's London headquarters (the rooms of this vast building that Fellows are allowed into amount to 'the library and a tiny airless room in the basement') is indicative of the attitude to Fellows. Springer does concede that: 'The fact you want to go from A to C is wonderful. That wasn't even being said a year ago.'

Bunt and Billings listen with the worn patience of parents who are watching their children throw food over the kitchen as they try to feed themselves. It's an ugly, messy thing, this feedback process. But once you've started down this particular road, it's hard to turn back.

Springer's comments are just the tip of an iceberg. There are others in the room who are also angry but remain silent. During the coffee break, I speak to a handful who are skeptical about the RSA's commitment to change. There's a feeling that the workshops, seminars and 'tasks' (from setting up a **Facebook** group to building a model with plasticine that represents 'the RSA you want to see') are simply a diversion from the real goal of getting this 250 year old organisation to genuinely open up.

The RSA is a charity, but it is dealing with the same problems faced by many businesses today: What does 'networked' actually mean? Just how networked do we need to be, and why? How do we become networked? How do we manage a networked organisation? Do we need designated 'leaders' or just 'facilitators'?

The situation at The RSA is interesting because it shows both the need for change and how traditional strong leadership can be a barrier. Change needs to be 360 degrees and holistic. That won't happen unless the people at the very top of the hierarchy are willing. How we can change individual mindsets is something I'll continue to explore in the chapters to come.

Mix it up

If this book were a circle, you could start at any chapter and the journey, I hope, would still make sense. I've begun with *co-creation* because it felt right to kick off with structure and the building blocks that enable the collaborative process. Innovation thrives in a loosely structured, dynamic environment. Leaders like Lee Bryant, Jason Fried, Lloyd Davis and Steve Moore understand today's need for **modularity** and portability: they want to empower, stimulate and engage – so they create formats (or software) which people can remix, mash-up and **customise** to suit their purposes. These open structures are great at enabling genuine dialogue between different stakeholders.

While *co-creation* is all about collaborating and connecting with others, the next chapter should encourage a little more introspection. *Passion* marks the starting point of your personal **social media** journey: because defining exactly what you want and knowing how to communicate that effectively is the key to building your community in the online world.

Notes

1. Peter M. Senge (1990), *The Fifth Discipline: The Art & Practice of the Learning Organisation.* Random House, p. 14.
2. C. K. Prahalad and Venkat Ramaswamy, 'Co-Opting Customer Competence', *Harvard Business Review,* January 2000.
3. Venkat Ramaswamy and Francis Gouillart, Draft manuscript, *The Alchemy of Co-Creation* (Simon & Schuster, FreePress, 2010) (via **Wikipedia**).
4. en.wikipedia.org/wiki/Co-creation
5. This kind of self-expression can be seen as belonging to the highest level of human needs: the need for self-actualisation. Psychologists Kurt Goldstein, Abraham Maslow and Carl Rogers all gave slightly different meanings to the term 'self-actualisation'. My preference is for Maslow's definition, the background to which is discussed in more detail in chapter 2.
6. Academic Clay Shirky has suggested we dispense with the division altogether: 'The days of making a distinction between internet and the real world are over. It's hard to imagine any model of popular culture for example that doesn't include YouTube or any model of a managerial organisation that doesn't include email.' (from podcast interview with blogger Nicole Simon, 2 June 2009: crueltobekind.org/dmmk-interviews-with-clay-shirky-599).
7. Davis told me he first heard 'collaboration' used in this way by John Varney, former Chief Technology Officer of the BBC talking at a Wealth of Networks conference.
8. In the 12 months since I met with Davis in August 2008, Tuttle clubs were started in Bath, Birmingham, Brighton, Cardiff, Cornwall, Hove, Lewes, Manchester, Newcastle, Oxford, Tunbridge Wells and Wolverhampton, plus Barcelona, Boston (Massachusetts) and Long Beach (California): tuttleclub.wordpress.com/2009/01/29/advice-to-a-new-tuttle-meister
9. tuttleclub.wordpress.com/2009/01/29/advice-to-a-new-tuttle-meister
10. Glocal is derived from glocalisation, a portmanteau word made up of globalisation and local. It has origins in the Japanese term with the same meaning, dochakuka.

11. www.creative-choices.co.uk/server.php?show=ConBlogEntry.150
12. Payne, Christian, 'PICNIC'08 – A meeting of creative minds', 4 September 2008: ourmaninside.com/2008/09/04/picnic08-a-meeting-of-creative-minds
13. www.thetuttleteam.com
14. According to the email Davis sent out on 5 May 2009: 'You're in this group e-mail because you're in my address book AND you've been to Tuttle AND I believe you either are freelance/self-employed OR your employment is flexible enough to allow you to take part in events like Tuttle and share your industry knowledge.'
15. Ori Brafman and Rod Beckstrom (2006). *The Starfish And The Spider: The Unstoppable Power of Leaderless Organizations*. Penguin, p. 112.
16. www.policyunplugged.org/social-conference
17. Read more at www.bensaunders.com
18. See www.colalife.org
19. NESTA website: www.nesta.org.uk
20. www.barcamp.org
21. See Harrison Owen, 'A Brief User's Guide to Open Space Technology': www.openspaceworld.com/users_guide.htm
22. Andrew Jones, Todd Sunsted and Tony Bacigalupo (2009), *I'm Outta Here: How Coworking is making the office obsolete*. Not An MBA: notanmba.com/blog/2007/12/meat-butter-and-jelly-sandwiches-a-co-working-manifesto
23. notanmba.com/blog/2007/12/meat-butter-and-jelly-sandwiches-a-co-working-manifesto
24. www.google.com/support/jobs/bin/static.py?page=about.html&about=eng
25. Vogelstein left *Fortune Magazine* before the article he was researching was finished but he published the interview with Schmidt on his **blog**: techblog.typepad.com/my_weblog/2007/04/my_other_interv.html
26. ask.metafilter.com/62624/Pros-and-Cons-of-Googles-20-percent-time-concept – comment
27. ask.metafilter.com/62624/Pros-and-Cons-of-Googles-20-percent-time-concept – comment
28. en.wikipedia.org/wiki/Bootlegging_(business)
29. K. Knight (1967), 'A Descriptive Model of the Intra-Firm Innovation Process', in *The Journal of Business*, Vol.40, pp. 478-496.
30. Lorraine Mawhinney, 'And on the 5th day...', *The Scotsman*, 15 July 2002, p. 6.
31. See, for example, 'The Public Domain: Enclosing The Commons of The Mind', Boyle's presentation to The RSA, London, 10 March 2009: www.thersa.org/events/vision/vision-videos/james-boyle
32. For a full exposition of these concepts see Otto Scharmer, *Theory U: Leading from the Future as it Emerges* (Berrett-Koehler, 2007).
33. Seth Godin (2008), *Tribes: we need you to lead us*. Portfolio.
34. Umair Haque, 'The Smart Growth Manifesto,' 30 January 2009: blogs.harvardbusiness.org/haque/2009/01/davos_discussing_a_depression.html
35. Umair Haque, in his session at 2gether08, London, July 2008.
36. Alan Cane, 'Architecture: if only we could start again from scratch', 13 May 2009: www.ft.com/cms/s/0/38900cf8-3e8c-11de-9a6c-00144feabdc0.html

2. Passion

Myth: Social networking is a time-waster

Reality: Building connections is vital to business

I once had an overbearing boss who made me cringe every time she walked into the room, but I've also had gorgeous colleagues who cheered me up just by saying hello. The emotional reaction others can cause in us, and vice versa, can have a lasting impact on our behaviour at work, especially when those reactions are repeated on a daily basis. Such day-to-day emotions are key to whether a workplace functions effectively.

The passion and commitment we all instill in those around us is crucial. Increasingly, in today's working environments, everyone has some kind of leadership role to play. From the CEO through to department heads right down to individuals who may be charged with running a project or even heading up the staff football team, it is rare for a person to be without responsibility.

As influencers, we will get more done if our behaviour is consistent and inspiring; in other words, if we 'lead' from the heart. That is the best way – and, in the long term, the only way – to win commitment from others.

The British academic, Tudor Rickards, picked up a story once told by Meryl Streep in an interview: the actress remembered when she was a student at drama school and a tutor asked the class how they would play a king:

> 'And everybody said, "Oh you are assertive," and people would say, "Oh you speak in a slightly deeper voice." And the teacher said, "Wrong. The way to be king is to have everybody in the room go quiet when you come in." The atmosphere changes. It's all up to everybody else to make you king.'[1]

Rickards posed the question: are drama and leadership really that far apart? He concluded that charisma can be related to on-stage presence and that 'schooling' can help us make a 'decent impact'. But it was his emphasis on the changing emotions of the 'audience' that was most intriguing: 'What [is it] about the leaders we (help) create which makes them special?'[2]

Certainly, a leader is nothing if no one is 'watching' them. Keith Grint, the Oxford Academic and former trade unionist, took this idea to its logical conclusion in *The Arts of Leadership*.[3] He compared leadership to various artistic disciplines and identified one key skill set as 'the performing arts':

> 'In this we can include the theatrical performances that leaders must engage in if they are to achieve the necessary mobilization of followers and it is also derived from the skills of rhetoric and the skills of negotiation. Thus having a persuasive message, delivering it effectively, and deploying negotiating skills to achieve movement [are] critical elements of leadership.'[4]

But don't confuse Grint's idea of 'performance' with putting on a show. It is all about persuading others to follow you through the strength of your actions. As illustration, Grint gave the example of Florence Nightingale, whose care for injured soldiers during The Crimean War (1853-1856) set the standard for modern nursing. Nightingale did not preach about her ideas: she enacted them.

What's your story?

Like Grint and Rickards, I agree that there is a highly reciprocal, interdependent relationship between CEOs and companies, managers and teams, leaders and followers. The way in which a manager behaves will have repercussions throughout the whole group. Actions speak louder than words and of course the best leaders should lead by example. Real-life 'narrative' and commitment will always be more inspiring than a list of bullet points.

Our skills of persuasion, rhetoric and negotiation can be exploited through **social tools** – but we should use these tools with caution. It's not about bravado: a subtle approach can be just as effective. As the **blogger** and co-author of *The Cluetrain Manifesto*, Doc Searles, said:

> 'What works best with **blogging** and **podcasting** is just being ourselves. Without artifice. Without performance. Without contrivance. No less talented, but far more relaxed, than what being "on stage" traditionally, reflexively, requires.'[5]

In *The Starfish & The Spider*, Ori Brafman and Rod Beckstrom take this point still further: they quote[6] the ancient Chinese philosopher Lao-tzu, 'a leader is best when people barely know that he exists; not so good when people obey and acclaim him; worst when they despise him'.

One of the great things about the web is that arrogance and hypocrisy are seldom tolerated – anyone displaying these traits will soon find a whole heap of commentators happy to take them down a peg or two.

Conversely, honesty and genuine passion are rewarded. Because of this inherent property, the web throws up unusual celebrities: shy and geeky Craig Newmark, whose multinational company, *craigslist*, started out as an events newsletter; single mum Lauren Luke, who launched her own make-up line after millions viewed her tutorials on *YouTube* – and the afro-American from a poor background, Barack Obama, who funded his successful US Presidential campaign (and his campaign for the Democratic nomination) through millions of $10 online donations.

None of these people conform to a conventional leadership 'type' – but they all have great stories to tell. And those stories have been true and consistent from the start. The repetition of such stories is something Grint noted when he analysed Florence Nightingale's fame back in the 19th century: he observed how the various accounts of Nightingale's good deeds in the Crimea had 'locked the past into a *rhetorically replayable present*' :

> '[Nightingale's] reputation would have had to have been transmitted – by word and print – to others for it to have assumed significance. In effect, therefore, Nightingale's leadership performance is inevitably reproduced, expanded, distorted and reconstructed through rhetoric of one form or another.'[7]

Through the internet, our past actions are forever recorded in this *rhetorically replayable present*. Stories are played out time and time again. If your rhetoric is believable and powerful enough, the reproductive, amplifying, viral properties of the web will easily disseminate your message for you.

Your passion – knowing where you come from, what you care about, and why you need others to care – is key. Once you identify what really matters to you, the tools are in place for you to repeat your message again and again: and your online and offline social networks are the perfect places to start spreading the word.

The people formerly known as the audience[8]

At co-working offices, *BarCamps* and *social media* gatherings everywhere, participants are united by a shared passion. At The Hub in Islington, the focus is social entrepreneurship. At Steve Moore's 2gether participants wanted to use digital technology to solve global problems. At *BarCamps*, everyone meets for the chance to swap ideas in an open environment.

Shared interests are the driving force behind online *social networks*, too.

The chances are that you already have a profile on a number of different sites. You might use *LinkedIn* for work contacts, *Facebook* for friends and family, and *Ning* for special interest groups. Perhaps you signed up to *Twitter* for some *microblogging*, *Spotify* to listen to new bands or *Dopplr* to share travel plans. Maybe you joined *Bebo* because your friends (or kids) were watching *Kate Modern*, or logged onto *MySpace* or *YouTube* for because someone sent you a link to a great video. Whatever your needs or interests, there'll be a *social network* that fits the bill.

The bulk of material on *social networks* is low cost and amateur, yet because this content comes from our friends, we find it compelling. Successful networks are cleverly designed and can become quite addictive. Each has its own distinctive character. Why is it that people keep returning to *MySpace*, *Bebo*, *Facebook* or *Twitter*?

'*MySpace*'s audience is very engaged with media,' says *MySpace developer platform evangelist* Chris Thorpe. 'The ties between friends are slightly weaker than, say, on *Facebook*, but weak ties are strengthened by a common shared interest in content – music, film and games...*MySpace* is more about friend discovery [and] about social discovery of content where you are looking at what your friends are interested in.'

'*Bebo* is actually pretty good in the sense that people tend to replicate their real social ties on the *Bebo* experience,' says *Bebo* marketing executive Ziv Navoth. 'There's really no hobby of "Who has the most friends?"; that doesn't really come to play in the *Bebo* culture...The way [in which] we are different...is [in] the whole capability for self expression.'

'*Facebook*...enables a huge range of images, text, and connections to be created,' writes marketer, Seth Godin. '[It] surfaces what some are calling the *social graph*. What you know, how you know them, who knows whom. It takes the hidden world of tribes and illuminates it with bright digital light.'[9]

'About December 2007 [*Twitter*] users stopped talking about lunch and started contributing interesting stuff,' says long-time *Twitterer*, Alan Patrick. 'And that behaviour radically transformed the service's utility from vacuous gossip to useful news filter. And the system's ubiquity has seen it used as a TV backpath, a machine2machine comms system and crowdsource search engine.'[10]

So, *MySpace* is all about discovery, *Bebo* reinforces your offline *social network*, *Facebook* is a kind of interactive address book and *Twitter* offers a *realtime* news service (among other stuff). But the really interesting thing about online *social networks* is not so much the purpose of each network as the way in which, once common ground is established, people begin to interact with each other. And these relationships take on a special significance in many people's lives.

Building social capital

'If you build up enough trust, people are prepared to help each other for free. It's a blend of the *experience economy* and *the attention economy*,' says musician and writer, Pat Kane, whose *Ning* network, Hue and Cry Music Club, has around 3,000 members. Through this community, Pat sells gig tickets, and encourages people to buy CDs and tracks of Hue and Cry's music, rather than download pirated copies.

This sense of trust can work in different ways. When UK-based musicians, Steve and Lobelia Lawson, played a series of gigs in the United States, they didn't spend a penny on hotel rooms or agents' commission fees; instead they funded and scheduled the tour entirely through the goodwill of contacts made on *Twitter*:

> '[I had] less than 1000 followers at the time,' remembers Steve Lawson. 'But it was enough that people were like, "Oh, I like what you do! How can I get to see you?". So we threw out [an update] that said, great... we're coming over [to the US], if you'd like to book a house concert, drop us a line...[It was much better than] trying to contact clubs and then ending up taking coffee shop gigs where they say..."we'll give you 10 bucks and a free coffee". Instead, we had people who were desperately grateful to us for playing.'

In Ivo Gormley's documentary film, *Us Now*, a 19 year old backpacker, Eric Tomczak, arrives in London for the first time to stay with a host he's met through the travellers' network, *CouchSurfing*. The camera follows Tomczak as he walks through unfamiliar streets, looking for the stranger's flat:

> 'I've never met him before except online,' says Tomczak. 'He's going to be hosting me for two nights. There [are] a lot of unknowns...it's not

as dangerous as you would think. I'm not too worried about what he's going to be like.'[11]

In the same film, mum Lorayn Brown sets off to meet a group of friends made on the online network, Mumsnet: 'I don't really know that much about them apart from the fact they've all got babies,' she admits. 'It can be a very lonely journey, parenting…so to try to get that community spirit that would have been there so many years ago, we have to find some other way of doing it – and Mumsnet is probably the best way.'[12]

Luckily, Tomczak's host turns out to be a cheerful-looking type who's just cooked dinner and Brown's fellow mums turn out to be nothing but friendly. Experiences such as these are all examples of *social capital*, a type of goodwill that has been around since humankind first began living in communities, but has more recently been applied to the internet. Clay Shirky describes it like this:

> 'When your neighbour walks your dog while you are ill, or the guy behind the counter trusts you to pay him next time, social capital is at work. It is the shadow of the future on a societal scale. Individuals in groups with more social capital (which is to say, more habits of cooperation) are better off on a large number of metrics, from health and happiness to earning potential, than those in groups with less social capital.'[13]

Today, the existence of *social networks* means that social capital has got itself a whole new growth engine. The tendency of online networks to organise in groups based around interest, location and other unifying factors, along with general tools such as *tagging* and search mean it is easier than ever to find and connect with like-minded people. As long as the appropriate safety mechanisms are in place, once you've found a community which shares your passions, it's almost inevitable that you'll start connecting, collaborating and helping out other community members. Trust builds from there. Reciprocation and shared experience are powerful catalysts.

There's no reason why this sort of behaviour cannot cross over from purely *social networks* into the workplace. Any such cultivation of social capital would ensure employees not only find work more enjoyable, it would actually reduce transaction costs – a huge factor in the financial outlay of any business.

Headshift's Lee Bryant uses the example of a cost of a sale made through a call centre to that of a sale made to a friend to illustrate why a more social approach, driven by unifying interests, can be so valuable to business:

'The transaction costs if you run a call center are huge: just the fact that you employ people on a low wage, with low levels of motivation, to have un-informed, frustrating, conversations with your customers, means that your staff hate you and your customers hate you – which means you increase the cost of doing business. Whereas if you go to sell something to a friend of yours, there's almost no transaction cost. You have trust, you have a context and you sell. You know that there will be reciprocity because you're meeting that person again and so on – and that's the way that business and trading had always taken place, with much lower levels of friction in the system, because it's never been abstracted from the personal. I think…on a large scale, we're now able, through technology, to return to that way of doing business.'

Of course, it takes time to build up friendships, and there is a cost involved in that. But increasingly we are seeing that social methods *work*. Over the long term, and in most of the tasks that we need to complete in our workplaces today, personal fulfilment is a key motivator.

The American author and business consultant, Dan Pink, describes it as the difference between intrinsic motivators and extrinsic motivators. Extrinsic motivation is a carrot and stick technique: you work hard and are financially rewarded for your efforts. Intrinsic motivation, on the other hand, is:

'The desire to do things because they matter, because we like it, because they are interesting, because they are part of something important: This is a new operating system for business.'[14]

Pink argues that the effectiveness of intrinsic motivation over extrinsic motivation has been proven time and time again in science, but, until now, has been largely ignored in business: he uses research backed by the Federal Reserve Bank of America and London School of Economics to make his case.[15,16]

Community spirit

The number one rule to remember is this: businesses *are* communities.

'There is no such thing as a core business,' says Arie de Geus. 'The US railroad system nearly died as a result of the motorway system being built – because they saw themselves as in the railroad business not the transportation business. A business identity does not lie in an industry, it lies in its human community.'

Although traditionally, the word 'community' is used to refer to a group of people living in the same location, it can also describe a group that is 'organized around common values and social cohesion'.[17] To be fair, successful businesses have always performed this function. And stakeholders don't simply include management, staff, contractors and freelancers – the broader community extends to investors, clients, suppliers and, indeed, any members of the public directly affected by a company's activities.

In the world's more developed economies, work often means more than simply putting food on the table: we have *careers* in which we hope to realise our potential, reinforce our sense of ourselves (or, at least, ourselves as others see us) and achieve some level of fulfilment. People don't just want to 'work' – they want to participate, collaborate and contribute. Savvy businesses can capitalise on this.

A unifying, meaningful vision adds value to a company in three ways: firstly, a shared belief system – evident in a happy, well-functioning community – improves loyalty and reduces staff turnover; secondly, the workplace experience becomes more satisfying, so the number of days lost through illness should be reduced, also saving costs. Finally, a shared sense of purpose creates goodwill – social capital – which is less directly measurable in terms of impact on ROI, but clearly desirable.

In 1943, the American psychologist Abraham Maslow (1908-1970) published a paper in which he set out his theory of a 'hierarchy of needs'[18] – a theory much beloved in **social media** circles.[19] Maslow argued that once 'deficiency' requirements were met (such as food, clothing and shelter), we would become more concerned about 'aesthetic' needs: the need for self-actualisation being paramount among these. Maslow described this need as 'the desire to become more and more what one is, to become everything that one is capable of becoming.'[20]

So, as a manager (or even, these days, a participant) in the workplace, how should we accommodate Maslow's concept of self-actualisation? Do we need to care about what drives our colleagues, or ask what their priorities are? Should we be thinking about building and reinforcing a community around individual values? Can we create social capital through the power of those ideals?

Of course, it all depends on how you view your fellow workers. In 1960, Douglas MacGregor (1906-1964), an American academic, used Maslow's hierarchy to identify two distinct management approaches[21]: in Theory X, employees were seen as inherently lazy and needed to be tightly supervised; in Theory Y, employees enjoyed work and were self-motivated. Theory Y was linked to the upper levels of Maslow's hierarchy (encompassing self-actualisation), while Theory X was linked to the lower levels.

Although both approaches are evident in management practice today, it goes without saying that a Theory X approach might put the dampeners on your community-building programme. Certainly, Theory Y was more evident among the businesses I spoke to for this book. When it comes to incorporating employee ideals into overall strategy, young companies, in particular, appear to be as ambitious about social change as they are about profit margins. **Huddle**, for example, has launched the Huddle Foundation, and gives its software away free to charities; Google has **Google for Good** and other altruistic projects.

Patronage, philanthropy and fund-raising have long been a part of corporate culture; what has changed is the social – connected – dimension. Remember how advertiser Russell Davies talked about no longer separating strategy from execution? Now companies don't have to simply donate a percentage of their profits to the arts, or sponsor developing world health programmes, they can engage their whole workforce in instigating social change. And this is a powerful shift.

People power

Maria Sipka is one of the most positive people you could hope to meet. Born in Czechoslovakia at the height of communism, she was smuggled out as a baby with her parents and elder sister. The family moved to Australia – Sipka's adopted homeland and the place where she learnt to believe that anything was possible. After making some money from B2B marketing in the 1990s, Sipka decided she wanted to do something more meaningful.

Now she lives in Sarrià, an upmarket district of Barcelona, Spain. From here she runs her new business, Linqia – a community-based advertising service – and travels extensively, speaking on *social media* and community-building. As part of her fairy-tale life, she advises some of the world's leading brands, including Procter & Gamble, Merck Serono and Glaxo Smith Klein.

It's a hot, sunny day in Barcelona, and the windows of Sipka's office are wide open. As we chat over *Skype*, I can hear the typically Mediterranean sound of mopeds speeding by in the narrow street outside.

Sipka always seems happy – but today she is on cloud nine. She's buzzing because of an event organised by one of her partners, Procter & Gamble, earlier this week: in the last 36 hours Sipka and her colleagues have raised more than £30,000 to provide Tetanus vaccines to women in the developing world – all as the result of a *social media* campaign that they set up in minutes.

Sipka was one of 250 people – mostly Procter & Gamble employees – invited to spend an evening in Geneva for an event called 'Digital Night'. Sipka had no idea what the event was going to be about – she thought it was a gala ball, so she arrived dressed up to the nines, only to be surprised to find nearly everyone else in suits, brandishing laptops. The element of surprise was intentional.

> 'It was an amazing experience,' she recalls. 'There were five different rooms with about 50 people in each room. We all walked into our assigned rooms and had to get started. I didn't know what was going on, no-one knew what was going on. [The group] was like a flock of sheep.'

On arrival, the teams were told simply that the aim of the night was to raise money for the Pampers 'One pack=one vaccine' campaign, an initiative from P&G that supports UNICEF in its goal of eliminating maternal and neo-natal tetanus. Each team had just ten minutes to define a strategy and everyone took responsibility for a different task. The excitement of live fundraising was intense:

> 'Every time something important happened it flashed up on a big screen. And we could also see the results [of the fundraising] in *realtime*. Someone called Salma Hayek and got her to donate. Someone else said "Hey who are the 100 most followed on *Twitter*?" And got on the phone to Ashton Kutcher. Every time there was a success we celebrated it. We raised £12,000 in two hours. We were trending on *Twitter*. People's heads were spinning...all as the result of a campaign which we invented on the spot – the great thing is that we got quick tangible results. That's the sort of uplifting experience that says to anyone "You can do it!"'

The event created a Eureka moment for Sipka:

> 'One of the biggest issues is getting people internally to evangelise. There's no better way to [raise awareness about *social media*] than to get people involved in an activity...this type of format works really well in convincing the cynics. It could be used anywhere.'

If engaging people and inciting their passion is the best way to instill learning, Procter & Gamble have found a great way to do it. Digital Night worked on many different levels: it united P&G employees in a positive shared experience (community building), it produced instant, marketable, results (brand building) and it taught people about the power of **social media** – by getting them involved in something that really mattered to them.

But community spirit doesn't have to be built on grand gestures – and it doesn't necessarily need to have a philanthropic dimension – small day-to-day activities also have an impact.

The Butterfly Effect

Stowe Boyd is something of a celebrity in **social media**. He describes his role as 'Front Man for The /Messengers' and, with his confident smile, trademark beret and goatee beard, you'd be forgiven if you mistook him for an ageing rock star. Boyd revels in the ambiguity.

> 'The /Messengers is not a band, although it sounds like one,' he says on his website. 'It's just the name I dreamed up for my consulting business back in 2007...I consider myself the front man of a constantly shifting collaborative network.'

Boyd and I are sitting in the Community Lounge at the **Web 2.0** Expo in Berlin. All around us, MacBooks are humming and **bloggers** are tapping away. We're all a part of Boyd's extended network (as he is of ours). To the right, Martin Koser (aka Frogpond) is chatting on **Jaiku** and **Twitter**; to the left, information architect Johannes Kleske holds court (offline and no doubt on as well) with likeminded geeks.

It's late afternoon and we've got dozens of sessions to report back on, and many new connections to follow up. Glance at any screen and you can see a whole range of **social media** in use – **Tweetdeck**, **Delicious**, **Dopplr** and **Xing** are just some of the applications on display.

Boyd is in his element, and so he should be – for it was he who coined the term '**social tools**' back in 1999. He's been watching the rise of **social media** for the last ten years and, like so many others, is evangelistic about its potential, especially in terms of its impact on the way we work:

> 'People are decreasing their involvement in personal productivity. If people give up personal gain for just one moment – even just a minute of their personal time – the network as a whole is more productive. Look at the **network effect** of one person having a willingness to help.'

One example could be the increased value of a **Flickr** photo someone has tagged which is then found and used by a high school student in a project.

Another might be a **Wikipedia** article that has been read through and corrected by an expert.

The Butterfly Effect was a metaphor used by chaos scientist and weather simulator Edward Lorenz (1917-2008) to illustrate the sensitivity of a dynamical system – such as the weather – to slightly varying initial conditions. He used the image of a butterfly flapping its wings in Brazil having the potential to influence the course of a tornado in a far distant place. It's clear that on the Net, one person's behaviour can cause all sorts of ripples. And the cumulative impact of millions of tiny, positive actions can be profound.

> 'We're moving away from a money-driven, hard capital mindset to a gift-driven, social capital mindset,' says Boyd, and he nods his head in the direction of the geeks and **bloggers** all around. 'The people here will always trade personal productivity for network connectivity. Above all, they want to remain connected with the people who are important to them.'

Between the physiological, safety and aesthetic needs of Maslow's hierarchy, there are two other layers. These layers: 'social needs' and 'esteem' – also known as 'the belonging need' – span emotional relationships. They represent the psychological importance of friendship, intimacy, love and respect – the desire for social affirmation, if you like. Boyd may be an idealist, but I agree with him on one thing: **social tools** enable us to talk about the things that are important to us with the people we care about – in this way, they become an intrinsic motivator, serving our deep need for connection extremely well.

Shiny, happy people

> '[It] was tremendous, a huge experience...there were lots of people... who are already hanging out on **Facebook**, **Twitter**, whatever...and **blogs**, and so forth, and there was just this general feeling that we were just having this massive, lovely, love-fest. Like "Oh my God, here you are! Oh, give me a hug!"'

It's July 2009 and it sounds like Luis Suarez might have just returned from a music festival. In fact, he's just got home from a corporate conference: Enterprise 2.0 in Boston. The conference took place over four days packed with panel discussions, seminars, workshops, parties, local gatherings and **tweet** ups – a great opportunity for **social media** diehards like Suarez to do what they love best: network.

Suarez is still reeling from the excitement.

> 'We know [each other] this way, because that's how we interact online
> – and then you actually get to see other people who do not know [each
> other] online: then you can actually see these weird looks, like "Are
> these people actually working for companies?"'

Suarez does work for a company – one of the world's biggest. His employer,
IBM, has a workforce of half a million and a presence in more than 200
countries. Suarez's role is to drive the uptake of social software across this
enormous corporate network. His job involves connecting with thousands
of people, many of whom he may never meet in person; he has become an
expert in relating to others online:

> 'When I started using [social software] I started to realise how I
> was building a community around me of people who shared the
> same passion for knowledge management, collaboration, learning,
> communities...all of a sudden I was finding a common ground.'

Today, these *social tools* don't only help Suarez IBM employees to connect
and collaborate, they also enable around half of the workforce to work
remotely – mostly from home. The company has employees based in Majorca,
Barbados, Bermuda and 'really cool places' in Brazil. Suarez himself lives
and works in a tiny village on Gran Canaria, a sub-tropical island where most
people still take a siesta in the afternoon and the only disturbance during our
Skype chat is a neighbour's dog barking in the distance.

> 'When people tell me, "I didn't know there was an IBM office there", I
> say "Yeah it's my house!"' chuckles Suarez.

Suarez may be the only IBM employee in Gran Canaria, but he is far from
isolated. Through IBM's in-house *social tools*: in particular, Blue Twit (a
Twitter clone) and *Lotus Connections* (a suite of tools including a *social
network*, *blogging* and *bookmarking*), he is 'always on' to his work-mates.

> 'My social software tools are actually becoming my virtual water cooler.
> My [boss], Gina Poole...actually shows off that she has one employee
> working and living in Gran Canaria [and] she knows more about me than
> of the team that lives in the same city where she lives. Because all the
> [online] places where she hangs out, I hang out.'

But when he's ensconced at home in Gran Canaria, tapping away at the
computer, doesn't he ever feel the slightest bit lonely? Suarez claims he gets
ample face time through attending conferences around the world and giving

seminars to IBM employees in other countries. Besides, he argues that any *cognitive dissonance* we might experience through enterprise **social media** (that is, the psychological discomfort caused by the fact that we think we 'see' people when in reality we're talking to a computer)[22] is far outweighed by the fact that a long-lost 'human' dimension is being brought back into the workplace.

> '[People] are no longer treated as resources, as assets, as animated objects that actually do work nine to five. They are treated as people again. And that basically means that when they come into work...[their colleagues] are no longer talking to a person who is doing a job, they are talking to a real person who has got emotions, who has got a private life, who has got plenty of hobbies, a pet, a spouse, a husband, kids or whatever and what social software is doing there is helping people to provide a much more accurate, in this case online, persona, that [shows] them as individuals.'

I agree with Suarez – people enter all sorts of details into online profiles and **blogs** that they may not necessarily give out in a conversation, and communication based on common interests means that relationships exist on non-work levels – thereby adding another dimension to corporate culture. These **rich connections** are especially important in a large company where daily, face to face contact between employees isn't always possible.

Work hard, play harder

We are witnessing a pull towards informality in business that is a confluence of many different trends: the break down of barriers between home and working life, the need to get things done quickly and effectively without ceremony, the rise of 'no-nonsense' marketing and the popular interest in psychology and what makes others 'tick'.

Social tools give us spaces in which to communicate in a friendly, intimate way. The non-serious, irreverent nature of many of these conversations, combined with the fact that they frequently relate to non-work topics, is the reason why many bosses choose to ban social sites altogether. But if we want to create a committed workforce, build social capital and focus on intrinsic motivators, these casual, enjoyable interludes are essential.

Behaviours typical of **social networks** – flirting, joking and poking – can all be interpreted as a manifestation of playfulness, and there are many who believe that play is crucial in working environments today. Commentators such as musician Pat Kane (*The Play Ethic*, 2004) and management consultant John Williams (*Screw Work, Let's Play*, 2009) argue that intelligent workers need an element of fun to enable them to remain creative and focused over time:

> 'The play ethic is an alternative belief-system,' says Kane. 'Which asserts that in an age of mass higher education, continuing advances in personal and social autonomy, and ubiquitous digital networks (and their associated devices), we have a surplus of human potential and energy, which will not be satisfied by the old workplace routines of duty and submission. The identity of a "player" – optimistic, willing to try and experiment, open to participating with peers in a multitude of projects – fits this new landscape, this new social order, much better.'[23]

Many of us are 'players' – we appreciate the opportunity to experiment and make things happen in a safe environment. **Social tools** can help us do this. But building an online community that inspires commitment and engagement, one in which it is safe to play, isn't always easy. The community has to be pitched at exactly the right level. And the online network needs to be a true reflection of the participants' lives offline: the activities relating to the community need to be relevant and not seem like an imposition.

Hitting the right note

In their book on social marketing, 'Groundswell', Forrester Research analysts Charlene Li and Josh Bernoff give a great example of a workplace community that chimes perfectly with the employee culture – Best Buy's Blue Shirt Nation.

Best Buy is a chain of consumer electronic shops in the US with around 155,000 employees. When Blue Shirt Nation was created in 2006, Best Buy's young sales associates had been begging for email addresses so they could communicate with each other properly. When Gary Koelling and Steve Bendt, creatives in Best Buy's **Social Technology** team, launched Blue Shirt Nation, employees got the email they wanted – and a whole lot more.

The site was originally intended as a research tool, but because it was up to Best Buy's employees to moderate and shape the network, it became something completely different. In many ways, Blue Shirt Nation is now similar to a consumer-facing **social network** like **Facebook**: employees build profiles, **blog**, make friends and share knowledge. But this is a corporate site, so the focus is work: employees talk about their day, post their feelings on changes in policy and solve problems together.

On his *blog*, Koelling remembered the fun he had as a child, *customising* bikes and cars with his friends, using tools from their dads' toolboxes. He wanted the employee network he'd created to spark just that kind of excitement:

> 'BSN is like that. A place to play and make. With all of us playing around, and bringing our stuff to the party including the collective experience of being Blueshirts , making friends and all that – what we end up with is kinda like a massively multi-processor distributed bionic computer. Capable of who knows what. Maybe capable of making stuff. Making ideas come to life. Making work more fun. Making friends. Making a mark.'[24]

I liked Koelling's idea of playfulness, and wondered how he had developed this concept through the BSN community: what, exactly, did he give the Blueshirts to play around and experiment with? In an email, he responds:

> 'I guess in the beginning they were given two key things: permission to try, we as administrators were very hands off about what the site could be used for – that was largely determined by the users; and an *open source* platform which meant that whatever they wanted to do, whatever tools they wanted to build/have built for them, we had the freedom to do that at low to no cost.'

Company-wide, Best Buy's staff turnover rate is 60 per cent – but the rate within the Blue Shirt Nation community is a fraction of this: 8-12 per cent. It is clear that the employees who are part of the online network are finding an extra dimension, further enrichment, to their working life. Blue Shirt Nation has been such a success that Koelling and Bendt are now transferring the lessons they've learnt into a process that can be used to build and manage other Best Buy communities.[25]

Does size matter?

One argument used against online *social networks* is that the sheer size of the communities means that efficient human interaction isn't really possible: instead of having deeply meaningful relationships with a small number of close contacts the fear is that we are tricked into having fragmented, inconsequential relationships with a vast, transient crowd.

Chat to anyone in *social media* for long enough, and the chances are that the Dunbar Number (150) will pop up. This figure, formulated by British anthropologist, Robin Dunbar (b.1947), is frequently cited as an indication of the ideal number for people to have in a their personal networks.

Dunbar's hypothesis was that: 'there is a cognitive limit to the number of individuals with whom any one person can maintain stable relationships.'[26] He set out to prove this by studying different varieties of primates and the extended family groups in which they lived. He correlated the group size and brain size of the different types of primate and came up with a mathematical formula illustrating a relationship between the two. Using this formula, he calculated an 'exploratory' figure of 147.8 to indicate a 'mean group size' for humans.

Dunbar's research into village and tribe sizes appeared to back this figure up: 150 was the estimated size of Neolithic farming villages, and the splitting point for Hutterite settlements;[27] it is also the basic unit size for British army battalions (which consist of 700 soldiers divided into five companies of 140). It's no surprise that 150 is also considered a good size in business.

The American academic Danah Boyd (no relation to Stowe), in a paper addressing the failure of early *social network Friendster*, noted how *Friendster* used 150 as a 'magical' number to cap the number of friends that users could have. This turned out to be a mistake, observed Boyd: 150 is not so much the number of people we know or have known, it is more specifically the number of people who are in our 'current' network:

> 'Dunbar was interested in how monkeys groomed each other to keep up their *social network*. What he found was that there was a similarity between monkey grooming and human gossip. Just as monkeys groomed to maintain their networks, humans gossiped to maintain theirs! He found that the *maximum* number of people that a person could keep up with socially at *any given time*, a.k.a. gossip maintenance, was 150. This doesn't mean that people [only] have 150 people in their *social network*, but that they only keep tabs on 150 people max at any given point.'[28]

The size of network that feels 'natural' to us is one issue, the amount of inter-user trust that can be realistically generated at scale is another. And mass uptake of any network is a factor. Speak to anyone who was around in the early years of the web and you'll find a bit of nostalgia for that pioneering time when all the engineers knew each other by name: even institutions like ICANN (the internet domain name authority) talk about the 'halcyon early days.'[29]

Size has always been a contentious issue in business. In the mid 20th century – manufacturing's heyday – economies of scale meant that biggest was best, but as far back as 1973, the British economist E. F. Schumacher was arguing that 'small is beautiful'; he proposed that large businesses would function better if they were decentralised.[30] Today, the emphasis on knowledge means that smaller units are perceived as ideal. Small and start-up companies are noted for having agile, innovative environments where everyone knows everyone else and levels of trust are naturally high. It's so much easier for small companies to be *passionate*. Once a business reaches a certain size, it might not be possible for every stakeholder to be involved in decision-making, have a say in corporate strategy or take part in regular get-togethers.

Applied and used correctly, **social tools** can go a long way to remedying these problems. But, in a large company, how do you persuade everyone to get on board? Social media evangelists have been looking at ways to promote uptake.

Finding your social media ice breaker

A recurrent issue for **Web 2.0** experts is why some executives, especially those at middle-level in large organisations, don't seem to 'get' **social technologies**. Common problems include a fear of losing control, confusion about the technologies available, over-reliance on email and/or expensive (but not always effective) IT solutions, and concern about the amount of time it might take for any new system to be assimilated. In addition, familiarity, ease-of-use and relative satisfaction with the status quo mean that **switching costs** are often higher than we might imagine.

Despite much of what has been written about the **Millennial Generation** (or **Gen Y**), age is not necessarily the issue: what is needed is a particular mindset. Without a doubt, managers have to experience the new technologies for themselves. Yes, chances are that they're statistically more likely to have had that experience if they're under 30. But there's no reason to say that the older generation can't start working in different ways if the motivation – the passion – is there.

Social website experts, Mint Digital, researched the online behaviour of the over 60s as part of a development project for Channel 4. Mint's Creative Director, Andy Bell, found that older people could be just as passionate about online communications as their younger counterparts:

'We found lots of pensioners who love email and **Skype**. Communication is fine, as long as is it fits closely with an existing mental model. If a pensioner can think "ah, it is just like sending a letter but quicker" or "ah, it is just like using a phone, but over the computer" then they get it.'

Although it is a relatively new technology, **Twitter** has proved a surprising hit with older users. Maybe because the functionality is simple, and lists of followers and followees are easy to control. Musician Steve Lawson told me that his mum uses **Twitter** – and loves it. For Joan Lawson, now retired and living in a remote village in Scotland, the promise of daily interaction with family and friends is a prime motivator.

At IBM, Luis Suarez has a special trick for engaging older executives, many of whom may have been with the company for 20 or 30 years.

'I ask them... "do you want to leave your brand behind? Do you know the second or third generation after you have left [will have] no trace that there was xyz person who actually did this, this and this at IBM?"...And they go, "Well, I never thought about it that way." And you say, "Well, it's up to you to do it". And they say, "I don't feel that I can contribute" and you say "There are millions of ways that you can contribute, it's just up to you to decide how you want to brand yourself."'

Suarez is always looking for ways to level the digital playing field. With his help, IBM has set up a handful of reverse-mentoring programmes where younger employees teach the older staff about **social technologies** and older staff pass down their knowledge of the company to newer recruits:

'It's no longer a question of whether you are young or old or whatever – this is just about putting yourself out there and sharing what you have and letting people know what you are good at.'

MT Rainey, CEO of online mentoring site, **Horsesmouth**, would agree. She found that older people were just as keen to volunteer their time to the site as a younger demographic, simply because the call to action was compelling. She thinks the age issue is something of a smokescreen:

'I don't think it's age dependent actually. I mean obviously you could generalize about age, but I think if you could give older people something to do online, and it's kind of **WYSIWYG** stuff, which most websites are, they'll go for it big time, because they've got time, and they are interested. With **Horsesmouth**, our older users really love it.'

The developer's dilemma

But are we really ready to collaborate?

E-learning expert, David Jennings, has been interested in co-operative, non-hierarchical ways of organising since he did an MSc in occupational psychology at Sheffield in the 1980s. He believes that technology has finally caught up with 'ideas that have been around for a generation':

> 'There are all sorts of challenges to co-operative working,' he says. 'The main problem with genuinely co-operative organisations is that they're simply not scaleable. Perhaps if [the co-ops of the 1970s] had had *wikis* and *microblogs*, and a more cellular structure, they would have been more viable.'

Of course, there are success stories, most notably the Co-operative, which was founded in the UK in 1873 and is now the world's largest consumer-owned business with a chain of supermarkets, two banks and many other business interests to its name, but the Co-op remains an admirable exception. The vast majority of co-operative businesses in the UK have collapsed under the sheer weight of their ambition.

Jennings cites Charles Landry's book, *What A Way To Run A Railroad*, (1985)[31] as a great analysis of why co-operative working often fails. The book argued that people create their own organisational 'cramps' (restrictive behaviours), which are counter-productive and cause the co-operative structure to be overwhelmed in trying to cater for them. The book also pointed to the lack of good management skills in many UK-based co-operatives.

> 'If you look at other countries, such as Sweden, you'll see a social democratic culture that looks more favourably on this sort of thing. Volvo, for example, experimented with semi-autonomous work groups in the 1980s...they were much more about putting the technology in the hands of a small group of people and saying "Here, look! There are the tools. There's the job. Get on and do it and we'll set the outcomes and exactly how you organise yourselves is completely up to you."'

Giving people ownership and allowing them the freedom to make their own decisions is a proven way of energising teams and creating passion – but that's something that doesn't always seem to come naturally to us. Maybe it *is* a cultural thing. But the UK cannot be considered to be running scared from what might now be considered to be *social* approaches.

The UK's digital sector has been at the forefront in developing landmark *social technologies* (examples include *Bebo*, *Last.fm* and *Huddle*) and we have a thriving *social media* scene that, while it may not compare to Silicon Valley in size, certainly has its own distinctive role to play.

Usability is one growing area of expertise. The technology we have today is far more user-centric than the online calendars and other early collaborative tools developed by software engineers in the 1980s: there is nearly always an incentive to participate. The key change between the 1970s co-operatives and enterprise *social technologies* today is that, now, the individual, not the organisation, is the focal point. But the end goal of sharing resources in order to create better products or services is the same.

Developers can now write software that serves the organisational greater good whilst also meeting the more immediately selfish needs of the individual user. As a society, we may consider ourselves to be increasingly motivated by ideals but, as Jennings points out, sometimes we're simply too busy:

> 'If you can make the social benefit a by-product of the selfish interest then it's much more likely to be sustainable than a cooperative ideology. You can't rely on people always being motivated by [high ideals]. For example we've just been talking about what it's like to have a newborn baby. You think, I know it'd be really good if I did all these socially valuable things, but I just haven't got the time!'

Defining the social object

The web's most successful networks have been built from millions of tiny actions by millions of individuals. While sometimes these actions are genuinely altruistic (contributions to *Wikipedia*, for example), many are, first and foremost, essentially self-serving.

Delicious is a global news archive; *Flickr* and *YouTube* are, respectively, the world's largest picture and video repositories; *Twitter* has become a *realtime* news service. But the participants in these networks aren't necessarily motivated by wanting to build something unique, they are more likely to be there because they want to *bookmark* an article, send someone a photo or video, or simply let their friends know what they are up to.

In 2007, Jyri Engeström, founder of the *microblogging* site, *Jaiku*, developed a theory of 'social objects'.[32] Engeström observed how successful online communities always focused on a specific 'social object' – a photo, video, status update or text message. This is a single point, a single currency, around which the community gathers. The social object is something that the network users care passionately about. Most importantly, the social object must be share-able.

All successful *social networks* are built around a distinctive object, observed Engeström. He hoped his theory would provide a useful starting point for anyone thinking about designing an online community. He gave the examples of *MySpace* (music tracks), *Flickr* (photos) and *Delicious* (*bookmarks*).

Often, the social object will be obvious – there will already be a community of interest or of practice around it. When IBM set up Developerworks in 1999, it was in response to the fact that software developers wanted to chat and collaborate about the products they were building – often with colleagues in other locations. Developerworks was born – with products as the social object.

But it's not always possible to build a network around a specific thing. Generalist networks like *Facebook* and *Bebo* have a whole host of meaningful items: photos, videos, *blog* posts, status updates etcetera – for users to share and comment upon. In these sorts of cases, individual, one-off campaigns can add an element of compulsion and interest.

Narrative can be a powerful catalyst, as we know, and in 2007, *Bebo* ran a competition encouraging people to contribute short stories. *Bebo*'s Vice President, Marketing & Business Development, Ziv Navoth, saw these 'social objects' as a great way to create excitement among existing users and drive new people to the network.

Compelling content

It's a late afternoon in October 2008 and Ziv Navoth is sitting in his office in AOL's posh new headquarters on Broadway, New York, chatting to me on *Skype*. Navoth is Vice President, Marketing and Business Development, for *Bebo*. Just six months ago, in March, AOL bought *Bebo* for £417m ($850m). At the time, *Bebo* was the world's third largest *social network* (45m registered users). Now it's fast losing ground to *Facebook*, *MySpace* and *Twitter*. AOL is none too happy. Navoth's priority is to make *Bebo* compelling again.

'Everybody wants to believe that things can get better, everybody wants to believe that they can win, everybody wants to believe that they can make a difference, whether they work for a start-up or for a 20,000 person organisation. What you have to do as a leader is to convince people...I'm a big believer in stories and storytelling as a way to convey messaging and to get people excited about what you're excited about.'

Navoth knows all about storytelling. In February 2007, *Nanotales*, his collection of short stories, was published in the same week he started at **Bebo**. His first task was to run a competition encouraging users to write their own 'nanotales' – short stories of under 1,000 words. The stories were uploaded to the web where they could be reviewed and rated by other users.

Navoth sold the competition idea to **Bebo** as a perfect fit with the ambitions of its core 16 – 24 year old demographic, and it proved effective in harnessing the viral power of the internet. Shortlisted writers promoted the competition on their **blogs**, asking readers to vote for them, and spread the word. The stories they'd written became a focal point – in effect, social objects – they were treasured items to be shared, read, commented upon and linked to.

> '**Social media** allows you to cross the barriers of space and time,' says Ziv. 'You can broadcast your story with zero investment and the only thing that will determine whether those stories get spread or not is if they are any good...if the story that you tell is powerful, it'll spread. You couldn't do that before.'

From the heart

If you want to motivate anyone, be it your friends, a business team or an entire company, it's good to start with a story. And it doesn't matter whether you're the CEO of a multinational or a teenager on **Bebo**: the internet is a great leveller. Craft your message in the right way, touch a chord, and your words will spread like wildfire. Add **network effects** to a well articulated strategic vision and you get a virtuous, ever-expanding, circle. If you create something others want to build on, you're really harnessing the power of **social media**.

Remember how Procter & Gamble's Digital Night engaged staff in a meaningful mission, sparking collaboration? Remember the enthusiasm of Stowe Boyd's geeks, Luis Suarez' hugging executives and Blue Shirt Nation's playful contributors? Whether it's driven by high ideals, the desire for self-expression or an innate need to belong, passion is something we all love to share.

If your business has a unifying, collective strategy at its core, your colleagues will be more motivated and the entire workforce more engaged and more productive. Passion is crucial in a fragmented world where **social media** runs like mercury through the gaps. It is this, more than anything, that will help you build a robust business community.

The next chapter looks in detail at why the concept of knowledge management is being replaced by enterprise **social media**, a far more fluid and dynamic approach. And I'll demonstrate how **social tools** are changing behaviour in every day working practices.

Notes

1. Meryl Streep quoted on Tudor Rickards' **blog**: leaderswedeserve.wordpress. com/2009/01/02/leaders-we-deserve-on-becoming-a-king
2. Tudor Rickards: leaderswedeserve.wordpress.com/2009/01/02/ leaders-we-deserve-on-becoming-a-king
3. Keith Grint (2001), *The Arts of Leadership*. Oxford University Press.
4. *ibid*, pp. 22-23.
5. doc-weblogs.com/2006/07/10#theFormerlies
6. Ori Brafman and Rod Beckstrom, *The Starfish & The Spider*, p. 115.
7. Keith Grint (2001), pp. 26.
8. This is a common idea among those who argue that the media has changed irreversibly, first used by Jay Rosen in a **blog** post entitled, 'The People Formerly Known as The Audience', 27 June 2006: journalism.nyu.edu/pubzone/ weblogs/pressthink/2006/06/27/ppl_frmr.html
9. Seth Godin (2008), *Tribes*. Piatkus, p. 46.
10. Alan Patrick in a **blog** post, 5 June 2009: www.broadstuff.com/ archives/1732-Twime-say-Twitter-will-Twange-the-World.html
11. Eric Tomczak in '**Us Now**', directed by Ivo Gormley (Banyak Films 2009).
12. Lorayn Brown in '**Us Now**', *ibid*.
13. Shirky, *Here Comes Everybody*, p. 192 – in writing about social capital, Shirky was building on the work carried out by Harvard sociologist Robert Putnam for *Bowling Alone* (2000).
14. Dan Pink, 'The surprising science of motivation', **TED** talk, July 2009 (www.ted. com/talks/dan_pink_on_motivation.html).
15. For example: an analysis of 51 separate studies of financial incentives announced in an event at the London School of Economics on 30 June 2009 found 'that performance-related pay often does not encourage people to work harder and sometimes has the opposite effect' (www2.lse.ac.uk/ERD/ pressAndInformationOffice/newsAndEvents/archives/2009/06/ performancepay.aspx).
16. Pink's ideas are not dissimilar to the work of Harvard business theorist Chris Argyris who put forward a concept of external versus internal commitment in the 1990s. External commitment is a type of contractual agreement, whereby management define specific work targets and processes and employees fulfils the minimum that is required of them, because: 'it is a fundamental truth of human nature and psychology that the less power people have to shape their lives, the less commitment they will have.' Internal commitment, on the other hand: 'is participatory and very closely allied with empowerment. The more that top management wants internal commitment from its employees, the more it must try to involve employees in defining work objectives, specifying how to achieve

them, and setting stretch targets.' Argryis makes it clear that internal commitment is preferable (and the participatory nature of enterprise **social media** seems a great way to drive internal commitment). For more on this see Chris Argyris: 'Empowerment: The Emperor's New Clothes', *Harvard Business Review* 76 (May-June 1998): pp. 98-105.

17. en.wikipedia.org/wiki/Community
18. A.H. Maslow, 'A Theory of Human Motivation' *Psychological Review* 50(4) (1943), pp. 370-96.
19. See, for example: Meredith Trottier, 'Your Customers' Hierarchy of Needs', 23 February 2009: www.ignitesocialmedia.com/your-customers-hierarchy-of-needs or Judith Wolst, 'Social media addresses the hierarchy of needs', 19 August 2009 (blog.twingly.com/2009/08/19/guest-post-social-media-adresses-the-hierarchy-of-needs).
20. A. H. Maslow, 'A Theory of Human Motivation', *Psychological Review* 50(4) (1943).
21. Douglas McGregor (1960), *The Human Side of Enterprise.* McGraw Hill.
22. Kathy Sierra addressed this comprehensively in her widely-read **blog** post, 'Is Twitter TOO good?': headrush.typepad.com/creating_passionate_users/2007/03/is_twitter_too_.html
23. Pat Kane in an interview with John Williams, 14 September 2009: www.theplayethic.com/2009/09/playethicoverview2009.html
24. garykoelling.com/node/343
25. www.businessinnovationfactory.com/weblog/archives/2008/09/best_practices.html
26. R. I. M. Dunbar (1993), 'Coevolution of neocortical size, group size and language in humans'. *Behavioral and Brain Sciences* 16 (4): 681-735 (via **Wikipedia**)
27. en.wikipedia.org/wiki/Dunbar%27s_number
28. Danah Boyd, 'Revenge of the Social Network: Lessons from Friendster', talk given at Stanford University, California, 4 February 2005.
29. 'ICANN: A Blueprint for Reform', 2002: www.icann.org/en/committees/evol-reform/blueprint-20jun02.htm
30. E. F. Schumacher (1999), *Small Is Beautiful: Economics As If People Mattered: 25 Years Later...With Commentaries.* Hartley & Marks.
31. Charles Landry; Dave Morely; Russell Southwood and Patrick Wright (1985), *What A Way To Run A Railroad.* Comedia.
32. I heard Jyri Engstrom present his ideas on social objects at the NMK Forum one-day conference in London, 13 July 2007. A great summary by Kevin Anderson is here: strange.corante.com/2007/06/13/nmkforum07-jyri-of-jaiku3

3. Learning

Myth: Email is the best way to share knowledge

Reality: Social tools increase productivity

Joel Spolsky, CEO of respected US software company, Fog Creek, served as a soldier in the Israeli army so has direct experience of a command-and-control environment. On his *blog*, Joel on Software (www.joelonsoftware.com), he argues why this management style can never work in knowledge-based businesses. With command-and-control, the leaders give the orders and people in the field execute them. With knowledge-driven projects, the norm is for everyone to work on their own specific – and complex – tasks. Spolsky once wrote how micromanagement, for example, can become counterproductive:

> 'You micromanage one developer in a spurt of activity and then suddenly disappear from that developer's life for a couple of weeks while you run around micromanaging other developers. The problem with hit and run micromanagement is that you don't stick around long enough to see why your decisions are not working or to correct course. Effectively, all you accomplish is to knock your poor programmers off the train track every once in a while, so they spend the next week finding all their train cars and putting them back on the tracks and lining everything up again, a little bit battered from the experience.'[1]

This type of management intervention can stall the creative process and have a negative impact on production. Instead, maybe we should all practice what Seth Godin referred to as 'micro-leadership' – a sort of gentle, hands-off guidance that advises without condemning and reassures without smothering[2] – a friendly 'nudge' rather than a castigating slap[3]. But that's often tough to do. Our traditional structures ensure that managers – especially middle managers – are expected to monitor progress and make decisions, often with inadequate information. As Spolsky observed:

> 'In a high tech company the individual contributors always have more information than the "leaders", so [the leaders] are rarely in the best position to make decisions. When the boss wanders into an office where two developers have been arguing for two hours about the best way to compress an image, the person with the least information is the boss, so that's the last person you'd want making a technical decision.'[4]

Spolsky paints a good scenario of how knowledge – or, to be precise, a specific lack of knowledge – works. And the larger the organisation, the more layered the corporate hierarchy, the further removed decision-makers are from principal players, the worse the potential for error. Multiply Spolsky's squabbling developers by ten, a hundred or a thousand, and you have infinite possibility for misinterpretations, bad judgment calls and knee-jerk reactions – leading to ill-informed decisions that can have ramifications throughout the business. This could be seen as a negative example of the **butterfly effect** described in the last chapter.

Enlightened managers know that good business is not so much about obtaining, creating and owning knowledge as learning from and applying that knowledge. It is about creating positive butterfly and **network effects**. It is about building virtuous circles. It is about maximising not so much your knowledge but truly realising the *potential* of that knowledge.

The Emperor's old clothes

A friend of mine is a head of sector in Her Majesty's Civil Service. The UK civil service, as we know it today, was established in 1855. Its meritocratic system was based on the Chinese version, which can be traced back to the Qin Dynasty (221-207 BC).[5] For the Chinese, and for Britain in the mid nineteenth century, it was completely acceptable for decisions to be made with incomplete information, especially when they concerned remote parts of the empire:

> 'So with foreign [regions], the civil service developed a culture where people didn't have constant contact with the embassies,' says my friend. 'You might send a letter saying, "I'm about to invade a neighbouring region, hope you don't mind, let me know". And…the letter would take two weeks to arrive. Parliament would find out and say "Don't do it!". They put that in another letter that, four weeks later, arrives back – but [by then] it is too late.'

With communication between different places based on the physical delivery of letters, the world of the mid nineteenth century necessarily operated in silos. But my friend was surprised to learn, during his recent recruitment to the Civil Service, that senior managers were still required to excel at making decisions with inadequate information:

> 'It was kind of like saying that I have a car that runs at 20 miles an hour, and at 21 miles per hour the wheels start to go a bit wonky and you

have to lean out of the window and bang it with a hammer and then you can go 22 miles per hour. So we're looking for a person to drive this car, so if you are good at leaning out the window at 20 miles an hour and hitting a wheel then we want you. I think that is absurd. Why don't you just say that the car is broken?'

My friend's frustration reminds me of the time I was studying for an MBA, a few years back. The course was laden with training in this type of 'confident guesswork'. In presentations, we were admonished for answering questions with 'Sorry, I don't know' – not knowing was a sign of weakness! Any answer was preferable and if it was wrong, well that would be a problem for another day. In the heat of the presentation moment, an untruth, especially a well-presented and credible untruth, was far, far better than an admission of defeat. Likewise, we were encouraged in business strategy sessions to 'pick a number, any number' when coming up with financial projections – this would give the team something to work around, towards, or back from.

While few businesses today may be as labyrinthine and bureaucratic as the UK civil service, guesswork in decision-making is standard practice. Why do we persist with those wonky old structures when brand new approaches are needed? Maybe it's because, as Joel Spolsky often points out, the command-and-control mentality still exists in many places.

Plugging the knowledge gaps

It makes sense to delegate decision-making to the people closest to any situation – preferably those who are directly involved. As far as possible, we should empower employees to truly 'own' their projects – and appreciate the tough choices that can go with responsibility.

JP Rangaswami, a senior executive at BT, puts it like this: 'why would you want to hire smart people and then tell them what to do? It sort of doesn't make sense. You want to tell them what needs to be done and then say, "well, you're smart guys and you figure out the best ways. And if you have a problem, then come to me."'

Even in an organisation as highly disciplined as the US army, command-and-control is now being mixed with other methods. For example, Special Forces based in Iraq and Afghanistan have been structured and specifically trained to work autonomously. The decentralised nature of Al Qaeda, The Mujahideen and other enemy networks has forced Western military leaders to think differently.[6]

In acknowledging that the most pertinent information often lies at field level, business leaders need to do more than simply (re)consider decision-making; they need to look at ways of making knowledge across *all* levels more explicit. It's not so much about managing the knowledge as about letting that knowledge breathe: storing it in a place where it'll be regularly accessed and updated, making it more useful and valuable. Ensuring that employees across the organisation are constantly able to *learn* .

Enterprise social software tools are not knowledge management systems – they are not even systems. They are lightweight tools that allow structures to emerge organically over time. Ideally they are used by everyone in the organisation: employees, co-workers, even partners.

The discipline of knowledge management (KM) was established in the early 1990s. KM was about eliciting tacit knowledge, such as best practice, and then storing it in vast, widely accessible databases. **Social tools** are an evolution of this: they record the actual behaviour of employees – what they do, how they do it – and make inferences based on the frequency of certain actions. From these inferences, an actual pattern of best practice might emerge – and not necessarily one that has been articulated by employees. The evolved pattern is better, because there's often a difference between what people say and what they do. In addition, employees may be inhibited about addressing certain issues explicitly, so this organic, bottom up structure can uncover latent issues and interests; for example, Headshift's Lee Bryant talks about one client where a gay and lesbian network quickly emerged around a certain set of **tags** – causing the network to be formally acknowledged by the organisation.

Re-use, repair, recycle

If knowledge were a fossil fuel, we would be appalled at the waste. Knowledge is literally leaking out of our buildings, being buried in landfill and being thrown out before its sell-by-date. It is common practice for IT departments to wipe the laptops and hard drives of employees who leave an organisation. Even if digital copies of documents are made, it's rare that there is a system for easily identifying the information they contain.

But knowledge is, in many cases, a non-renewable resource. Often people leave a company with many years of experience and knowhow that was generated in a certain time and place – and could be invaluable to those who follow. Imagine how much better it would be if people could deposit knowledge in a secure place where it was reachable and searchable – a **wiki**, for example – rather than leave everything buried in the 'my documents' folder on their soon-to-be-wiped computer desktop.

The most profligate consumer of information – the biggest energy-waster – is email. Once received, our email sits solidifying in individual inbox silos, becoming less digestible by the minute, more impenetrable over time. Email may be categorised by date, name and subject, but how many of us are thwarted when we try to track down a long-lost message using those labels? And how about the time wasted in simply reading emails that aren't relevant to us?

> '[Email] has turned into a nuisance that's costing companies millions,' reported Suw Charman-Anderson in *The Guardian*. 'We may feel that we have it under control, but not only do we check email more often than we realise, the interruptions caused are more detrimental than was previously thought.'[7]

IBM's Luis Suarez was receiving around 40 emails a day when he decided to give it up in 2008:

> 'I became tired of my usual morning ritual of spending hours catching up on e-mail,' he wrote in the New York Times. 'So I did something drastic to take back control of my productivity. I stopped using e-mail most of the time. I quickly realized that the more messages you answer, the more messages you generate in return. It becomes a vicious cycle. By trying hard to stop the cycle, I cut the number of e-mails that I receive by 80 percent in a single week. It's not that I stopped communicating; I just communicated in different and more productive ways.'[8]

Now Suarez finds a focal point of his job is persuading his colleagues at IBM that email does not have to be the centre of their working universe:

> '[There is] this whole culture around everything being on email. When you're trying to introduce a new set of tools to help people be more productive and share knowledge and establish themselves as thought leaders, and you find out they don't use these tools [simply] because they're not integrated with their personal email systems, you go "OUCH! That hurts!"'

Suarez has found that ***social technologies*** such as instant messaging, ***blogs*** and ***wikis*** (combined with old technologies such as the telephone) are a more than adequate replacement. The time spent on the new technologies is less than that of wading through an inbox because the information is organised in useful, relevant, more semantic ways.

Tweeting chickens

Carlton House Terrace, on The Mall leading to Buckingham Palace in London, is thought to be one of the finest creations of Regency architect John Nash. Since 1968, the East Terrace basement has been occupied by the Institute of Contemporary Arts, the UK's home to avant-garde culture. It's a Friday morning in November, and Benjamin Ellis and I are sitting in the foyer of this impressive institution. We're surrounded by the very latest in film, art and music, and we're having a heated discussion – about chickens.

Ellis has six bantam hens and they don't want to go outside now that the first frosts of winter have arrived. Also, they've stopped laying eggs. Of course, the bottom line solution would be to gently put the creatures out of their misery, and have a nice chicken curry for dinner. But Ellis doesn't think this is ethical. The chickens provide more than just eggs, they offer company (of sorts) and entertainment for his children. They represent six little lives. And the fact that they're no longer laying doesn't directly correlate to the Ellis family going hungry.

I'm interested in chickens because my country-dwelling sister keeps them, and it's great for Lila (my urban toddler) to get a real-life demonstration of where eggs come from. Ellis and I didn't really come to the ICA to discuss chickens – we came to swap thoughts on *social media*. But I follow Ellis on *Twitter*, and he's been talking about his bantams: now a whole new area of common ground has opened up for us.

Social tools are great at delivering that arbitrary information you never knew you wanted. And once information is explicit and reachable, it is far more useful. As Ellis puts it:

> 'A lot of creativity comes from randomness but it's hard to construct randomness in a useable way. That's really what *social media* does: it's constructive randomness...it enables the information to get to where it's needed.'

A former marketing executive at Cisco and Juniper Networks, Ellis now runs Redcatco, a consultancy that focuses on solving the communication problems within organisations.

> 'The biggest challenge in any organisation is the asymmetrical nature of information. You have a piece of information. I have a need for that piece of information. But how do we know? Email doesn't really work because it's predicated on the fact that you know who your information

is useful to...most of the information assets of an enterprise are placed carefully out of reach: in people's in-boxes, or stored on their hard drives as documents. If you're really progressive you go "well, we've got an **Intranet** and we'll put it up or we'll use **SharePoint**". [But] people have moved from individual information pockets to information enclaves.'

The break-through comes when there is habitual creation of meta-data: the type of data that Ellis refers to as 'the semantic wrapper':

'Information about information is what you really need. It's a contextualisation. That's kind of what the **semantic web** is all about [and that development is] a journey that has been going on for 10 years, because it's a really hard problem: getting computers to understand context is really hard. And getting people to **tag** stuff is hard. And that's again where things like **blogs** and **wikis** and **social media** are crucial to an enterprise because it's all reasonably lightweight, semantic, information.'

The **semantic web** was envisioned by director of the World Wide Web Consortium, Tim Berners-Lee, in 1999. He saw it as a web in which computers become so capable of analysing data that a lot of the stuff we search for today (information, products, entertainment) will be automatically delivered to us in easily digestible forms, while more mundane, administrative tasks (signing up to a website, for example) will be routinely completed on our behalf. Berners-Lee has described the **semantic web** as a key component of the next generation of the web:

'People keep asking what Web 3.0 is. I think maybe when you've got an overlay of **scaleable vector graphics** – everything rippling and folding and looking misty – on **Web 2.0** and access to a **semantic web** integrated across a huge space of data, you'll have...an unbelievable data resource.'[9]

If you've seen Steven Spielberg's *Minority Report* (2002) and remember Tom Cruise standing in front of his giant computer screen, reaching out and pulling down every bit of information he needs, you'll have an inkling of what it all might look like.

This new, intuitive web may still be some years away, but many of the technologies that will create it are here today. Already, we need to run in order to keep up – and it's not possible to sprint when you're plodding through email messages one by one. **Social tools** enable organisations to respond quickly and effectively to events, and to learn from and apply knowledge in the most relevant ways. And the cost of embracing these new *social technologies* is chickenfeed compared to the damage that missed opportunities could cause your business.

Land of daydreams

Of course, none of this is to say that traditional classification and record keeping measures aren't valuable. Paper-based filing systems such as filing cabinets, folders, microfiche and index cards are still useful and relevant, especially when used in conjunction with digital information storage. But if you're over-reliant on offline, linear, methods, it might feel like using a tea tray to surf a tsunami.

Author Frank Baum reputedly got the idea for the magical Land of Oz from staring at the bottom drawer of his filing cabinet (O-Z). But what could be less magical, more awe-quashing, than the sight of a metal drawer stuffed full of dusty, bulky, manila folders – especially if they've been scrawled on in someone else's illegible handwriting? It's no wonder Baum day-dreamed.

Technicolor Oz resembles the internet while Kansas is more like the offline, paper-based office: on the 'Net, we're still the same people, trying to achieve the same goals (results, profits, a good working environment), but instead of a four-walled, analogue reality, we're in an intense, brilliant landscape where strange, random things happen, all connections are possible and it's the way we interpret our journey that matters.

But it's all about knowing how to get the best from the system – and making it work for you. Mis-tagged **bookmarks**, badly constructed **wikis** and online communities with tumbleweed blowing through them will be just as demoralising – and stressful to deal with – as a roomful of dusty old filing cabinets.

Hollywood or bust?

When Vincent (John Travolta) and Jules (Samuel L Jackson) talk about French names for hamburgers ('They call it a "Royale with Cheese"') on the way to commit another violent crime in Pulp Fiction (1994), the film's writer/director Quentin Tarantino was heralded as a master of unconventional story-telling.

But the non-linear, broken narrative of a film like *Pulp Fiction* – and other post-modern classics such as Christopher Nolan's *Memento* (2000) or Alejandro

González Iñárritu's *21 Grams* (2003) – is a great representation of how we all experience life: cultural commentator (and ICA Director of Talks) James Harkin called it cyber-realism, 'a new kind of storytelling that deliberately engages our restless, cybernetic imagination.'[10]

It's a part of the human condition to be restless and, when we actually do settle to focus on a task, it is inevitable that we're beset with distractions and interruptions. Projects veer off in unexpected directions, clients change their minds, colleagues call in sick, an external event can change the course of everything. Often, things simply don't go according to plan. Life can be anything but 'linear'.

If enterprise *social media* can capture conversations, linear and non-linear, and enable us to later make connections where we wouldn't have otherwise, then that has to be enriching at least – and, overall, value-adding. *Blogs*, *wikis* and *social networks* (whether they be focused on products, photos, news updates or *bookmarks*) help us create an online repository of information that should become increasingly useful over time. The new way in which these tools are structured – fluid, modular, *customisable*, remixable – means they have great potential to inspire and challenge us – just as powerfully as an Oscar-winning movie.

Playing tag

Back in the early 1990s, Headshift co-founder, Lee Bryant, worked in media relations for the Bosnian Government. From 1992-5, during the Bosnian War, he edited a daily briefing document on the Government's behalf. He developed a way of making the briefings honest, informative and useful. The reasons for the conflict were complex, but Bryant's bulletin was straightforward, and always contained links to other sources; Bryant believes it gained traction with news editors because of this.

As a linguist (he picked up Serbo-Croat after studying politics at University, and also knows French), Bryant is something of an anomaly in the English-speaking world. But his background helps explain why so much of Headshift's work has a strong appreciation of language, and linguistics, at its core. *Tagging* – the labelling of information using key words – is central to many projects.

> 'Social *tagging* is fascinating for many reasons,' says Bryant. 'One of my big drivers to get involved in [*social media*] in the first place was the concept of self representation; the idea that we can represent our own

identity and form our own networks with people who are interested in that identity or share some values rather than trying to communicate through mass media...we can negotiate our own meaning through our own labels and combine them to understand each other better and also to solve very practical problems like finding information and finding the right things.'

In a non-linear world, *tagging* is a great way to recall and search for information once it has been stored. When data is tagged, ideas and issues can be tracked easily across different parts of the organisation. And trending topics can be identified. So, for example, the *tags* 'newoffice', 'Brussels' and 'thingswedontlike' might be an indirect way of employees telling management exactly what they think of a particular relocation plan. Over time, folksonomies (naming systems) and ontologies (belief systems) emerge – the unique language and values of your organisation, developed from the grassroots up.

Bryant is enthusiastic about the way *tagging* can enhance understanding. Headshift built a successful prototype for BBC News that incorporated user *tagging* of news stories – part of a bid to overcome the corporation's rather rigid existing classification system.

In another project, for the policy think-tank, Demos, staff profiles were made more dynamic by the addition of a 'recently used *tags*' section – these *tags* were updated as and when the staff used new ones. As Bryant points out, the conglomeration of *tags* that an individual has used over time can be a more accurate representation of their interests than anything they would declare themselves.

Because some clients fear a loss of control ('They believe a formal taxonomic structure might enable them to solve their problems in a manageable way'), Headshift has created a bipartite system that combines fixed classification with social *tagging*. The formal classification will start with aspects that are universally accepted, such as locations and department names. If a specific *tag* becomes popular in the social realm, it can be 'promoted' to the formal system.

When this type of meta-data is collected properly, the rewards are proven. Bryant gives an example from work carried out for the English National Institute of Mental Health: two key terms ('early intervention' and 'psychosis in youth') didn't have a place in the formal family tree but emerged from the social *tagging*. The official adoption of these terms led to a deeper understanding and appreciation of the situations they described.

Bryant stresses that he and his Headshift co-founder, Livio Hughes, seek to avoid any kind of 'management' and believe in allowing consultants and technical staff to work as autonomously as possible – maybe it's no surprise that he constantly seeks to enable people to say specifically what they want, in exactly the manner they choose.

Not long after our meeting, Bryant and Hughes throw a party to celebrate moving into their new offices (a penthouse complex on the edge of London's stylish Butler's Wharf, a zone of refurbished warehouses on the bank of the Thames). It's there that I meet consultant Penny Edwards, who's just written her MBA dissertation on *wikis* at work. Edwards tells me the one person I really must speak to is Ross Mayfield – the man who founded 'the world's first *wiki* company'.

Mixing business with pleasure

SocialText founder Ross Mayfield works out of an unassuming office in downtown Palo Alto, California, a couple of blocks away from the Caltrain station (if you listen hard, you can hear the train bells clanging) and a stone's throw from the sprawling Stanford University campus. Like just about everywhere else in Silicon Valley, *SocialText*'s low-tech surroundings are a foil for the hi-tech business taking place. People talk on the phone about 'mikis' (mobile *wikis*) and 'webinars' (online seminars) as if these were common words in the English language. '*Wiki* Wednesday across the way' is scrawled in faded marker pen across the reception whiteboard. So, this is the unassuming site of the world's first *BarCamp*!

After a few minutes, Mayfield appears. He's the first company chairman I've seen wearing shorts. Admittedly, it's around 28°C on a September afternoon. We go outside to sit in a shady spot under a couple of Cypress trees, partly so I can make the most of the weather, partly so that Mayfield can have a cigarette.

Mayfield co-founded *SocialText* to build *wikis* for business in 2002. What made him feel that this type of *social media* could work as an enterprise solution?

> 'So much interesting stuff was happening in the social space [at that time]. Adrian from Ryze was putting on loft parties in San Francisco and wanted to connect all of his friends in between parties; Dave Siffery created *Technorati*, because he had a problem while he was *blogging*, trying to track and follow all the conversations. Ben and Mena Trott from

Six Apart, Evan Williams from **Blogger**...they all created tools to scratch an itch, to interact with their friends and their community. Even the guy who invented **Trillian**, which is a multiple instant messaging client, did it because he had met this really hot girl on a beach who was using a different network.'

'We had just had the tech bubble collapse and there were a lot of people who were unemployed and that contributed to the amount of people making really cool innovative hacks to solve their own problems. We saw an opportunity because these new tools had much better social dynamics than those we saw in traditional enterprise software. They were lightweight, web native, and it was, in effect, a different platform, compared to the heavy clients.'

Mayfield and his co-founders were keen to take that simplicity and apply it to business. The **SocialText wiki** platform was developed, although initial uptake was confined to the highly tech-literate.

Six years on, Mayfield has seen a massive change in the consumer markets – the growth of **Wikipedia**, **open source** software and **blogging** have meant that 'on the consumer side, the bar is raised higher'. Consumer products genuinely have to work for people, otherwise they won't be used. And issues around intellectual property, libel and confidentiality are beginning to be resolved, 'with thousands of **blogging** policies up on the web for corporate lawyers to pull down and adapt.'

The **SocialText** platform has grown and developed in many ways since 2002. **WYSIWYG** editing, introduced around 2004, was a step forward. But the real tipping point came in 2006, when the rise in popularity of **Wikipedia** meant that there was a surge in demand for **wikis** inside companies. Today **SocialText** has served over 4,000 customers and employs 50 people in offices across the world. The whole user experience is far more transparent and participatory, meaning that 'non-techie' types can access and use the platform with relative ease.

It's important to Mayfield that the development of any corporate **wiki** is in itself collaborative:

'You're trying to keep [any] complexity up on the "social" level rather than baking it down into the software. You're trying to get a really good mix of people sharing and then patterns emerge out of all that sharing and collaboration. The old way that you'd do that is by structuring work flows in enterprise software, where people would fill in the form, click the button and go to the next step in the process. Now what you are trying to do is not have that structure...but let structures emerge as a by-product of people getting their work done.'

Go with the flow

This 'in-the-flow' approach is one I found echoed repeatedly in interviews. It's clear that where people use a tool as an integral part of their work, adoption is a great deal easier. '*Wikis*', '*tagging*' and '*bookmarking*' are still not, quite, every day terms. This sort of behaviour is outside many of our usual workflows. Even if, for example, we already use tools for **bookmarking** (like **Delicious**) or photo-sharing (such as **Flickr**), we might not be all that familiar with the idea of adding *tags* whenever we upload new material; it might be a while before we settle on the nomenclature that feels right for us. Likewise, if we have important information to share, most of us are still more likely to send it in an email rather than put it onto a **wiki**.

'People [are] very much set in their ways of how they actually collaborate and share knowledge,' says Luis Suarez at IBM. '[My team] realised that we needed to move away from the focus on the tools per se, and say "OK, we'll focus on the way that people work. Let's watch and study their behaviours and their patterns and how they actually get things done – focusing on tasks opposed to tools". When we did that switch, man! That was like opening up the people. It was like, "wow! I could have never believed that it was so easy to change this!"'

'The problem with previous approaches, like knowledge management,' says Headshift's Lee Bryant, 'is that we tried to tackle the problem head on explicitly. It was like we were saying to people "you've got these things in your head, please get them out of your head so we can write it down and we'll store it". And people resist! That's "above the flow" knowledge sharing. What you need to create is in the flow, so that knowledge sharing becomes a secondary output of what you do anyway. For example, I'm reading a vast amount of stuff from my **RSS** network and then I write about that stuff or **bookmark** that stuff – all of which takes place in an open configuration. Really what I'm doing is that I'm working, it's my work. Yet now it has the additional consequence of making available a rich body of data for other people to see so I am knowledge sharing but I never sit down and explicitly knowledge share.'

Bryant uses the example of an international law firm where several thousand people may read the same thing and research the same material. Just by connecting these individual tasks together [using Enterprise **RSS**] common interests will surface and connections will be made between what people are doing. Bryant calls it 'a really practical form of collective intelligence.'

Stewart Mader, a **wiki** expert based in San Francisco, believes that once employees get used to these new, social, ways of working, they won't want to go back:

> 'Rank and file employees are often afraid that if they put all their knowledge into a **wiki**, they won't be needed any more – but the opposite is true. If you hold onto your knowledge, all you are is an overpaid security guard. Once you start sharing your knowledge and collaborating with other people you become more valuable to your company. In fact, you're more likely to have your job outsourced when you're not contributing knowledge.'

Are we there, yet?

Mader's point is, on the surface, hard to argue with. But many of us have invested years building up a power base within our company and/or industry. Consciously or unconsciously, this power is usually rooted in some kind of control: of information and of decision-making. Once we feel we've earned the right to this control, we have a natural tendency to keep a hold of it, especially where it matters: we might be happy to give advice to a student, for example, but would we willingly share information with someone who was likely to compete with us for a promotion?

In *The Fifth Discipline*, MIT academic Peter Senge argues that there are a number of 'learning disabilities' which prevent companies from reaching their full potential. These include 'I am my position' (where people only do that which their job description requires), the illusion of taking charge (where 'proactive' behaviour is simply reactive behaviour in disguise) and the myth of the management team (where a team's collective strategy is often focused on maintaining the *appearance* of a cohesive team). These disabilities need to be seen and recognised clearly – but sadly they are 'often lost within the bluster of day-to-day events'.[11]

Senge cites the work of Harvard business theorist Chris Argyris, who observed that management teams, even when composed of intelligent, highly skilled people, could be extremely dysfunctional. The desire to protect the reputation of the team at all costs could lead to the phenomenon of 'skilled incompetence' whereby teams would block out any new learning that was threatening.[12]

As far back as the 1970s, Argyris, working in collaboration with philosopher, Donald Schön, observed a marked difference between people's *espoused theories* and *theories-in-use*. Argyris noted that while people might genuinely believe that they wanted to share information and empower others, the reality was that, in practice, other factors came into play that prevented them from doing so.[13]

An example might be the CEO who says 'Sure, I'd love my workforce to be more empowered and effective!' when, on the ground, a desire to suppress negative emotions, combined with the urgency of short-term goals and a familiarity with doing things the traditional way, cause our CEO to say something like 'I know Jane has some great new ideas but I just need her to reach her sales targets for the week'. The reality here is that working processes continue more or less unchanged, the only difference being Jane's increasing dissatisfaction as she feels, rightly, that her CEO gives out contradictory messages.

A more overt example comes from the need of individuals to instinctively protect their own power bases – reinforcing the knowledge silos. In the 1990s, I worked for a television production company specialising in 'reality' formats such as docu-soaps and talkshows. There was intense rivalry between the teams on different shows as to who got the best stories (and ratings). All the producers and researchers were dependent on the general public to provide interesting, gritty real-life story-lines so, when the Head of Programmes decided we needed a central contacts database, individual programme editors agreed this was a great step forward. In reality, while the editors loved the idea of getting contact details from other teams, none of them wanted to share their own contacts. Predictably, the database flopped because no-one kept it updated.

Senge uses the term 'mental models' to describe the factors that might underlie these contradictory behaviours; Argyris prefers to refer to 'mental maps'. Both terms aim to encapsulate our personal belief systems, thought processes and the way we approach problem-solving. It's clear that we need to be aware of pre-existing mental models. Our theories-in-use, the way we actually plan, review and implement our espoused theories, might provide a key as to why new technologies and tools aren't being assimilated as smoothly as we'd like.

A combination of in-the-flow adoption, intrinsic motivators (as outlined in Chapter 2) and consistent management support would be a great way to drive *social media* uptake internally. I looked at two very different companies, Dresdner Kleinwort and IBM, to see how these ideas had been applied in practice.

Beautiful things

It's October 2008 and I'm in Berlin for the **Web 2.0** Expo Europe. I'm sitting in the auditorium at the Berlin Congress Centre alongside IBM's Luis Suarez and Swiss **blogger**, Jens-Christian Fischer. We're listening to JP Rangaswami talk with passion about how **Web 2.0** is changing the way we communicate at work.

For the past year, Rangaswami has been managing director at BT Design, heading up strategy and innovation. But it was during his previous incarnation as CIO for the British-based investment bank, Dresdner Kleinwort, that he made his mark. In 2007 and 2008, Silicon.com named Rangaswami as one of technology's 50 most influential individuals, describing Dresdner Kleinwort as 'an aggressive leading-edge adopter of innovative and disruptive technologies' – not bad for a company whose roots could be traced back to 1786.[14]

We are living in information-rich times, says Rangaswami. In the past, people didn't bother to set early video cameras (time, date etc.) because it was such a complex process, and certainly nobody bothered to **tag** their videos. Today, you get information about everything – the type of camera, the time, the place, the content. In addition, there's not just the option to post the video online and have a persistent record but you can also share that record with the wider community, so that record gets enriched.

Sharing a work conversation, for example, and moving it around becomes valuable today, Rangaswami is saying. Embedding that within your workflow becomes immensely valuable: 'it's a malleable object you can do beautiful things with'.

Rangaswami is a familiar face to this crowd, as well as a great speaker, and it seems everyone wants a piece of him. After his talk I wait a while before he finally wends his way down to the community lounge for our interview. He's still in reflective mode:

> 'In low attrition, low job-mobility environments, there was a genuine covenant. It made sense to have a consensual style of management. You learnt to take a bullet for the team. And your team would remember. Over time, everything evened out. It was thick ice that you skated over. Consensus was built over long-term relationships.'

This 'covenant' did not only affect teamwork, it also impacted on performance reviews and appraisals. It was all a part of 'institutional memory', as Rangaswami puts it. And this memory was responsible for deciding whether or not the time was right for a pay rise, or if a minor misdemeanour might be overlooked.

> 'Nowadays you get moved around. How do you get that information to be valuable? How do you deal with this new world? The silo structures of the past don't always allow us to access information from wherever we are. Maybe you need to have a *wiki*-like construct, where knowledge becomes a cloud asset?'

In 2001, Rangaswami had just started working as CIO at Dresdner Kleinwort when he started to look at enterprise social software in order to 'solve some leadership problems'.

> 'I found that email was appalling – there were so many "broken trust" implications in it – bcc was evil: "I trust you so much that I'm going to have a conversation with you, with your boss watching, but I'm not going to tell you"; cc was "cover your arse" – the behaviour was appalling again.

> 'I realised this way of records being attached to messages was the wrong way round. We want messages to be attached to the records. Because we'd started getting into this world where email was being characterised by these huge file attachments. Instead, invert that.

> 'So I started looking at the problems I had and ways to find solutions to them. How can I build consistent communication? How can I make it shareable across the globe? How can I allow for cultural and linguistic differences? Could I use a *Wikipedia* type construct so that I can translate, so that I could have multi-lingual definitions of the same term? Could I use IM to capture conference talk in such a way that the linguistic risk is reduced? Could I use *blogs* as a way of opening up conversations?'

As Global CIO, Rangaswami was responsible for a communications network of 6,000 employees across 35 countries. The way he saw it, the problems at Dresdner Kleinwort were caused by four key things:

1. Attrition (the high rate of staff turnover)
2. The high mobility of staff in roles and locations within the firm
3. Cultural differences – the same word meaning different things
4. Linguistic differences – the meaning of words being lost in translation

In 2002, Rangaswami started a *blog* internally, which he used to champion *wikis* and other *social tools* as the new way forward ('I felt the school of leadership that I wanted to follow was a soft-spoken influencing style rather than dictatorial'). By 2005, he had overseen the company-wide rollout of an internal **blogging** tool, **wiki**-building software (using the **SocialText** platform) and a group messaging software that combined email with instant messaging to facilitate ongoing collaboration over projects.

These were significant changes and Rangaswami believes he was successful for four reasons: Firstly, Dresdner Kleinwort's management had a reputation for being reasonably enlightened: the company had 360 degree performance reviews for example, so there was already a culture of 'listening', where feedback was encouraged. Secondly, Rangaswami decided to introduce just one central **wiki** so that connections were made that wouldn't have happened otherwise – private workspaces were available only on special request. Thirdly, he persuaded a handful of key groups and individuals to start **blogging** and creating **wiki** pages so that interest gently built up by word of mouth (electronic or actual) over time, rather than in a formal, company-wide roll-out. Finally, Rangaswami ensured he had strong support from senior management, many of whom did what they could to get the ball rolling.[15]

Darren Lennard, Dresdner Kleinwort's managing director, initially tried to get employees involved by starting a new **wiki** page containing a mission statement, and then emailing everyone to tell them about the **wiki** and suggesting they added content. When nothing happened, Lennard had to rethink his approach:

> 'I realized that I had to be a lot more directive if I wanted behaviours to change. And I also had to put up **wiki** content that required users to get involved.'

Lennard then posted an agenda and action items for a meeting, inviting responses via the **wiki** and not forgetting a crucial point: he told his assistant to inform people that he would no longer be reading email on certain topics.[16]

For Rangaswami, the approach was instinctively hands-off: for example, he was happy to allow employees to set up a poker club and ask each other for advice on camcorders, as long as it meant they were using the new tools. He also felt there was no need for any kind of formal policy on conduct as the wider organisational culture would have already set boundaries for employees.

While the impact of the internal **blogging** system was gentle rather than revolutionary (in the first year there were just 200 posts and 330 comments),[17] Rangaswami won numerous accolades for his work. As well as recognition from Silicon.com, he was named Waters Magazine CIO of the Year 2003 and The European Technology Forum's CIO Innovator of the Year 2004.

Rangaswami was at Dresdner Kleinwort for nearly ten years. He became CIO in 2001, around the time of the global stock market downturn, and was tasked with cutting the IT budget by 40 per cent. People looked to him to bring radical change to the organisation. His views were experimental for the time – not dissimilar to those of consultants like Ellis, Bryant and Mayfield – but because of his position, Rangaswami was able to put his ideas into practice. Like Davis and Moore in Chapter 1, Rangaswami behaved much in the way of the 'catalyst' described in *The Starfish & The Spider*: the 'inspirational figure who spurs others to action'.[18]

Rangaswami was a relatively new member of staff at Dresdner Kleinwort when he began his programme of change. In other cases, the catalyst can be an established voice within the organisation. One example is IBM – a massive global company that has moved forward in leaps and bounds because it has proved willing to allow individual employees to experiment.

Inverting the pyramid

IBM is a sponsor of the **Web 2.0** Expo in Berlin, so maybe it's no surprise that members of its **social media** team pop up all over the place. On the first day, Vice President of Social Software Programs and Enablement, Gina Poole, is running a session on **Web 2.0** at work.

It's standing room only in Poole's session and I'm a few minutes late so I get to perch on some steps behind a pillar and listen to her voice. Luckily her voice is great – maternal, soothing and full of enthusiasm. Poole is telling the story of Jeannette Browning, an IBM employee who was singled out and praised for adapting social software (**Lotus Connection** Activities/**Lotus Notes**) to help her sales team, and then was so chuffed by the recognition/acknowledgement of her efforts that she started creating lots of 'enablement' materials to help other IBMers do similar stuff.

When Poole and I chat over lunch in the Community Lounge afterwards, it becomes clear that this kind of 'social pyramid selling' is something she loves to orchestrate. In her time with the company (and there's been 25 years of it – she started out as a programmer in 1984), Poole has set up various **social** *media* programmes (BlueIQ, which promotes social software internally, is the latest); and launched a start up, the developerWorks community.

Like Rangaswami, Poole uses evangelists to create a positive buzz about a tool before it becomes corporate-wide. A common factor behind Poole's projects has been the use of volunteers in driving things forward. The BlueIQ ambassadors, for example, are 700 people who've offered to promote social software throughout the organisation, simply because they believe in it. Poole loves to build momentum and consensus by using champions to introduce something new.

> 'Taking risks is really important. Try an idea out by getting some early adopters, some enthusiasts. Then if it's a success, communicate that broadly to those early adopters – they're going to want to talk about their success story. Make them the "poster children" of your campaign. Make them the rock stars. Don't just evangelise the project, say "look at what it did for this individual". Success breeds success.'

Poole is softly spoken and exudes charm; she clearly enjoys her job and loves meeting people. So, how would she describe her leadership style?

> 'More pure leadership than command-and-control…in the old management era, knowledge was power. Now in the social era you want to unleash the knowledge. The powerful person is the one who can lead by influence. You don't need a big budget and lots of direct reports. I can lead more effectively by influencing others, getting them excited and having them join my movement. It feels like you're managing more of a matrix. Listening is very important.'

And why has *social media* become so important?

> 'People like to share – that's one of the most powerful things. This sharing creates "weak ties" you can build on. I'm interested in helping people get outside of their inboxes [echoing the IBM mantra kicked off by Luis Suarez]. People start mixing and matching things in ways that management would never dream of. The end result of bringing projects together, that serendipitous stumbling across things is very powerful. Like connecting the dots. It's a great way to break down silos: "oh, you're doing that, so am I. Let's work together"…things tend to go in directions you'd never expect.'

Life was very different when Poole started at IBM back in the 1980s:

'When I joined IBM it was very hierarchical and things moved very slowly. It was tough for good ideas to bubble up. We went through a near-death experience. Then Lou Gerstner came in [as CEO]. That was a great catalyst for a change in focus. Since then, management has become more participatory. We turned the management pyramid on its side and then on its head. Now we're really harnessing creative capital and social capital.'

One of the ironies of social software is that, even at a technology company like IBM, people consider it to be 'new' and therefore potentially scary and difficult to use, but the beauty of **social tools** is that they're actually quite intuitive and simple. The premise of most **social networks** – 'only connect' – taps into that primitive need to share, contribute and belong identified by Abraham Maslow (and discussed in Chapter 2). **Social tools** simply help us do what we've all been doing for a very long time.

The birds and the bees

It's 1862, and the naturalist Charles Darwin is in his kitchen garden at Down House in Kent, South-East England. Darwin is standing stock still between the beds of orchids, primroses and cowslips, observing a honey bee which has landed softly on one of the flowers and is now busy gathering pollen grains from the petals.

In a few moments, he will turn and make his way back up the garden path, through the back door and into his study, where he'll add the finishing touches to the manuscript of his soon to be published book, *The Various Contrivances by which Orchids Are Fertilized by Insects*. This book has been written as evidence to support his theory of evolution outlined in *The Origin of Species*, which he's published three years previously.

Through his research at Down House, in the place he calls his 'experimental bed', Darwin has found that many species of orchid owe their elaborate flower structure to natural selection – these structures have evolved to facilitate cross-pollination. Furthermore, he's discovered that orchids and the insects that carry their pollen have evolved by interacting with one another over many generations – this process he refers to as co evolution.

It's another hundred years until the world's first computer network will be established, but Darwin is practicing an early form of **crowdsourcing** to help his research. Despite spending nearly all his time at Down House, either in his study or in the kitchen garden, he is in constant communication with the outside world. Darwin claims to write eight to ten letters a day (around 7,000 of these survive and are held in an archive at Cambridge University). He uses these letters to co-ordinate international research, exploring everything from plant reproduction to human origins for *The Descent of Man* (1871).

In 1831, Darwin had been recommended by his tutor at Cambridge for a self-funded place on the second voyage of HMS Beagle, a scientific expedition to South America which took nearly five years to complete. During the voyage he befriended a number of diplomats, missionaries and fellow scientists. Now he is able to write to this network of friends around the world — and ask them to tap into their own networks.

This research covers all countries in the British Empire (approaching its peak in the mid nineteenth century) as well as the Americas. For example, the Brazilian-based botanist, Fritz Muller, sends Darwin exotic seeds, which he then sends on to contacts in other parts of the world for comparison and comment. Bizarre objects are frequently attached to the letters (there is one in the archive in Cambridge University Library from New Zealand; it still has squashed bees taped to the paper).

One scientific discovery concerns dried specimens of a long-tubed white orchid native to Madagascar (it is to presume that Darwin received these dried flowers in a package via his network); the orchid's flower has a 30 cm long tubular spur with a small drop of nectar at the base. Darwin is convinced that this orchid has been pollinated by a moth with a foot-long tongue, a claim which is ridiculed by some of his peers. But many years later (around the turn of the century), a Madagascan moth with a foot-long tongue will be discovered.

Thus correspondence (the *social media* of its day) was immensely important to Darwin's scientific discoveries. And Darwin was impressed by the quality of the information that his contacts gathered and delivered to him. They were motivated not by financial reward, but simply for the sake of reciprocation and communal discovery (sound familiar?). Darwin's biographer, Jim Moore, notes that he was very good at getting people to do what he wanted simply by being extremely appreciative of the help they offered him.

As Darwin writes to his friend, John Jenner Weir in 1868: 'If any man wants to gain a good opinion of his fellow men, he ought to do what I'm doing, pester them with letters.'[19]

It is not only his global network that Darwin uses for *crowdsourcing*. He also makes full use of his *social network* at home. Whenever a baby is born in the Darwins' circle of friends, it's Darwin (not his wife, Emma) who sends the card of congratulations – a questionnaire contained within it. This questionnaire asks about facial emotions, which Darwin then relates back not only to the origins of racial differences but also to expressions of sorrow and fear in young animals.

'Science obsesses itself with trifles', observes geneticist Steve Jones during BBC Radio 4's season to celebrate Darwin's birth. He describes Darwin's central theme as 'the enormous power of small means'.[20]

This theme ties in nicely with **Web 2.0**'s emphasis on **network effects**. We can only wonder, if Darwin had had the sort of data possessed by Google at his fingertips, what else he might have discovered.

Keystone corps

It's a bright, sunny afternoon at the Googleplex, Google's headquarters in Mountain View, California. In between the white and glass buildings that house the offices, swathes of green grass and neatly trimmed hedges offer relaxing spaces to chill out or eat lunch in. Red, blue and yellow umbrellas and seating add a Google-branded completeness to the landscape.

Every so often a Googler speeds past on a bright yellow JacMac Scooter, off to the next meeting or, possibly, one of Google's many free talks – maybe a 'Google University' lecture, a 'TechTalk' or an Authors@Google seminar (this week it's Sci-fi writer Neal Stephenson). You won't see many cars here. But there is space for nearly 2,000 of them underground. The 26 acre Googleplex includes public trails and a 5 acre public park – a spirit of space and leisure pervades.

I'm looking out on all this from the corner cafeteria of 'Building 47', where I'm sitting with Matt Glotzbach, Product Management Director, Google Enterprise. Even indoors, it's impossible to forget where you are. Red, green, blue and yellow prevails – cups, plates, notice boards, chairs…even the lava lamps are all 'on message'. All this is exactly as you might expect.

> 'We've become a strong brand, a household name,' agrees Glotzbach. 'We're a mainstay, a staple, in all our users' lives. Most people know about and use Google in some form or another.'

Google makes great **Web 2.0** products, but it's also the definitive **Web 2.0** company. Its structure and strategy are built on the principle of **network effects**.

Google exemplifies what Harvard academic Marco Iansiti and consultant Roy Levien have described as the 'keystone advantage' – this term is taken directly from biological ecosystems where 'keystone' species are those that maintain the healthy functioning of the entire system because their own survival depends on it. Google is positioned not only to help foster the health of the system, its lynch-pin role means that it benefits more than most from that system's good health.

> 'Because every transaction is performed through the Google platform', write Iansiti and Levien, 'the company has perfect, continuous awareness of, and access to, by-product information and is the hub of all germinal revenue streams. There's no need for Google to do market surveys and statistical analyses to forecast trends in the ecosystem; the information is already in Google's database.'[21]

Its usefulness means that Google is in the enviable position of being seen as trustworthy by consumers, and it doesn't need to do anything underhand to obtain this invaluable information. Unlike other large monopolistic companies, Google is unusual in that it is generally liked and respected by its user base ('if we ever lost user confidence, we'd cease to exist in a very short time', agrees Glotzbach).

Today, says Glotzbach, Google's sheer weight of users and its advertising income combine to enable it to watch – and follow – virtually every trend on the horizon. The business looks – at this stage – invincible. In the foyer of Building 47, a monitor suspended above the welcome desk displays key words being typed into Google as we speak: Lehmans...Britney Spears...Kentucky... Goats cheese...Indian Monsoons...Motorcycle. You get the sense that the thoughts of the world are ticking away – and they're all passing through Google's search engine.

Knowledge permeates every aspect of Google: whether it is in the information fed into the company by consumers or the ideas generated and added into the system by employees. The '20 per cent rule' discussed in Chapter One and Google's infamous 'don't be evil' mission statement have both been part of the culture from day one. Google is a textbook innovator, and a key part of its strategy is to make sure its employees love working there.

> 'One of the things embodied at Google is empowerment,' says Glotzbach. 'And that doesn't mean that a governance model and a decision making structure and process don't exist, they do, they're just not strictly top-down dictated. People respond well to empowerment,

they rise to the occasion. Google is lucky that we weren't starting out with decades of legacy. We were a new company, 10 years old. We got to start that way and then maintain [the empowering structure] as we got bigger.'

Now Google is turning its innovative focus to 'apps' – software applications – and specifically those that can be used within the enterprise. As Glotzbach and I talk the web community is buzzing with talk about Chrome (Google's new web browser) and Android (its mobile phone operating system); in a few months time **Google Wave** (a **realtime** communications tool) will launch – creating a whole new surge of hype and anticipation. It's hard to imagine that just a few years ago, when Glotzbach started at Google, search and advertising (**AdWords** and **AdSense**) were the only products.

'When I talk to Eric [Schmidt, CEO] and Larry [Page, co-founder] and Sergey [Brin, co-founder], they say that Enterprise has always been in the plan. It arguably got delayed a few years while the ads businesses really sky rocketed to success but it's always been part of the core strategy. Now there's been a refocus. Enterprise is now the second largest business at Google, behind the ads. And I like to say that we're going to create the second "large" business.'

Glotzbach believes the time is right. Internet connectivity is near ubiquitous in developed countries, and **cloud computing** has hit a maturity point. He points to the fact that, four or five years ago, if we used an application in a web browser, there was a heavy penalty. The application was less stable, slower. Now not only is web based software arguably as good as software based on a desktop, in a lot of ways it's better, because what you do is enabled by the processing power of the web:

'It's just a better user experience,' says Glotzbach. 'If you use Gmail, like I do for work, I have 14 gig of email and I can do a search on my email and find messages from the day I started at Google in less than a second. I couldn't make 14 gig of mail work on my local computer, let alone search and find the right things.'

General problems of email aside, Gmail's search capability and anti-spam software has certainly made it one of Google's most popular applications. Again, Google has 'keystone advantage' – it is simply so ubiquitous in the consumer world, especially for teenagers and students, that corporate clients now want a Googlesque 'flavour' to their IT infrastructure:

'[Business culture] is naturally changing as the new workforce comes in. My new project manager is straight from university...the only model he knows is the open-based, collaborative sharing type. We talk to a lot of companies who say one of the reasons they want to bring Google apps into their environment is because they are trying to attract a certain type of talent to their company, and one aspect of attracting that younger talent is giving them the kinds of tools that they would already use on their own.'

Everyone at Google's primary-coloured complex seems young – from the receptionist, to the press officer that accompanies me, to Glotzbach himself. Maybe it's just the setting, sunshine and pervasive optimism, but there is a touch of *Logan's Run* (the 1976 sci-fi film where people die at 30) about the place. Still, the company is only ten years old, and if Google is about to embark on the Next Big Thing, it's no surprise that the world's brightest technology graduates flock here.

Glotzbach loves the correlation drawn by technology journalist Nicolas Carr between electricity and **cloud computing** in his 2008 book, *The Big Switch*:

> 'The ubiquity of electricity fundamentally changed the way we live and **cloud computing** has the opportunity to do that again. We no longer work in silos: we're constantly sharing information whether it be through email or through multiple people collaborating on a document or a web page. It's all about collaboration and team work. Even just 10 years ago, people spent a lot of time asking, I've got a company here and a company over here and they want to work together? How do we share IT systems? How does this company send mail to this company? Obviously standardisation has solved that problem. Now information flows easily: if I want to send a document to you, I can do it from my phone, for God's sake! The corporate boundaries are fading away.'

If Google Enterprise produces anything even half as successful as **AdWords** (which generated £12.5 billion revenue in 2008), Glotzbach and his colleagues will no doubt be very happy. Although **cloud computing** has its disadvantages – there are still unresolved security issues, for example – the move from pc-based to online or **Cloud** working is seen as the next phase for the internet industry. From what Glozbach says, the data contained in the cloud is going to spark the next big workplace revolution. And, what's more, the web visionaries seem to agree.

The house that Tim built

When Tim O'Reilly's colleague Dale Dougherty coined the term **Web 2.0** back in 2004, and O'Reilly picked it up as a useful meme to throw out to O'Reilly Media's conference audiences, they had little idea how the concept would spread like wildfire through the digital media world. With the onset of global recession, a handful of 'Web 2.0 Expos' were cancelled in 2009, but in 2008 they were still in full swing, attracting tens of thousands of delegates from across the world.

When I bump into O'Reilly in the Javits Centre foyer at the **Web 2.0** Expo New York in September 2008, he invites me to come with him as he heads to the main hall to rehearse his keynote. After the run-through, we get some time to sit and chat in front of the stage. O'Reilly says that **network effects** are the real game changer when it comes to corporate learning:

> 'You design applications that get better the more people use them, then the applications that work get the most user data. The winners are those that harvest collective intelligence: Amazon, Google...Google is actually harvesting the intelligence of all users.
>
> 'When I started looking at all the companies that had survived the .com bust, they had all in one way or another harnessed collective intelligence. So, for example, eBay, they built a marketplace with buyers and sellers where the users were the application. Amazon worked harder than any other e-commerce vendor to get their users to annotate their database with comments, reviews and ratings. Google, they realised that there was literally hidden meaning on every link on the web. Google is harnessing the intelligence of all the users. '

So, what does O'Reilly think business needs to do, today, to make the most of the web's capabilities?

> 'Enterprise needs to learn about **realtime** responsiveness to its users. Banks have a tremendous amount of data about their users – but they don't share it with us. They actually have data that is continually updated. For example, every time you go to a merchant and swipe your credit card, you're adding to your database in the same way that every time that someone clicks on a link they're adding to Google's database. So what's the difference? Banks have big data centres and the fact is they do not make **realtime** user facing services against that data. For example, when you swipe your credit card, it doesn't say, "Hey, you've spent enough this month!"'

O'Reilly tells me about Wesabe (a kind of personal finance **wiki** – where you upload your entire bank account and credit card info, and get advice from other users on your spending habits). He believes every business needs to be thinking about what data assets it owns and how it can use them:

> 'One of the things that I suggest to any company is what data assets do you own and how can you build new fresh data services against that data? I think a lot of traditional businesses have enormous data assets, they just need a slightly different mindset.'

What's wrong with the current business mindset? O'Reilly believes that a great deal of time is being wasted on tasks that could – and should – be automated.

> 'First of all it's the idea that you do things [manually] in the back office. For example, you may have your people who are studying the analytics for your business and making decisions. But if you look at how Google operates, you realise that you can't operate at that level; it's got to be automatic.'

Who does O'Reilly really admire in business today?

> 'Wal-Mart is a great example. Some people haven't put this together, they might say that you are stretching **Web 2.0** too far, but Wal-Mart has immense automation. If you take something off the shelf at Wal-Mart it triggers something. They're automated in the same way that Google is automated. I guess the point I would make is IT is a central competency of corporations like these – it changes from being a back office function to really being the nervous system of the entire operation.

> 'Look at the growth of Zappo's [the online shoe store]. It recently hit revenues of $1billion. Tony Shieh, the CEO, has become a hero...Jeff Bezos [Amazon.com] is also very strategic. He's thought a lot about how the world is going to change. Who'd have thought that getting into cloud services would make sense, but Amazon web services (providing hosting to **Flickr** etc.) has become a great sideline.'

O'Reilly inspired the **BarCamp** phenomenon and triggered worldwide uptake of the 2.0 meme. I wouldn't want to argue with his predictions on business.

It's true that Amazon has done a great job in reinventing its competitive edge through **Web 2.0**'s Silicon Valley renaissance. Even eBay has managed to sustain itself, despite being criticised in the industry for lacking imagination. Among the three surviving giants of the last dotcom boom: Yahoo! is the one most considered to be a poor relation. Yahoo! came out of Stanford University, the same stable as Google, but has somehow fallen by the wayside, a victim of early success and over-fast expansion.

Like Google, Yahoo! spent the mid 2000s on the acquisition route, buying up small successful *Web 2.0* companies like Kelkoo, *Flickr*, *Upcoming* and *Delicious*. Unlike Google, it doesn't have cool knowledge management sprinkled quite so liberally through its DNA, but it nonetheless employs some very smart people.

Looking for the next big thing

It's only 9am Pacific Standard Time but Tom Coates is having a stressful day. He relocated to San Francisco from the UK six months ago and this weekend his entire family are coming to visit. Last night, his parents flew in from London. In a few hours, he has to pick up his younger brother from the airport. In between he needs to tidy the whole apartment. And then he has to find the time to speak to me.

I only know all of this because I've been reading Coates's *Twitter* updates. During our *Skype* chat, Coates is politeness personified, and there's no mention of all this other stuff. Maybe because he's already vented his stress via *Twitter*. Still, it's weird, seeing a 360 degree picture of someone you've never met.

Coates is not only busy at home; he's working flat-out at Yahoo!, where for the last 18 months he's been developing start-up projects. He is currently head of product on Fire Eagle, a location monitoring application. Needless to say, he still finds time to *blog* (www.plasticbag.com), and to think about 'being progressive and doing something new', which is how he loosely describes his role at Yahoo!

Coates puts the whole *Web 2.0/social media* phenomenon into context:

> 'There is always something going on which is really exciting, but under the surface, most of these next big things are part of a larger trend... There's always been social software of a kind, from message boards on *Telnet* through to email and mailing lists...human collaboration and communication have been big questions since the dawn of time. The only novelty here is that every few years we find an interesting new angle, a new way of approaching it.'

While Coates feels that social software is 'kind of exhausted' in terms of industry development, he thinks Glotzbach's and O'Reilly's points about data are bang on the money:

> 'Web of data stuff is newer. A website is just a front page for the creation and organisation and distribution of data beneath it. What we're seeing now is that data can be sent from one area to another and be re-purposed and connected together and we're seeing how information can flow through that…we've seen a different model appearing that has really kicked the collaborative possibilities further.'

Social media are just the thin end of the wedge. And the cracks we are seeing in rigid organisational structures today are only the beginning. There's no such thing as too much data, says Coates, and it's inevitable that traditional hierarchies will buckle under the weight: a 'weblike' system is essential for good information management – the sooner we start moving in this direction, the better.

Harvest time

The fact that all this potential for exponential learning is now at our fingertips is tremendously exciting. The idea of us all contributing meaning as we work is quite liberating – especially as the data we contribute will create genuinely useful processes and structures rather than ones that have been assembled, in retrospect, somewhat haphazardly. Within organisations, we need people in the mould of JP Rangaswami and Gina Poole – people who genuinely get a kick out of empowering others, and then have the confidence to sit back and let things happen.

With the boom in data-based services, we will face other issues: who owns the data, for example – doesn't the customer have rights to the information they create? It's likely that we'll see further convergence and blurring of boundaries as our world becomes more fluid, says Matt Glotzbach at Google: 'These days, especially in technology, your partners are also your customers, are also your competitors – all at the same time. It's a much more dynamic environment.'

Will the prosumer (people who produce as well as consume) soon be eclipsed by some other hideously portmanteau character – the 'boss-tomer', for example? Or maybe Headshift's Lee Bryant is right and it's all okay: the fact is we will have just come full circle: we'll all be selling to our 'friends'. In that case, what might we possibly have to hide? And what might be the benefit in holding anything back? That's the question I'll explore more fully in the next chapter, 'Openness'.

Notes

1. www.joelonsoftware.com/items/2006/08/08.html
2. Seth Godin (2008), *Tribes*. Piatikus, p. 48.
3. In *Nudge: Improving Decisions About Health, Wealth and Happiness* (Yale University Press, 2008), Richard H Thaler and Cass R Sunstein argued for a greater use of 'nudges' in public policy – interventions that encourage rather than mandate certain types of behaviour.
4. www.joelonsoftware.com/items/2006/08/08.html
5. The examination system for British civil servants was based on the Chinese imperial examination system – this is discussed in more detail in Derk Bodde (1948), *Chinese Ideas in the West*. American Council on Education.
6. Art Fritzson; Lloyd W. Howell and Dov S. Zakheim, 'Military of Millennials', *Strategy + Business* magazine, Issue 49, Winter 2007.
7. Suw Charman-Anderson, 'Breaking the email compulsion', *The Guardian*, 28 August 2008 – see chapter 6 for an interview with Charman-Anderson.
8. www.nytimes.com/2008/06/29/jobs/29pre.html
9. Tim Berners-Lee quoted by Victoria Shannon: 'A "more revolutionary" Web', *International Herald Tribune*, 23 May 2006.
10. James Harkin, 'Losing The Plot', *The Observer*, 22 March 2009 (www.guardian.co.uk/film/2009/mar/22/21-grams-memento-pulp-fiction).
11. Peter M. Senge (1990), *The Fifth Discipline: The Art & Practice of the Learning Organisation*. Random House, pp. 17-25 and p. 26.
12. *ibid*, p. 25.
13. The distinction between espoused theories and theories-in-use was first outlined in M. Argyris and D. Schön, *Theory in Practice: Increasing professional effectiveness* (Jossey-Bass, San Francisco, 1974) – and has informed much of Argyris' work since.
14. Dresdner Kleinwort was formed in 1995 when Dresdner Bank (Germany) acquired Kleinwort Benson (UK). The roots of Kleinwort Benson date back to 1786 when Hinrich Kleinwort and Robert Benson set up their respective financing companies. The bank suffered in the global economic downturn 2008 and some units closed; it was acquired by Commerzbank in December 2008. Dresdner Kleinwort's remaining businesses were rebranded as part of Commerzbank in September 2009 (en.wikipedia.org/wiki/Dresdner Kleinwort).
15. These four points are adapted from the key points outlined by Harvard academic Andrew McAfee: Andrew P. McAfee, 'Enterprise 2.0: The Dawn of Emergent Collaboration', *MIT Sloan Management Review*, Spring 2006, Vol.47, No.3 (PDF downloaded from sloanreview.mit.edu/the-magazine/articles/2006/spring/47306/enterprise-the-dawn-of-emergent-collaboration).
16. *ibid* (Lennard quote).
17. *ibid.*
18. Ori Brafman and Rod Beckstrom (2006). *The Starfish And The Spider: The Unstoppable Power of Leaderless Organizations*. Penguin, p. 93.
19. BBC Radio 4, 'Life After Origins' (Darwin: *In Our Time*, episode 4, broadcast 8 January 2009).
20. All the information about Darwin came from the BBC Radio 4 series, *In Our Time*, during the Darwin season, and from the science website: science.jrank.org/pages/5389/Pollination-History-pollination-studies.html
21. Bala Iyer & Thomas H. Davenport, 'Reverse Engineering Google's Innovation Machine', *Harvard Business Review*, Article, 1 April 2008, pp. 5-6.

4. Openness

Myth: We don't need to be transparent

Reality: Your competitors are more open

Consultant Dominic Campbell lives what he calls a 'declarative lifestyle'. With a presence on multiple *social networks* (he uses *Facebook*, *Twitter*, *LinkedIn*, *Flickr*, *YouTube* and *Last.fm*, among others), Campbell is the first to admit he holds little mystery. It's easy for anyone who might be interested to go online and find out what he did last night, where he goes on holiday, what he studied at university and the names of his closest friends.

> 'There's no longer a need for false identities now,' says Campbell. 'Why can't we just be the one person that we're really comfortable with? Currently, work makes you act differently and pretend that you're someone else. These tools are helping us to break down those barriers and start being human beings again at work, which can only be a good thing.'

It's a steamy summer evening at The Royal Society of Arts, London, and Campbell is getting a little hot under the collar. He has been invited to defend his position in front of a panel of cultural experts under the topic 'Private Lives – A Thing of The Past?' The panelists: Matthew Taylor of the RSA, Claire Fox from the Institute of Ideas, political commentator Iain Dale and journalist Stephen Whittle take it in turns to pick holes in his argument.

The conversation goes something like this:

> **Whittle:** In a previous life you might have been described as an exhibitionist. Why don't you care?

> **Campbell:** There are major benefits through revealing yourself online like this. I'm the kind of person who tries to live a really honest lifestyle. I'm trying to break down the barriers. Everyone goes to work and 'acts', but I don't feel I have to be a different person at work to the one I am at home.

> **Taylor:** You're young, idealistic and pure – can you not see any moment in your life when you won't want to be like this?

Campbell: I can see that once you've started on this path, you're effectively trapped and there's no way out later. I guess it's unlikely I'll ever get to be a politician.

Fox: One of the great advantages of our modern cities is that we've moved away from the 'curtain-twitching' of the village. You seem to be doing your best to replicate village life – with yourself as the village idiot. Do you really have to grow up in front of the rest of us?

Campbell: No-one has to look at this stuff if they don't want to. I'm talking to my friends. No-one else needs to care. *Tweets* [updates on *Twitter*] can be inane and pointless.

Dale: If they're pointless, what's the point?

Fox: Don't you see that this is demeaning to yourself?

Campbell: I probably don't have an answer to that. In many ways it's about being a micro-celebrity – and that's the celebrity of the modern world.

Each panelist seems to be at least ten years older than Campbell, so maybe that's the reason why they simply don't seem to understand why he's doing this. When the debate opens up to comments from the floor, the generation gap is palpable.

A young man with an asymmetric haircut, who looks in his early twenties, says he uses *social media* for self-discovery: 'I guess I represent *Generation Y* – I'm searching for an identity, for love and affirmation'.

Meanwhile, an elderly man in a grey suit is agitated: 'We've crossed the boundary between public and private in such a way that we're heading for calamity!'

The reality lies somewhere between these two extremes. The web may not be as benign – or as regulated – as a sixth form disco, but nor is it a vipers' nest. Some argue that the trajectory is circular rather than perpendicular: we are returning to the village culture of the past, now it's simply on a global scale. They believe this is a positive step because it means people will watch out for each other.[1] Others say that there is nothing to be afraid of – they point to the fact that Millennials like Campbell are actually developing a sophisticated understanding of what distinguishes a 'public personal life' from the genuinely private.[2]

It's true that there are reasons to be wary. We might be happy to display all sorts of personal information online, but we feel uncomfortable and threatened when third parties collect similar information for their own purposes. In the workplace, for example, there has been a huge increase in employee monitoring: in 2008, spending on security software rose by nearly 20 per cent – and the global security software market is expected to be worth more than £13 billion in 2010.[3] For some years now, groups such as Privacy International have lobbied governments and businesses across the world in an effort to ensure our right to personal privacy is protected. In an article entitled 'The Dark Age of Transparency', mobile consultant Benjamin Joffe expressed deep concern about surveillance and privacy invasions and warned that even people 'with nothing to hide' need to be vigilant.[4]

But in the words of another 'witness' at the RSA debate, Tom Ilube (CEO of online identity company, Garlik), we need to accept that this futurist scenario tinged with elements of George Orwell's 1984 is already here: our energies should be focused on managing it constructively: 'The debate about whether it can be stopped, reined in, or whether it's good or bad, is irrelevant.'

The real-life panopticon

Campbell works as a consultant, so an 'open' approach makes him appear friendly and accessible while garnering him plenty of free publicity. Most of his clients already know him in a social as well as a professional capacity, so the revelation that he enjoys a drink and loves dance music, for example, will come as no surprise. Moreover, we appear to be at a point in history where mistakes, misdemeanours, and indiscretions are becoming an accepted part of everyone's make up: when the leader of the UK Conservative Party, David Cameron, chose to neither confirm nor deny that he had taken illegal substances during his youth,[5] a minor turning point was marked in British politics. Cameron is media-savvy enough to know that if he denies anything, the hunt will be on to 'expose' him; if he simply shrugs his shoulders as if to say 'so what if I did?', the majority of people won't actually care enough to pursue the issue further.

At times, a shoulder shrug is all that's needed, in other situations a full apology – or more – may be required. The trick in today's all-seeing media environment is not to be good at 'burying bad news' – we all know that's fighting a losing battle – but to be skilled at responding appropriately when bad news surfaces.

In 2005, the writer and futurist Jamais Cascio made a pertinent prediction at the MeshForum conference in Chicago: soon we will be living in a world of near omniscient surveillance, he said, and the sooner we accept that, the better.

> 'This won't simply be a world of a single, governmental Big Brother watching over your shoulder, nor will it be a world of a handful of corporate siblings training their ever-vigilant security cameras and *tags* on you. Such monitoring may well exist...but it will be overwhelmed by the millions of cameras and recorders in the hands of millions of Little Brothers and Little Sisters. We will carry with us the tools of our own transparency, and many, perhaps most, will do so willingly, even happily.'[6]

Cascio called this world the 'participatory panopticon', after the circular prison designed by English philosopher Jeremy Bentham in 1785.[7] Bentham derived the name 'panopticon' from the Latin: observe (-opticon) all (pan-). The intention behind his design was that guards could see everything the prisoners were doing, without the prisoners being aware that they were being watched. In *Discipline and Punish: the birth of the prison* (1975), French philosopher Michel Foucault saw the panopticon as a metaphor for modern authoritarian society. Foucault argued that all hierarchical structures (the army, school, hospitals, factories) resembled the panopticon. He believed that the 'docile bodies' produced by discipline were perfectly suited to the modern industrial age.[8]

Luckily, we no longer live in an age where total compliance is so desirable. In the 21st century, argued Cascio, we are not only subjects of surveillance, we are also the active engineers of our own *'sousveillance'* – literally, 'watching from below'. Today, as far as communications and publishing are concerned, the means of production are in our hands. Anyone who owns a mobile phone or digital camera can capture and upload images and video footage. Anyone who can work a keyboard can go online and make their opinions known. So, yes, CCTV and digital databases may be recording our everyday movements, but we also have the power to contribute our own points of view. Wouldn't we all like to play a part in that? If we are all being watched, isn't it time we learnt how to handle our role as participants and 'co-watchers'?

Keep calm and carry on

The term *'digital shadow'* was coined in an IDC report in 2008[9] and refers to the data you leave unintentionally as you browse online (leaving *cookies*), make a purchase using a credit card, or are filmed on security cameras. A presence on any public records, including those of the local police department, would make up a part of this shadow. The shadow is the passive part of your *digital footprint*, which is the overall mass of digital information there is about you, including details you might actively post online via *social networks*, discussion forums or *blog* posts.

Alessandro Acquisti and Ralph Gross, academics at Carnegie Mellon University, defined online *social networks* as 'the eternal memory of our indiscretions'.[10] And it's true that, (to appropriate the UK's 1940 wartime propaganda slogan), careless talk costs livelihoods. Today, it's standard practice for employers to enter potential employees' names into Google's search engine. And in many cases, the personal information you actively leave on *social networks* can be just as damaging as unintentional information.

The marketing expert Seth Godin once told the story of a friend of his who was looking for a housekeeper and advertised on the classified advertising site, *craigslist*. Three CVs came to the top of the pile, and the friend ran the names through Google:

> 'The first search turned up a *MySpace* page. There was a picture of the applicant, drinking beer from a funnel. Under hobbies, the first entry was, "binge drinking."...The second search turned up a personal *blog* (a good one, actually). The most recent entry said something like, "I am applying for some menial jobs that are below me, and I'm annoyed by it. I'll certainly quit the minute I sell a few paintings."...And the third? There were only six matches, and the sixth was from the local police department, indicating that the applicant had been arrested for shoplifting two years earlier.'[11]

It's no surprise that managing personal brands online is big business: an online search of the term will bring up a million results. While it makes sense to be consistent and opportunistic if your focus is building a personal brand (for example, decide on your message and repeat it as often as possible), many managers and CEOs are looking for more nuanced approach: the tone on a corporate *blog*, for example, might be quite different from that on a personal one, while your 'followers' on *Twitter* might be more work-orientated than your 'friends' on *Facebook*.

Multiple profile (dis)order

If you choose to publish a variety of information online, the best way to keep certain aspects of your life relatively private is to maintain more than one online identity, either by using different email addresses for different accounts, or by setting up very distinct profiles, and keeping them separate. As musician

Dean Whitbread wrote in response to an online discussion on the merits of **Twitter**:

'What I *love dearly* about **Twitter** is that you can have multiple accounts. So, on my personal account, I stick to the Dunbar concept – [the idea that] our brain size limits the amount of meaningful social interactions we can maintain – and my other account is totally open and more public.'[12]

Whitbread's approach is typical and there are many who follow this example, often with one account in the name of their business or consultancy, and another in their own name. Another way of doing things is to use different platforms to segment your audience: take, for example, the BBC's Director of Global News, Richard Sambrook, who has a very public, accessible, profile on his **blog**, but keeps his **Twitter** updates private.

This method makes sense because you may want to have a different type of conversation on different networks. **Blogger** Rob Vanasco described the problem like this:

'Someone heavy into the tech industry who uses **Twitter**, or a service like it, might not want their **Twitter** post automatically updating their **Facebook feed**. Their family and friends might not want to be inundated with post after post about what article they are reading, up to the date tech news, or what sites they've just bookmarked or added to their **RSS feed**. This could potentially turn their friends/family off to reading their updates, and could be a good way to lose friends on **social networks**.'[13]

It's a good idea to show sensitivity to the views of your online connections, whether they be friends, family or work colleagues. Developer Chris Thorpe at **MySpace** thinks that, given time, we will all become more adept at managing personal privacy settings and developing different profiles for different aspects of our lives:

'What we have to realise is that these things ebb and flow over time,' he says. 'I used to be a research scientist, now I work in social software. Those [identities] are both authentic at the time. When I was an immunologist, my record of my research papers was the thing that you could say defined me and authenticated me at that particular time. Now, not necessarily quite so much. They are just facets of our personality over the years.'

One size fits all?

But keeping up multiple identities can be tiring and time-consuming. The faster we work, the more we need simplicity. People with a single online persona, managed across various outlets, are arguably able to work more efficiently. This potential merging of work, social and family identities, and the issues associated with blurring these boundaries, is known as 'social convergence'.

Alex Hoye, CEO of digital agency, Latitude, admitted he found it difficult when he first started *microblogging* to the world on *Twitter*, but he now feels a sense of freedom in having one 'voice':

> 'One of the first struggles I had was that my work persona, my home persona and my family persona all had to be one and the same and initially that meant some filtering – and there is some filtering in there – but on the other hand it means that you're actually more natural in all three now which is a real cultural revolution in some ways.'[14]

Education consultant Tessy Britton had a similar experience: 'The transparency of that kind of joined-up-ness was a bit unnerving,' she commented on my *blog*. 'It lasted about two months. Now it actually feels more natural, and warmer... less formal, even if less private.'

Headshift's Lee Bryant agrees that some kind of convergence is taking place, and feels this is having an impact on the way employers approach *social networking*:

> 'I think the barriers are becoming more blurred, certainly in smaller companies...in many forms of collective action that we have today, commercial or non-commercial, [the working environment] is much more collegiate and cooperative. That doesn't mean that there shouldn't be "leaders" or "managers" but then I think they need to operate in a different way.'

Certainly a degree of 'openness' is expected. Some employers may be natural *bloggers* and communicators, while others may find that line a little more difficult. The trick is to find what feels natural to you. Nic Price, a former IT manager at the BBC, puts it like this: 'It doesn't have to be a *blog*. You could just sit in the canteen on a Friday afternoon and buy people coffee. That's participative. That's "*Web 2.0*"'

Managing the transition

As home-working and flexi-working become more common, and work seems to blend more readily into other parts of our lives, a hard and fast division of work/social personas seems less relevant. At the same time, our ways of working are becoming, generally, more meritocratic: presentation and status are often less important than content and commitment: it's not so much the way you do something, it's what you contribute that's important.

In his research around defining the exact nature of 'public' service for Channel 4 (for 4IP – a public service programming initiative launched in 2008) Channel 4 commissioning editor Matt Locke argued that there's no such thing as 'private' any more, only appropriate behaviours. He proposed some initial thoughts around six 'spaces' of *social media*: these formed a segmented continuum that included secret, group, publishing, performing, participating and watching.

> 'I'm sure there are many, many variants of this kind of analysis around the web,' wrote Locke on his *blog*. 'But I've found it really useful as a way of helping people think of the 'register' [their] project is operating within, to design from the point of view of the user, and to make sure we don't cross implicit boundaries that will offend [those users] or discourage participation.'[15]

So, the implication for management would be that while one type of language and behaviour could be used in a 'secret' space –via locked updates on *Twitter* to a privileged group of friends, for example – quite another voice would be appropriate in a 'publishing' space – such as a corporate announcement on *YouTube*. Your 'identity' can remain the same across all platforms. Locke's breakdown is helpful because it suggests that the online world is much the same as the offline: most of us know instinctively whether or not a joke we share in the pub with friends is suitable for telling on stage at a conference. Online, it might be harder to distinguish the different environments, because we simply don't, yet, have enough relevant experience – but this is something that will change over time.

Like Locke, web designer and *blogger* Priya Prakash has observed that we are only just at the beginning of this new space (or spaces), so, therefore, it's no surprise that we find it difficult to learn the appropriate stance to take:

> 'We're in a transitional phase; that's why it's so stressful. The tea ceremony [in Japan] has a tradition, an etiquette, of hundreds of years. In twenty years time we won't be worrying about how to behave on

MySpace or *Facebook*. It's like road traffic safety – 150 years ago, no-one knew which side of the road to drive on!'[16]

Genuine social responsibility

While personal indiscretions or embarrassing activities may be increasingly forgiven or, at least, consciously ignored, people are far less tolerant when it comes to business behaviour. Social, demographic and economic factors are conspiring to force a change in the way businesses present themselves to the world. A new generation of customers and employees demands more openness – and companies must adapt if they hope to sustain a competitive edge.

While businesses such as Cadbury's and Rowntrees (influenced by the Quaker beliefs of their founders), and the Co-op (with its policy of ethical investment) practiced genuine corporate social responsibility as far back as the mid 19th Century, corporate codes of ethics only became commonplace in the late 1980s, following a wave of business scandals like the Union Carbide gas leak in Bhopal, India (1984) and the Alaskan Exxon Valdez oil spill (1989).

But it wasn't until the early years of this century, with the revelation of unethical decision-making in world-renowned companies like Andersen, Enron and WorldCom, that the public perception of business was altered drastically. The release of films such as *The Corporation*, *Super Size Me*, *Black Gold* and *Wal-Mart: The High Cost of Low Price* – all questioning the legitimacy of business practices in corporate America – have done little to reassure the public. More recently, the near-collapse of the global economy triggered by the behaviour of leading banks has caused people to question the efficacy of a bonus culture. Consumers now expect a far higher standard of ethical conduct from business. Companies are being closely watched to ensure that they don't 'trip up'. And in the *blogosphere*, any mishap is likely to be magnified a hundredfold.

In a paper for *The Journal of Business Ethics*, South African academics Gedeon J. Rossouw and Leon J. van Vuuren identified an 'ethical growth process' or 'spectrum' of corporate behaviours with regard to ethics. These behaviors include an immoral mode, a reactive mode, a compliance mode, an integrity mode, and a totally aligned organisation mode.

In immoral mode, a company focuses entirely on maximising profits, to the point of excluding its stakeholders. When stakeholders press for change, the company moves into reactive mode. Once the importance of a good reputation is realised – and desired – the company enters compliance mode. As the company becomes proactive in ethical behaviour, and its relationship with stakeholders is marked by genuine engagement, integrity mode is achieved. Finally, a totally aligned organisation is one in which the transformation is complete: the company lives and breathes through communication and understanding with its stakeholders.

Rossouw and van Vuuren's spectrum is simplistic: the transition from 'bad' to 'good' sounds idealistic and improbably smooth; the underlying assumption is that all stakeholders have the same interests and that these are aligned with increasing 'morality' on the part of a company (when, of course, an investor in a company who is interested only in maximising ROI has very different interests from an environmentally aware consumer of a company's products). Nonetheless, this model is useful in that, at all levels, we can see how *social technologies* might help: both in enabling engagement with stakeholders and in disseminating information about ethical corporate behaviour. If a company genuinely wishes to move up through this spectrum, *social tools* can play a key role.

In cyberspace, everyone can hear you scream

So, we know *social media* has the potential to facilitate a dramatic improvement in business conduct. Sadly, on the whole, businesses have not been quick to grasp this opportunity. A common mistake made by companies is to see the web as simply another marketing channel. They leap onto the web without taking a moment to understand the medium: they broadcast a familiar message, carry on with business as usual, apply old world methods to a new world audience.

I came across several examples in researching this book, three of which are discussed below: they concern marketing rather than internal communications, but they're all in the public domain and are good case studies in how businesses need to learn to speak in a more focused, engaged language instead of continuing with the broadcast, scattershot approach.

Falling off the bandwagon

In June 2009, the UK high street furnishing retailer, Habitat, ran a short-lived marketing campaign on *Twitter*. The brand programmed its *Twitter* account to spot trending topics of discussion on the network, and then to automatically issue a *Tweet* urging customers to buy its discounted Spring collection, containing a *hashtag* for each top trending topic – the idea being that any user searching for content relating to that topic would automatically see a marketing message from Habitat. The campaign resulted in updates such as:

> HabitatUK: #iranelection Our totally desirable Spring collection now has 20% off!

and

> HabitatUK: #iPhone Our totally desirable Spring collection now has 20% off!

As *bloggers* like Redcatco's Benjamin Ellis were quick to point out, these type of links are 'at best tenuous, and at worst a blatant bit of opportunism.'[17] Certainly someone looking for information on the Iranian Election is probably in a serious frame of mind and unlikely to be in the mood to choose a sofa. Likewise, an iPhone enthusiast will not necessarily be interested in lighting ideas. Ironically, the error quickly created a buzz in the *blogosphere* and the list of 'followers' on Habitat's *Twitter* account soon mushroomed from a handful to around 1,000.

Habitat was in a great position to make amends with its online community by eating humble pie and admitting its mistake. Instead, it deleted the errant *Tweets*, and for a few days sat on its hands, acting as if nothing had happened. Eventually, after complaints through the *blogosphere* reached fever pitch, Habitat's management got the message and issued a formal apology[18] – implying that a third party had been responsible for the mistake. This apology was treated with suspicion by *bloggers* who then started an online campaign for Habitat to reveal the identity of the 'intern' or agency responsible.[19] Habitat ignored this campaign, which continued to bubble under, causing prolonged harm to the retailer's brand. While it might not have been appropriate to reveal individual names, some kind of response, however vague, might have helped allay the anger.

Less bang for your buck

'People often treat the *blogging* environment as a sort of game that they can play,' says Yahoo!'s Tom Coates. 'As if, "it's not real people, it's just the Internet"'. Coates is remembering an experience he had with Reckitt Benckiser, the manufacturer of the household cleaning product, Cillit Bang.

'I basically had decided a while ago to look for my biological father and started looking for him and then found him...I was writing this whole *blog* post about the story, which I hadn't told my mother and she found out much later and was very angry about. In the comments a guy posted, "Oh I understand how this is". I was a bit suspicious: his name was Barry Scott and I thought, "this is a bit weird, I wonder what's going on here."

'I don't know why I thought it was suspicious but I sort of explored it a bit. It turned out that Barry Scott was a marketing vehicle for Cillit Bang. He's the guy in the adverts who stands up and says "Bang, and the dirt is gone!" The *URL* that he posted for his *blog* was in fact the Cillit Bang website and I thought, "this is extremely dodgy."

'So I wrote this huge, angry rant about it. Because the problem with these people is that they don't understand that you also have an audience. If they [upset you], the things that they are approaching you for on the good side can really backfire...If they understood what I wrote about, that would be one thing; if they had contacted me because they thought that I would be interested in [their product], that would be another thing...My argument here is that with the *blogging* environment, talking to people in general: the most important thing is that people are open and honest and reasonable.'

There's nothing more heinous in the *social media* world than faking it. Any brand that impersonates an individual and proceeds to respond to *blog* posts in an insensitive way is effectively asking for trouble. It's a tactic that will only cause harm in the long term.

Online community: handle with care

Nestlé is a 150 year old multinational specialising in packaged foodstuffs including baby food, coffee, dairy products, breakfast cereals, confectionery and pet foods. In recent decades, the company has suffered from a great deal of negative publicity; for example, the controversy surrounding its marketing of formula milk to mothers in the developing world.[20] Despite this, Nestlé is a household name and continues to produce a number of well-loved brands such as Nescafé and KitKat.

A friend who works with Nestlé tells the story of how a 16 year old Chinese boy set up a fan page on *Facebook* for Nestlé products. As soon as it found out, Nestlé contacted the *social network* and asked to be assigned full control of the community; **Facebook** acquiesced. Nestlé started by taking a step in the right direction – it appointed the fan page's creator as a moderator.

But within weeks of Nestlé taking ownership of the page, the content became increasingly corporate. Instead of listening to the language of the fans, Nestlé chose a conventional path – putting up company reports and financial results. This approach quashed the natural enthusiasm of the community and began to alienate its members.

Eventually, Nestlé reconsidered its stance and stepped back from direct interference. The fan page recovered much of its earlier, homespun feel, even allowing the odd negative comment to be posted. According to my friend, Nestlé's traditional, top-down, approach is the root of the problem: 'They don't have the internal [**social media**] evangelists,' she says. 'If this happens you create fear and you create hesitation.'

We, the media

Incidents like these show how businesses continue to make the fundamental error of allowing someone to **tweet**, **blog** or comment in their brand name without properly thinking through the ground rules for engagement.

Of course, the relationship between personal and corporate brand has always existed with regards to the CEO and to some extent other senior staff, but it's now becoming common throughout the corporate hierarchy. As corporate accountability and legitimacy become increasingly important, the conduct of a company's ambassadors is critical.

While consultants and freelancers may be fully committed to their own personal 'brand-building' and are happy to spend non-billable days polishing their online profiles and **social networking** as and when they fancy, corporate employees are far more restricted in what they can and can't do. Many organisations (including some of the 'enlightened' ones I spoke to for this book) restrict access to **social networking** sites from work, or during working hours.

Any employees that do keep a high profile online may either have to be sure to keep their social personas (if they happen to be outrageous or lairy) somewhere where their bosses won't find them (under a nickname, for example) and/or be careful that whatever they say about their employer, or even area of work, is towing the line with company policy.

Whereas *social networks* like *Facebook* and *LinkedIn* are, by default, private – only your 'friends' can see your full information, and you can make the privacy settings still tighter if you wish, sites that are, by default, 'public', like *Twitter*, can be more problematic. *Twitter* plays host to an increasing number of sales and marketing executives, all *tweeting* publicly, ostensibly as themselves, but – effectively – on behalf of their employer. This is new territory for corporate communications – both internal and external. What do businesses need to do?

In blog we trust

> 'All businesses are media businesses,' wrote Clay Shirky in *Here Comes Everybody*. 'Because whatever else they do, they rely on the managing of information.'[21]

This is my favourite Shirky quote and I'm reminded of it when I meet Arseniy Rastorguev, a Russian *blogger*, who is in London researching *social media* as part of his job at MMD – a leading corporate communications firm in central and eastern Europe.

I first meet Rastorguev at Lloyd Davies' Tuttle Club and a few days later we're sitting in the bijou surroundings of an anteroom of the Hospital Club in central London, sipping coffee and swapping stories. Shirky's argument was that every business, now, more than ever, needs to learn how to handle all data with sensitivity. Rastorguev puts this from a different perspective:

> 'In this new environment where everyone is a media outlet, you have to be as thoroughly good as you can,' he argues. 'I don't expect all companies to become fluffy and nice: they're a business, they have to earn money, they have to pay out to shareholders...I don't have any idealistic illusions, but I do think that companies are becoming more and more genuinely transparent and moving ethics further and further into the core.'

Rastorguev cites the Fair Trade movement as a good example, and points to an increasing environmental awareness that is born out of competitiveness rather than altruism:

> 'the whole green thing...it's not just conducting a tree planting event once a year and getting some coverage in the press, you have to actually

make your products greener...at least a tiny bit. So PR and corporate social responsibility stretches from being a front end function right into the core of the business.'

Again, that echo of Russell Davies (from Chapter 1): we can no longer separate strategy from execution – if a company wishes to project a wholesome image well, then, it probably needs to start being wholesome.

'You can no longer count on your PR department to do your PR for you. Because if one employee posts something you're in trouble or if one consumer posts something you're in trouble and just because of the ways [in which] it spreads...posting in a small **blog** to several dozen readers can become a mass issue.'

More than anything else, says Rastorguev, the **blogosphere** is 'a stock-market for trust'. And we need to champion our position in that market as aggressively as we nurture our share-price.

As it might not be possible to rein in all those **Tweeting** executives, a far easier alternative is to let them speak – and ensure your organisation is equipped to respond quickly and effectively to any possible controversy. One thing is certain: whatever you say and how quickly you say it will be picked up and monitored by the **blogging** community. Handle things properly, and a PR or HR disaster can just as easily become a coup: when the US electronics retailer, Best Buy, proposed a reduction in the discount employees received on company goods, the change provoked a torrent of negative comments from staff on the Blue Shirt Nation community. Three days later a member of the management team posted an announcement letting staff know that they had re-considered and the discount would remain unchanged.[22] A potential HR disaster was averted; instead, management was praised for valuing staff feedback.

Speak no evil

At the RSA event on private lives, both Dominic Campbell and Tom Ilube were agreed on one thing: in the future, there will be suspicion over anyone who doesn't appear to have an online presence, dodgy photos notwithstanding. The same might be said for companies who aren't seen to be engaging directly with their community – what might they have to hide? But regulatory concerns mean that attaining a culture of transparency is something of a sector lottery.

Maria Sipka advises leading pharmaceutical companies on using *social media*. Change is an uphill struggle, because there is good evidence, borne out by recent scandals and fines, that 'Big Pharma' are anything but open and above board in their business practices. In 2004, pharma giant Merck withdrew its painkiller, Voixx, from the market after a number of people had suffered heart attacks and died as a result of taking the drug. Merck's management was accused of covering up research which showed that Voixx significantly increased the risk of heart attacks and strokes; at least 28,000 lawsuits were filed against the company.[23] In 2009, both Pfizer and Eli Lilly were asked to pay record fines (£1.5 billion and £894 million respectively)[24] for marketing some of their drugs for uses that had not been approved by the US federal government.

The first phase of any *social media* strategy should be listening, says Sipka – subscribing to monitoring services and finding out what people are actually saying about your brand and products (however bad it may be); the second phase is all about generating content. But pharma companies are severely restricted in what they can and can't say. Sipka is frustrated that the sector's US-based watchdog, the FDA (the Food and Drug Administration), has yet to define a digital strategy.

> 'The FDA is watching every single move they make, telling them "you can't say this, you can't say that". But the regulators haven't realized that the nature of the medium is that it needs to be transparent. Companies are getting slammed for using *Google AdWords* because they haven't fully explained the [side effects] of something – but the amount of text you can use in *AdWords* is limited!'

It could be argued that if the side effects of a drug can't be described in *Google AdWords*, then it's a good reason not to use that medium. Sipka says that companies are taking on specialist legal teams to advise on 'how to work around the grey areas.' Meanwhile, the more knowledgeable players have realised that a simple approach is best. Positive information is beginning to circulate, because some companies have thought imaginatively: they are beginning to talk frankly with their communities about the issues they face.

> 'Pfizer, for example, are reaching out to their most vocal stakeholders – physicians and patients who are *bloggers*, for example – and inviting them to participate in a round table. And they *blog* positively about this experience. What does this indicate? Listening! This is great, because the image of pharma companies is so bad.'

Pfizer, the producer of Viagra, has long struggled with its online presence, particularly in respect of its famous 'performance enhancing' drug. The round table is a great innovation – relatively cheap to set up and run, and generating favourable results.

Another pharmaceutical company, GlaxoSmithKlein, has taken a different approach. It has created branded communities around specific topics, such as obesity[25]. There is nothing underhand about these communities – there is full disclosure regarding the company behind the sites – the interesting thing is that they're proving to be compelling to the demographics that GlaxoSmithKlein wants to reach. Conversations are generated around GSK's products, but contentious areas are avoided.

The lesson to learn from these two examples is that a degree of transparency is always possible, it's just that the route may not be an obvious one. The most important thing is not to be seen to be censoring your community in any way. History has shown, time and time again, that censorship doesn't pay.

You can't keep a good story down

It's Spring 1622 and Nathaniel Butter is thrilled to hear that the authorities have at last answered his pleas to be released from prison. With his wife pregnant and three young children at home, the short time he has been incarcerated has been extremely difficult. Under the Stuart monarchy of the time, rules on censorship are strict; Butter is a publisher and has been imprisoned for producing a pamphlet criticising the 1619 accession of Ferdinand II, the new Holy Roman Emperor. His situation has been made worse by the fact that the printer of the offending booklet, William Stansby, has also been imprisoned, and has been filing his own petitions to the authorities, blaming Butter for everything.

Butter's friend, Thomas Archer, has also recently been released from jail. He was found guilty of printing news bulletins without permission in 1621. These single page bulletins, an innovation of the time, are inspired by the 'Coranto', a news sheet printed in Amsterdam by a small group of maverick publishers. But N.B., widely presumed to be Butter, has been granted a license to publish these bulletins. In 1621 the Corante, the first English newspaper appeared on London's streets.

On his release from prison, Butter returns to his shop at the Pied Bull, London, and immediately sets about looking for a new and exciting project. Butter excels in printing pamphlets on contentious, topical subjects and his shop operates like an 'early news agency'.[26] On May 23, 1622, Butter publishes the first edition of his *Weekly News*. Although its full name changes on a weekly basis, the small, quarto-sized booklet is the first of its kind, and a further variation of the single-sheet corantos. The *Weekly News* is printed regularly, contains a miscellaneous mix of news from other European countries and is 'regarded as the true forerunner of [today's] English newspaper.'[27]

Butter's pamphlet sparks controversy. Ben Jonson is derisory, and mocks Butter in his 1625 play The Staple of News. Another critic dismisses the booklets as 'Batter' that 'besmear each public post and church door.'[28] The booklet remains contentious and publication ceases in October 1632, when the Star Chamber bans all 'gazettes and pamphlets of news from foreign parts.' The edict is lifted in 1638 and Butter returns to publishing news pamphlets until the start of the English Civil War in 1642.

The war brings with it a collapse of censorship, and a huge expansion in the amount of cheap printed pamphlets. According to **blogger** Nick Poyntz, who studies early modern history:

> 'For a penny or two nearly anyone could buy a pamphlet giving a hugely diverse range of views about politics, religion and pretty much anything else. A huge range of people started participating as authors of cheap pamphlets too. Successive governments in the seventeenth century spent a huge amount of time trying to put the lid back on the box, and confine the public sphere to where it had existed previously – via royal proclamations and edicts, within the court, and within parliament.'[29]

Many commentators have drawn parallels between the birth of newspapers and the burgeoning of **social media** today (as the internet itself has been likened to the printing press due to its powerful, information-disseminating qualities). The early **blogging** site, 'Corante' (launched in 2000) took its name directly from Archer and Butter's newspaper.

As with **social media** now, the authorities of the mid to late seventeenth century tried to control the news that was being disseminated, and the new conversations that were springing up. Seventeenth century governments were appalled by the idea that news could be generated and circulated between people they had little control over. As we now know, their efforts at censorship were, in the long term, futile.

The virtuous circle

We don't know if 1638 editions of Butter's international news pamphlets contained any notice of a book published the previous year in France by the

French philosopher, René Descartes. The book, *Discourse on The Method*, is often considered to mark the start of the European Enlightenment – an era that continued until the beginning of the Napoleonic Wars in 1804. The Enlightenment focused on the rights of the common people and challenged traditional institutions and morals, and in particular, the religious authority of the Middle Ages. The values of freedom, democracy and reason were championed, as were concepts like republicanism, liberalism and modernity.

While it's impossible to say if we're at the start of a new 'enlightenment', it's clear that a great deal of the enthusiasm and anger of the mid Seventeenth Century is present today. Back then, the authorities learnt to their cost that a distributed, grassroots, guerrilla movement is ultimately impossible to control.

Today, sensible leaders know that if they really try to control everything that is said about their business online, they would spend so much time micro-managing that any other work would be impossible: insanity – and insolvency – would beckon. But the level of intense communication enabled by *social media*, combined with consumer demand for increased accountability, mean that a certain degree of openness is essential: the only way to deal with this is to relax, jump in, and go with the ebb and flow.

In *Theory U*, Otto Scharmer talks about the learning capacity of 'sensing', a process of letting go where a group actively opens up and becomes fully aware of future possibilities. This process involves what Scharmer defines as 'the tuning of three instruments: the open mind, the open heart and the open will': it is not so much a passive action as an active refocus.[30]

> 'I once asked a successful top executive at Nokia to share her most important leadership practices,' wrote Scharmer. 'Time and time again, her team was able to anticipate changes in technology and context. Time and again, they were ahead of the curve. Her answer? "I facilitate the opening process."'[31]

Scharmer interviewed psychologist Eleanor Rosch at the University of California at Berkeley who told him that action resulting from this kind of unconditional awareness 'is claimed to be spontaneous, rather than the result of decision-making; it is compassionate, since it is based on wholes larger than the self; and it can be shockingly effective.'[32]

Opening up our minds to others inevitably involves a degree of reaching out, sharing and transparency – on our part. If our 'openness' lets whistleblowers lead a charge, then so be it; if our 'openness' uncovers scandal and corruption, then let's use those same *social tools* to publicise the fact that we are addressing it.

And trust creates a virtuous circle. Maybe it's something to do with the goodwill generated by a nice stock of *social capital*. Maybe it's to do with respect – treating others the way you yourself would like to be treated. Or maybe it's about gaining a great reputation. Sometimes, if we demonstrate honesty, humbleness and self-awareness, we can be surprised at the positive response.

Truth will out

'You can lie, but then you have to make sure you tell the same lie everywhere. You can only really throw truth into that stream.'

Christian Payne (aka Documentally) is a photographer and *blogger* now making a name for himself as a *social media* expert. For any CEOs hoping to turn their back on corporate lobbying and spin, Payne sums up the dilemma in a nutshell: the transparency of *social media* is such that you either tell your story consistently, or you don't tell it at all.

Payne's reputation precedes him. When I first start researching this book, people keep telling me he's the one person I have to interview. It's a Friday morning and we've arranged to meet at Lloyd Davis' Tuttle Club. Only, Payne's dog walker can't make it and he has to stay home to look after his Border Collie, so we're talking long distance (London – Boondocks) over *Skype*.

Six years ago Payne 'downsized', leaving full-time employment at a London newspaper to live and work in a small village in Northamptonshire. Payne was driven to opt out of the rat race by a series of bad bosses. He's candid about his disillusion with command-and-control style management.

'The leadership [in newspapers] is terrible. People sit there shouting like something out of a *Spiderman* movie. You've seen *Spiderman*, right? Well, the relationship Peter Parker has with his editors, who are always shouting at him – that's a completely accurate representation. There's no end of bullying.

'As a result you end up having no respect for either these people or the organisation that employs you. You just want to get back at them in whatever way you can. For example, when it came to expenses at the newspaper, people would calculate expenses to and from the office for every story, even though they would go direct from job to job. They could probably earn another £4K on top of their earnings annually through that. Most people did it, and the newspaper was completely unaware.

'[The managers would] just turn around and say, "you're staying tonight". You might have someone at home on a deathbed for all they'd know! There's no way to talk yourself out of it because you don't have that, "let's sit down and talk about this" relationship that you should be having...This is where *social media* needs to permeate into these kind of larger companies.'

Payne feels that far too many businesses treat their staff appallingly. He believes that *social media* can help managers to 'listen' more, be more open, and ultimately more inclusive – and he calculates this will have a positive effect on the bottom line of any organisation: he estimates his former employer was ('and still is') losing 'tens of thousands of pounds per year' because of false expenses claims. Engagement with staff might not only have uncovered this practice, it might also have eliminated the need for it in the first place.

Open for business

In his new role as a consultant, Payne advises organisations who wish to integrate social web technologies into everyday working processes. One of his clients is The Open University. He praises Ian Roddis, The OU's Head of Online Services, for being a senior manager with a particularly progressive attitude.

'The Communications Department are all on *Twitter* – they use it as a kind of *intranet*, but it's a kind of transparent *intranet* because obviously their conversations are visible to everybody. So, as they're talking about practices, it's visible to the outside world and the students. It's inadvertently advertising what they're up to as well as being open about the issues they have...because it's all in the public domain it gets sorted out quicker.

'The other day Ian sent a *Tweet* at lunchtime: "I'm working from home and having a beer, does that constitute drinking at work?". The thing is, he's not just talking to his employees but also to his clients and his sponsors. He's communicable and being honest. That's what's so likeable.

> '*Social media* has enabled there to be a massive corporate meeting taking place 24/7 at all levels of management, and that's really enabling. People can see directly what I'm doing at any point: for example, they can see if something's my idea. That's good, it gives me ownership.'

In addition to his work as a consultant and photographer, Payne is a campaigner for the human rights watchdog, Privacy International, so he is more aware than most of the implications of 24 hour surveillance – and 100 per cent openness. He argues that we are much more in control of our *digital footprints* – and shadows – than we think:

> 'You control exactly how many bits of data you want to throw into the stream. You are in control of that. I can turn *Skype* off any time I want...If you look at my *blog*, you will see absolutely no talk of my family. I'd say 95% of the people in my *social networks* don't even know whether or not I'm married. I've chosen to keep my personal life outside: I'd like it to be private.'

Closed-circuit leadership

In 2008, an established training organisation, Common Purpose, came under attack in parts of the British media for its 'secretive' working practices, which included holding meetings under the Chatham House Rule of non-attribution.[33] There were critical posts by *blogger*s, vitriolic videos on *YouTube* and even a BBC Radio documentary[34]. The campaign against Common Purpose was led by former naval officer Brian Gerrish, who believes the organisation is 'a secret society for careerists' operating 'a highly political agenda, which is to create new chosen leaders in society.'[35]

Blogger and journalist David Wilcox reported mixed feelings when he attended a Common Purpose workshop a few years ago:

> 'It definitely wasn't in my experience a very "bottom-up" sort of organisation. There was an online system which Common Purpose "graduates" were occasionally exhorted to use, but it was (and is) very Web 1.0 and behind a login...I did have some discussion with staff about how *blogging* might be useful as part of their communications and work with groups ... but the open style didn't appeal. I said I couldn't see how you could develop innovative projects for public benefit unless you were prepared to engage publicly.'[36]

In March 2009, in the wake of the broadcasting of the BBC Radio 5Live documentary, Wilcox was again approached by the organisation. This time, it seemed, it was keen to listen. Wilcox gave some advice on engaging with the wider community and the organisation now runs a number of **blogs** and has profiles on various **social networks**, as well as a **Twitter** stream.

As a training company which markets itself as forward-thinking, Common Purpose needs to radically change its image if it is to be seen as progressive, but it remains to be seen whether or not ingrained working practices can be reversed.

Common Purpose is an educational charity founded in 1989 by Julia Middleton. Although the not-for-profit claims on one of its websites to have 'no alignment with any political party, religion or other organisation whatsoever',[37] Middleton's background working for left-leaning organisations such as the Industrial Society (now The Work Foundation), The Media Trust, and the think tank Demos appear to give her impeccable New Labour credentials.

The public image of Common Purpose is a mirror of the British Establishment. As an organisation which charges up to £5,750 for its executive courses, Common Purpose clearly needs to demonstrate added value to its alumni: the exclusive online community and elite profile of graduates (clients include the Metropolitan Police and the BBC as well as '70 per cent of FTSE 100 companies', according to the website[38]) are part of its competitive advantage.

But Common Purpose tends to use a slightly pompous and jargon-filled tone across its media outlets. This language and approach means that, despite its **social media** presence, it still comes across to outsiders as something of an 'old school' gentleman's club.

Captain Marlow and Mr Kurtz

Open or closed? In the war-torn jungle of the argument between **social media** evangelists and the defenders of corporate identity, this disagreement lies at the heart. The legacy systems and cultures are Mr Kurtz, ailing, battle-worn, powerful and – possibly – corrupted. **Social media** represents the uninvited rescuer, Marlow – a civilising influence, the future, the opportunity for a freer, more democratic workplace.[39] But for those who have built their empire around a closed approach, there are tremendous costs to be borne in adapting to a new way of doing things.

Consultant Euan Semple alerted me to this split during a discussion about politics at a social media event. In a **BarCamp** style debate, one group was arguing that participative, **Web 2.0** approaches were natural (but unclaimed) territory for the UK Labour Party. Political allegiances were increasingly irrelevant, said Semple; the real issue was that, across the board, some people simply preferred locked down, hierarchical solutions while others would always choose more fluid ways of doing things.

A 'them and us' situation has developed, with a gulf in understanding between the two sides. For advisors like Semple, keen to see the transformation that good enterprise *social media* can bring to business, it's important to identify the 'open' people on the inside and work with them. For the 'open' thinkers within organisations, friends need to be made beyond the corporate boundaries. There is no doubt that the costs will be massive for organisations that don't start to enable genuine conversations. To their credit, most of the world's big brands seem to realise this.

To find out how established, well-loved brands were coping with the demand for increased transparency, I spoke to two keen corporate *bloggers*: Scott Monty at Ford in Detroit, and (through the recommendation of Euan Semple) Richard Sambrook at the BBC in London.

Back to basics

It's November 2008, and I'm reading through newspaper reports on the US car industry. The outlook is bleak: '100 days to save the American car industry' (*Guardian*), 'The end of Detroit: Shape up or ship out' (*Economist*) and 'Detroit's big three near the brink' (*Time*) are three typical headlines.

The high price of oil, coupled with environmental concerns, has caused a sudden slump in demand for the large, 'gas guzzlers' which the American car manufacturers have excelled in producing. In the last few months, sales have hit a 25-year low. The banking crisis means credit – for business as well as consumers – is increasingly hard to secure. Profits have collapsed, along with market values. Two of the three companies, General Motors and Chrysler, face potential bankruptcy [and several months later, in June 2009, the US witnesses the biggest manufacturing collapse in its history when General Motors does indeed file for Chapter 11]. Due to the interdependence of the US auto industry – Detroit's car manufacturing giants share 90 per cent of their suppliers – the third American auto-giant, Ford, also risks being brought down if GM and Chrysler fail.

At Ford, Scott Monty may not be able to save the US car industry single-handedly, but he's sure as hell trying. Just three months ago, Monty was working for Crayon, a small but reputable digital marketing agency based in

New York. Monty had established himself as someone who knew **social media** inside out, and who firmly believed in its potential for revolutionising public relations. Now he is filling a newly-created role at Ford where he's essentially responsible for the communications behaviour of over 4,000 people worldwide.

If any one company represents the heartbeat of the American Dream during the last century, it's Ford. Henry Ford's first factory was the cradle of the production techniques that turned the United States into an industrial powerhouse, while Ford's cars – in particular, the Model T and Lincoln – have played a leading role in America's popular imagination over the years.

Monty is under no illusions as regards the significance – and challenge – of the role he's been given. When he speaks to me on the phone from Detroit, he's typically upbeat:

> 'The Ford way of doing things is putting our heads down and moving forward with our plans. Alan Mulally [Ford's new CEO] spent a great deal of time pulling together a team and we'll put together our plan – with or without financial help from government. At the same time we're also having to support existing projects – it's like changing tyres on a car going at 60 miles an hour!'

Monty is tasked with creating a **social media** strategy that will then be a roadmap to help Ford become 'a leader in digital communications' five years from now. In the meantime, he continues to run digital marketing, recently launching sites for the Ford Mustang and a new media relations portal.

So, times are hard and there are cutbacks across the board. I ask Monty if there wasn't the tiniest bit of resentment when he walked in the door. On the contrary, he says: 'I was completely thrilled at how receptive people were to **social media**. It was like, wow, you're finally here!'

Monty says he's already detected a 'natural interest' in mainstream tools such as Google Docs and **wikis** and feels that enough 'cohesive teamwork' is being fostered through **Microsoft SharePoint**. However, he admits the current climate doesn't make it an ideal time to invest in a raft of new technologies: 'We're fortunate that **social media** is not as heavy in production costs, but we're also aware that we're constrained by human capital.'

Monty will need all hands on deck if he's to combat Ford's current challenges effectively. Part of his plan is to find a way of keeping on top of every story that breaks. He knows it will be tough: 'in corporate communications things move extremely fast. We think in terms of hours and minutes. We're a news organisation, essentially.'

Monty would like to help Ford turn the conversation outwards and not make the same mistakes as, for example, GM – whose **blog** has a reputation in the industry for being over-corporate and 'on message' – but Monty admits he is frustrated by his new employer's existing protocols on **blogging**:

> 'We need an army of ambassadors. But there's a pervasive attitude of fear – [Ford] employees can't say what they like on **blogs**. But would you stay quiet at a dinner party if someone was disparaging your company and you knew them to be wrong?'

Monty wants to humanise the company by building connections between Ford employees and the wider community. As part of his **blogging** offensive, he plans to launch a raft of distinct **Twitter feeds**, with the people behind each account clearly identified. Monty himself already has tens of thousands of followers on **Twitter** (@scottmonty) and is a master at treading a fine, conversational, line between personal opinion and corporate message. His approachability and enthusiasm have to be an asset for Ford in the tough times ahead. Whether this is all too little, too late, remains to be seen.

The audacity of hope

Richard Sambrook is sitting in his office on the first floor of Bush House, television blaring. It's 6th November 2008, the day after the US election result has been declared and the BBC's world news machine is going into overdrive, broadcasting minute-by-minute reports of President-elect Barack Obama's every move.

Sambrook's is the sort of character-filled room that you imagine should be featured in a lifestyle magazine or, at the very least, an episode of *Through The Keyhole*. Cartoon caricatures mix with modern art on the walls. A large comfy maroon sofa sprawls at one end of the office, a self-contained network of high tech communications (plasma screen, laptop, TV monitor, fax machine) at the other.

Sambrook himself seems relaxed, given that the last few days have been hectic. As Director of the BBC's Global News division, Sambrook is in charge of all the BBC's international news services, across radio, television and digital media. Guiding and monitoring the US presidential election coverage in 32 different languages can't be easy.

Before we meet, I check Sambrook's *blog* to see what he's thinking. The most recent post is 29th October, over a week ago. Sambrook admits he's not posting as frequently as he was when he launched his internal *blog* in 2004. Back then, he was the first senior manager at the BBC to do such a thing.

> 'I'd moved into my new role and I thought it would be an interesting communications tool. The BBC can be very insular and inward-looking: it's not just about journalism, I wanted to communicate with the new staff. After about three months I was getting 6,000 unique visitors each month. People I didn't know would stop me and talk to me in the corridor, just because they'd read something of interest on the *blog*.'

Sambrook is refreshingly honest about the things that bothered him at the outset. His editor's mind identified four areas of contention:

1. Am I going to be taken to task for something I write?
2. Am I going to offend a specific constituency or community?
3. Is anyone going to be interested?
4. Can I do it?

While he found the *blog* relatively easy to write, he was concerned about the way his audience would react:

> 'Being a journalist, the actual writing wasn't a problem. Finding a personal tone was. As well as issues like transparency, honesty and frankness. If you take all the contentious stuff out, will it be interesting?'

So far, the most awkward moment has been during a dispute between the BBC and the unions:

> 'I said the only way forward is through negotiation. And then found out the official BBC position is not to negotiate.'

Hmm. So would he extol the virtues of *blogging* to all senior managers?

> 'I wouldn't say everyone should do it. It only works for some people. You need to get the right mix of informality and openness. Otherwise it won't work. It's good to have a very clear purpose.'

When Sambrook, encouraged by Euan Semple (then the BBC's head of knowledge management), went to his bosses with the idea of setting up a *blog*, they must have thought it would be relatively safe. Sambrook was a BBC man through and through – he'd joined the organisation in 1980 as a sub-editor in the radio newsroom and worked his way up the ranks, becoming

News Editor and head of newsgathering, then Director, BBC News, before moving onto his current role. The BBC's then Director General, Greg Dyke, may well have imagined that Sambrook's editorial experience would create some kind of Pavlovian reaction if he ever thought about writing anything too edgy.

In 2006, two years after launching the internal **blog**, Sambrook moved his ideas into the public domain with the launch of *Sacred Facts* on Typepad. The site currently averages a modest 2,000 visitors a month.

> 'Because I'd already done it inside and [senior management] had seen my **blog**, it was okay. They clearly thought that I, more than anyone, should know the risks.'

Sambrook was Director, BBC News, in May 2003 when BBC Radio 4's Today programme ran a report claiming that the British Government had knowingly exaggerated claims over Iraq's weapons of mass destruction in a dossier published in 2002. The government's vehement rebuke of the accusations made in the piece led to a British judicial inquiry, chaired by Lord Hutton. The report Hutton eventually published was highly critical of the BBC and forced the resignations of the BBC's Chairman and Director-General.

Sambrook regrets that he was unable to comment on the affair:

> 'Part of my experience of going through the weapons of mass destruction incident motivated me. If I'd been **blogging** at that time, it would have been an opportunity to say something, to speak out against the spin – although the corporate line would have been tight.'

Sacred Facts has clearly given Sambrook a great feel for **social media**. BBC News now has an impressive presence across platforms as diverse as **Twitter**, **Flickr**, **Facebook**, Seesmic, Threadz, 12seconds and Qik. And Sambrook is already on the look out for the next big thing.

> 'The whole drift of the web at the minute is to move from static and text [which is where it was ten years ago] to being video and live, and it's right in that transition. Clearly in the next two years that's where the innovation is going to be. And for news that's hugely profound because anybody with a camera phone can broadcast live to the world, which is what we used to do.'

It's good to talk

In any discussion of the leadership we need for the future, openness and transparency are often cited as pre-requisites. While openness is the softer attribute, suggesting an overarching philosophy or belief system, transparency is more focused; it directly refers to accountability and inclusive decision-making and is called for when people feel they have a right to comprehensive financial disclosure, a declaration of business interests or a statement of intent.

Blogs and online communities are a great place to start when putting this type of information into the public domain – certainly an ideal way to test the water. Scott Monty and Richard Sambrook have improved the relationship with their respective audiences simply because of the two-way conversation that **blogging** and **microblogging** have opened up. Meanwhile, companies such as Nestlé and GlaxoSmithKlein have found that online communities create discussion around their brands, giving them a whole new life (although these communities still have a Pollyanna feel about them – it would be nice to see their incumbents push a little harder for genuine debate).

Openness is a state of mind. Yes, it's about truth and honesty, but it is also about receptiveness, sociability and friendship. It is about believing that people are, on the whole, good – forgiving misdemeanours and focusing on what matters: working towards a meritocracy, being optimistic. It's about being accessible and wanting to speak in a language other people can easily understand.

If we can combine genuine transparency with true openness, we'll make good progress. On the whole, people love to hear real-life stories, especially when emotions are used that they can relate to. **Social media** seems to be just one part of a bigger wave of social *stuff* – confessional journalism, celebrity culture, popular psychology and self-help manuals are all increasingly popular – the participatory panopticon is alive and kicking.

Maybe it is because we are inundated with stories and revelations: it seems that, generally, we are becoming more tolerant of a wider spectrum of human behaviours – social convergence in action, perhaps. It is this increasing acceptance of diversity, and the growing realisation that we may not always be 'right', that is constantly fed into and supported by the **social media** revolution. But just how much are we really *listening*? This is what I want to discuss in more detail in Chapter 5.

Notes

1. For example, this view was expressed by RSA CEO Matthew Taylor at the 'Private Lives: a Thing of The Past' debate at The RSA, London, on 19 June 2008.
2. Developer Chris Thorpe observes how *MySpace* users happily 'shed' identities they have outgrown: 'They will get to a stage where [a profile] is no longer "them" and they will close that profile down or leave it open and start a new one afresh.'
3. Ruggero Contu and Matthew Cheung, 'Forecast: Security Markets, Worldwide, 2008-2013, 3Q09 Update' (Gartner Research, 28 September 2009); The total figure for the 2010 market in security software was given as $16.3 billion.
4. Benjamin Joffe, 'The Dark Age of Transparency', *Asian Business Leaders*, August 2008 (www.plus8star.com/2008/09/25/the-dark-age-of-transparency).
5. See 'Revealed: Where the MPs stand on the drugs question', 14 October 2005, *Mail Online* (www.dailymail.co.uk/news/article-365395/Revealed-Where-MPs-stand-drugs-question.html) and 'The drugs questions that won't go away', 15 October 2005, *The Guardian* (www.guardian.co.uk/politics/2005/oct/15/uk.conservatives).
6. www.worldchanging.com/archives//002651.html
7. Thanks to Adriana Lukas for first alerting me to Bentham's concept of the panopticon and its use as a metaphor for the internet.
8. Michel Foucault (1977), *Discipline and Punish: The Birth of the Prison*. Trans. Alan Sheridan. Vintage.
9. John F. Gantz (Project Director); Christopher Chute, Alex Manfrediz; Stephen Minton; David Reinsel, Wolfgang Schlichting and Anna Toncheva, 'The Diverse and Exploding Digital Universe: an Updated Forecast of Worldwide Information Growth through 2011', (IDC White Paper sponsored by EMC, March 2008); thanks to Simon Perry for alerting me to this paper at Amplified08.
10. Acquisti & Gross in interview with A. George, 'Things you wouldn't tell your mother,' *New Scientist*, September 2006.
11. sethgodin.typepad.com/seths_blog/2009/02/personal-branding-in-the-age-of-google.html
12. Dean Whitbread in a comment on Lloyd Davies' *blog*, 27 February 2009: perfectpath.co.uk/2009/02/24/twitlash
13. itechmo.wordpress.com/2009/01/28/social-convergence
14. www.guardian.co.uk/media/audio/2009/feb/13/twitter-twestival-voxpops
15. test.org.uk/2007/08/10/six-spaces-of-social-media
16. Priya Prikash, audience comment in a debate on 'Digital Health' at the offices of Demos, London, 27 January 2009 (with regard to the example of road traffic safety, it's instructive to know that, 150 years on, there have been a number of successful experiments in removing traffic signs altogether – for further information see: en.wikipedia.org/wiki/Shared_space).
17. redcatco.com/blog/marketing/creating-a-bad-social-media-habitat
18. www.socialmediatoday.com/SMC/104490
19. See *blog* post by Benjamin Ellis (redcatco.com/blog/marketing/habitatintern) and *tweets* from Daren Forsyth (e.g. twitter.com/DarenBBC/status/3164690459).
20. For an update on the continuing controversy, see Joanna Moorhead, 'Milking It', *The Guardian*, 15 May 2007 (www.guardian.co.uk/business/2007/may/15/medicineandhealth.lifeandhealth).
21. Clay Shirky (2008), *Here Comes Everybody: The Power of Organizing Without Organizations*. Penguin, p. 107.
22. Charlene Li and Josh Bernoff (2008), *Groundswell: Winning in a world transformed by social technologies*. Harvard Business Press, p. 218.

23. www.independent.co.uk/news/business/news/merck-faces-renewed-legal-threat-over-vioxx-scandal-458007.html
24. Eli Lilly was fined $1.415 billion on 30 January 2009, the highest fine ever awarded to a pharmaceutical company; Pfizer broke this record on 2 September 2009 when it was fined $2.3 billion.
25. GSK has built a community around the topic of obesity, promoting its weight loss drug, Alli. (www.myalli.com)
26. en.wikipedia.org/wiki/Nathaniel_Butter
27. Bob Clarke (2004), *From Grub Street to Fleet Street*. Ashgate, p. 15, (via ***Wikipedia***).
28. J. B. Williams (1908), *A History of English Journalism*, Longmans, Green, p. 14 (via ***Wikipedia***).
29. Comment by Nick Poyntz on Lloyd Davis' ***blog***: perfectpath.co.uk/2009/02/24/twitlash/#comments
30. Otto Scharmer (2007), 'Executive Summary' in *Theory U*. Berrett-Koehler, p. 9.
31. *ibid*, p. 9.
32. *ibid*, p. 10.
33. The Chatham House Rule was devised at Chatham House, London, in 1927 and states that 'When a meeting, or part thereof, is held under the Chatham House Rule, participants are free to use the information received, but neither the identity nor the affiliation of the speaker(s), nor that of any other participant, may be revealed.' (www.chathamhouse.org.uk).
34. 'The Investigators: Secret Society?', BBC Radio Five Live, 8 March 2009.
35. Brian Gerrish quoted by David Wilcox: socialreporter.com/?p=531
36. socialreporter.com/?p=531
37. www.commonpurpose.net
38. www.commonpurpose.org/home/countries/uk.aspx
39. Mr Kurtz and Captain Marlow are the main protagonists in *Heart of Darkness*, a 1902 novella by Joseph Conrad. Marlow is sent on a mission to fetch Kurtz, an ivory trader, back from the jungle, where he has persuaded the local tribespeople that he is a demigod. The book explores the nature of civilisation versus barbarism and is a classic text taught in schools, colleges and universities; it was the inspiration for Francis Ford Coppola's 1979 film, 'Apocalypse Now'.

5. Listening

Myth: Management knows best

Reality: The truth is out there

It's January 2009 and the BBC is broadcasting a reality show called *Million Dollar Traders*. It's a three part series which takes eight 'ordinary people' (such as a vet, a soldier and a boxing promoter) and gives them basic training followed by a two month period during which they are expected to run their own (£1m) hedge fund. The two months happen to be September and October 2008 – possibly the worst period ever to be a hedge fund manager, let alone to be learning about the business from scratch.

In one scene, the two self-made millionaires who are running the experiment (one of whom, Lex Van Dam, came up with the TV format and is contributing his own funds to make it happen) discuss the lacklustre performance of a highly intelligent but nervous rookie – they decide it's time to 'let her go'.

The discussion between these two powerful men – 'she's going to cry, I know she is' – is fascinating, as is the interplay between the rejected girl and her fellow rookies in the minutes following her unceremonious dismissal.

In an emotional scene, three other novice traders decide to leave with their sacked colleague. The two 'bosses' stand in their glass-fronted office and look on awkwardly as the walk-out takes place, agreeing that it's best not to 'interfere'.

Of the three 'contestants' that are left at their desks, one, the ex-soldier, seems genuinely perplexed that there should be any gesture of solidarity. 'What's going on?' he asks, repeatedly, of no-one in particular.

Another (an entrepreneur and single mum) is later called in by the millionaire fund managers and congratulated on her 'impressive' (i.e. lack of) reaction to the entire episode. She is praised for her cool-headedness and told that such an approach is essential for City success. There is much talk of how emotions, and emotional ties to others, will only interfere with the single task in hand: making money.

In a separate incident, another novice – an environmentalist – despairs at his inability to turn a profit through ethical trading. He is singled out for criticism

– the suggestion is that his fixation with ethics is rather unnecessary and self-indulgent.

The timing of Million Dollar Traders couldn't have been better: a revealing portrait of City traders as the towers of mammon begin to topple. It should be set viewing for business studies students everywhere. I wonder if the two men who led the show have reconsidered their stance since? There's no doubt that many tears were shed on and off the trading floor in the turbulent months following the public collapse of Lehman Brothers on 14 September 2008.

Second that emotion

Tears and other displays of emotion have long been considered anathema to getting things done in the workplace, but there are signs that this entrenched belief could be changing. IBM's Luis Suarez is one of those leading the charge. He's convinced that social software is 'slowly, but steadily humanising' the corporate world, and has been writing all about it on his **blog**.

On 1 February 2009 Suarez, along with millions around the world, was glued to his television set, watching the final of the Australian Open tennis tournament. It was an all-time classic for tennis fans. After a dramatic five set clash, Rafael Nadal became the first Spaniard in history to win the championship, and Roger Federer was unable to hold back the tears. During the trophy presentation, Nadal put his arm round Federer and used his podium speech to heap praise on his defeated rival.

Luis Suarez found that the epic battle contained 'something rather unique and compelling that speaks about what these giants are capable of.' The display of emotion, wrote Suarez, 'would melt everyone even in the toughest situations'. Most importantly, it proved that the two tennis champions 'are also human'.

Suarez posed the question: 'Can you imagine your business re-gaining that human side of things? Those feelings? Those emotions?'[1]

An appreciation of emotion doesn't mean we all need to become tree-hugging hippies. It's about all the things discussed so far in this book: an appreciation of and desire for change, the wish to engage and collaborate with others, the nurturing of passion, a readiness to learn and willingness to open up. Most of all, it means that we are listening to – and noticing – what others really want. The facial, physical manifestation of an emotion is one way in which others communicate how they really feel. Admittedly, we should be sensitive as to whether or not the displayer of any emotion is simply acting but, more often than not, these expressions are a good indication of what a person is thinking. And that's useful knowledge to have.

The evolution of business

Diverse voices, thoughts and interpretations are crucial in corporate governance today. Expressions of sadness, joy and the whole gamut of other emotions are all a part of that new reality. Having someone in your team who suddenly gets angry when a specific change is proposed, or who bursts out laughing at a new product idea, may cause irritation (or worse) at the time, but monotone acquiescence is worse. Governance by a cohesive but diverse group of people, with differing reactions and varied opinion, could be a surefire way to futureproof your business.

While the strategy of diversification – having investments or products in different markets – has long been a credible way to make your portfolio more profitable or your company more robust, diversifying your board and senior management might seem a more inward-looking tactic. But such diversity is critical if we are to survive in a fragmented, global marketplace. A number of studies have shown that companies with at least one female director, for example, are more successful than those with all-male boards.[2]

Why are diverse boards more effective?

Charles Darwin, the father of evolutionary theory, discovered that variability was the bedrock of evolution through natural selection. In his studies of flowers, Darwin found out that a whole number of variables were necessary for successful pollination – not just the interaction between plants and insects: for example, he observed that primroses didn't simply have male and female flowers, but that these distinct flowers would have either 'long-styled' or 'short-styled' structures.[3]

Darwin's ideas were instrumental in informing the understanding of heterosis or 'hybrid vigour', a term used in genetics and selective breeding to describe the possibility of obtaining a genetically superior individual through cross-breeding. Corn hybrids, for example, substantially outyield conventional corn crops, and respond much better to fertilisation.

It makes sense that the need for diversity and hybrid vigour should also apply to business systems: both internally, with regard to the make-up and culture of a company, and externally, with regard to the market in which a business operates.

This chapter is about business ecosystems and how to keep them thriving and healthy.[4] Diversity is an important measure of the health of an ecosystem, and **the long tail** of the internet is rich in diversity: listening and responding to the fringes, not just by exploiting niche markets but also by learning from them, is increasingly important.

In this book's introduction, I referred to Craig Newmark (**craigslist**) and Barack Obama as leaders who have displayed a high level of emotional intelligence. The reason for this is that both men have made a huge virtue of listening: Newmark because he enabled the dedicated community behind the world's largest classified ads site, and Obama because he built his campaign war chest not via the pockets of a handful of wealthy donors but from $10 micro payments from millions of ordinary Americans. I'll look in detail at their approaches in the second half of this chapter.

Ways of seeing

Diversity is something we should strive towards. That could be to do with the blind spots we encounter. Remember Arie de Geus and his interest in Francesco Varela's theory of cognitive objects? Varela proposes that we need to recognise something neurologically before we can process it. De Geus is concerned that companies, as a rule, tend not to recognise anything unfamiliar and will therefore carry on with redundant practices, however much lip service they might pay to 'fashionable' ideas such as empowerment, change or innovation.

> 'We human beings can only see what we already have in our brain,' says de Geus. 'This is absolutely vital for the survival of companies, that they realise they have this inability to see what is happening in the world.'

De Geus believes that companies can protect themselves against this blinkeredness by adopting various approaches and tactics to ensure they are constantly living, learning and open to new ideas. In *The Living Company*, he argues that the most successful businesses display great sensitivity to the environment around them: they are tolerant, decentralised and they have the ability to build constructive relationships with others, both within and outside the boundaries of the company.

De Geus' concerns echo the concern of the former Wall Street trader Nassim Nicholas Taleb who talks about 'our blindness with respect to randomness'[5] in his 2006 bestseller, *The Black Swan: The Impact of The Highly Improbable*.[6] In the book, Taleb uses numerous anecdotes to illustrate how we can actually predict very little in life. He argues that we should keep our businesses as diversified, networked and agile as possible. Although *The Black Swan* was published a few years before the global financial collapse of 2008, Taleb's words are prophetic:

> 'Globalization creates interlocking fragility, while reducing volatility and giving the appearance of stability. In other words it creates devastating Black Swans. We have never lived before under the threat of a global collapse. Financial institutions have been merging into a smaller number of very large banks. Almost all banks are interrelated. So the financial ecology is swelling into gigantic, incestuous, bureaucratic banks – when one fails, they all fall...we have moved from a diversified ecology of small banks, with varied lending policies, to a more homogeneous framework of firms that all resemble one another.' [7]

That keystone advantage

Taleb's biological metaphors are interesting. Like de Geus, he paints a picture of an interlinked ecosystem where every entity has a specific role to play. Collaboration is crucial, yes, but at the same time, differences should be optimised and jealously guarded: too much inter-dependence is counter-productive.

Harvard academics Marco Iansiti and Roy Levien first drew attention to the relevance of biological systems to the networked business world in 2004 with the publication of *The Keystone Advantage*.[8] In this book, they argue that the basis of competition has changed from battles between companies to battles between networks of companies: 'strategy is becoming...the art of managing assets one does not own.'[9]

A number of people I interviewed for this book talk about 'ecosystems' when referring to markets or market patterns. In Chapter 3 I looked at Google, whose 'keystone' role in the internet means it not only helps foster the health of the system, it also has most to gain from the system's good health. Google's Matt Glotzbach believes that this position has helped ensure that the company's culture has stayed vibrant and innovative, despite its size (currently around 20,000):

'I think there's always a risk as a company gets larger that that gets watered down and I see it going the other way...the Google culture and what we've been able to maintain and grow, even at our scale, is amazing.'

The MIT academic, Otto Scharmer, agrees that a shift is happening. He believes we are witnessing a change in the way industries are organised as diverse views become more important:

'We see a shift from organising around one single institutional logic towards organising around whole ecosystem logics,' he says. 'That's where the web, among [other things], provides a critical infrastructure for organising, that can allow us to develop a way of organising that really is centred around the whole ecosystem rather than just the logic of [a] single institution which is... using the large ecosystem...for a particular purpose.'

Linqia CEO, Maria Sipka, sees her consulting work as holistic: 'Our approach is completely decentralised. It's a waste of time to work with one single client, it's much more important to create an ecosystem.'

When Sipka talks about fostering an 'ecosystem' rather than a single client, she's not implying world domination for Linqia (although that would be a pleasant side-effect), she genuinely wants to see a functioning unit of interdependent companies which partner and share information, thereby maximising available resources. The richer the ecosystem, the more voices and strategies it contains, the more robust and enduring it will be: so much the better for its inhabitants.

It's no coincidence that many '**Web 2.0**' organisations have elements of randomness built in to ensure that any network(s) created will be as diverse as possible. A key criticism levied against **social technologies** is that it's easy to find yourself in an 'echo chamber' where everyone more or less agrees with you. In the modular, decentralised, networked world, each individual can decide just how reassuring or challenging they'd like their own personal network to be (although, to be fair, this behaviour already exists in the offline world where we tend to marry, make friends and employ people from our own social group, or buy a newspaper whose views we already know we're predisposed to agree with).

One example of default, inbuilt, 'randomness' is the public timeline or '**feed**' of **Tweets** on **Twitter**'s home page. It's possible for anyone in the world to read your status updates (unless you actively make them private): because of this you're likely to attract a hugely diverse group of 'followers'. The **Twitter** interface prioritises trending topics so it's easy to click on a topic and find something interesting by someone you don't know, and then start following them. No wonder co-founder Biz Stone called this particular feature the 'Discovery Engine' when **Twitter** launched it in April 2009.[10]

Anything but 'normal'

Increasingly, we learn that it's not so good to find the social norm and pin everything on it. The big hit, mass market, have-it-all culture that defined the developed (and, to some extent, the developing) world in the 20th Century now looks out-dated. In 1960 we all wanted to live in white picket-fenced Suburbia with our heterosexual partner, 2.4 children, dog, cat, gas-guzzling car, TV and washing machine. Today, virtually anything goes: it's normal to want to be 'different'.

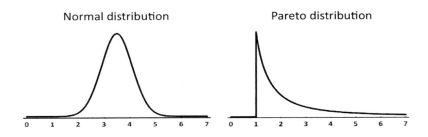

In 1733, the French Mathematician Abraham de Moivre discovered that a pattern of 'normal distribution' existed in certain groups of numerical data. When drawn on a graph, the normal distribution is completely symmetrical with a peak in the middle (around the mean or average figure) – this distribution is commonly known as the 'bell curve'. The normal distribution occurs in many natural phenomena including height and blood pressure, and is frequently assumed in science and statistics as a basis for testing and generating data. However, in the human-made world in which we live, any occurrence of the normal distribution is actually quite rare.[11]

Far more frequent in every day life is the Pareto distribution. This distribution, identified by the Italian economist, Vilfredo Pareto (1848-1923), represents Pareto's '80-20 rule' which he used to describe the fact that 20 percent of any given population tend to control 80 percent of the wealth. When shown on a graph, the Pareto distribution starts with a fat body to the left, and then slopes gently into a **long tail**. The Pareto distribution can be seen in the size of human settlements (few cities compared to many towns and villages) and in the type of files distributed over the internet (many small files versus fewer large ones).[12] It can also be seen in the buying patterns of consumers in markets where there is high freedom of choice: customers tend to favour 20 per cent of products over the other 80 per cent.[13]

In 2004, the Editor of *Wired* magazine, Chris Anderson, published *The Long Tail*, and threw the spotlight onto people whose needs and desires were, by definition, anything but 'normal'. Anderson was the first to pinpoint economic value in **the long tail** of the Pareto distribution curve. Instead of concentrating on the top 20 per cent of items, and selling large amounts of this limited number of products, Anderson argued that businesses could just as easily turn a profit by selling a larger number of niche items (the bottom 80 per cent). He pointed out that the internet, with its propensity to dramatically lower transaction and distribution costs, made this possible.[14]

This is quite exciting, because there has always been an inherent inequality in 'free' markets in that there was a physical limit to what shops could actually stock – which led to an over-dependence on the more popular items. Now, after years of focusing on the mass market, the common denominator and the creation of popular 'hits', whole industries are suddenly being told that profits can be made from selling to people who like quirky, odd stuff.

The Long Tail concept has been applied across a broad range of disciplines, from fund-raising (Barack Obama's US presidential campaign) and micro-finance (Grameen Bank, Zopa) through user innovation (where consumers and end users develop and refine a product, as opposed to suppliers) to **social technologies** such as **crowdsourcing** and to **peer-to-peer** distribution. Quintessentially **Web 2.0** businesses such as Amazon and eBay draw the bulk of their revenues from niche markets. This **Long Tail** is relevant to business leaders because, now, it's not only easier to *sell* to niche customers, it's also possible to listen to them. And they might actually have something of interest to say.

The cutting edge

'On the edge' or 'edgy' are terms which have long been associated with emotional instability or immaturity – these are the adjectives we use to describe provocative rock stars, satirical comedians or mouthy social commentators. Recently, however, we've seen an increasing focus on people at the edges – of our businesses, our marketplaces, even our conventional wisdom – as harbingers of economic and social change.

Since the early 1990s, the phrase 'edge of chaos' has been used in science as a metaphor for the way in which some systems (physical, biological, economic and social) exist somewhere between order and either complete randomness or chaos, where there is the greatest possible complexity.[15] The 'edge of chaos' is on the margins, but it is also the most creative place: the emergent beginning of something else. Like the tectonic plates that make up the Earth's surface, everything shifts – today's South-East Laurasia could be tomorrow's Himalayas.[16] **Complexity theory**, a relatively new academic discipline, attempts to address this mind-boggling stuff.

> 'The critical information is always on the margins,' says consultant Benjamin Ellis. 'In most businesses, what tends to happen is that the information that propagates is the meme: it's the lump of the big tail, late majority, whatever you want to call it. The interesting stuff you need to know as a business happens at the margins: it's what the little early adopters are doing, it's what's happening on **the long tail** with the exiting customers...that information is usually lost in a business and that's when you get Taleb's Black Swans – the events your risk assessment models would not have predicted.'

It was Ellis who first told me about Nicholas Nassim Taleb's book, and it seems he finds Taleb's ideas useful as a framework when consulting. Through **social tools** such as **blogs**, **wikis** and enterprise **RSS**, it's now easier than ever to capture and process information from the far reaches of your business: now you can practise 'mass listening' as opposed to mass marketing.

While Ellis values opinion at the 'edges' of business, fellow **social media** expert Stowe Boyd sees the edges as crucial for cultural and social change. For some years now, Boyd has been championing the online musings of ordinary people (as opposed to the mainstream media) – a group of individuals he likes to refer to as 'Edglings':

> 'I favor the term Edgling because I want to move away from media metaphors, and use economic or sociological ones. This...is about control moving from the central, large, mass-market organizations – which includes media companies, but also other large organizations, like government, religious organizations, and so on – out to the individuals – we, the people – at the edge.'[17]

Boyd sees these 'bottom up, egalitarian' people as incredibly important:

'[They have] a common base of perceptions about the world and our place in it that transcend the media market, and form what I think of as the basis for a future metaphysics, or, at the least, a new worldview.'[18]

Marketing expert Hugh McCleod would agree; in a series of *blog* posts entitled 'The Edges', McCleod recalled a key piece of advice from his mentor, Seth Godin: 'The edges. Always keep pushing on the edges'.[19] Godin was advising him in strategic terms: if you position yourself on the leading edge of a market, you're more able to change and adapt than the mass market majority.

But it seems that the edges are generally a sensible place to look for new forms of any kind of 'wealth' creation, especially at a time when our current sources are so depleted. In his Harvard Business School *blog*, appropriately named 'Edge Economy', economist Umair Haque argues that our old model for economic growth has reached its limits, and we need to start looking beyond those boundaries – to the edges – for new ideas:

'20th century capitalism is eating itself,' he wrote in January 2009. 'Today's leaders are plugging dikes, bailing out industries and banks as they fail. Yet, what negative global growth suggests is that the problem is of a different order: that we have reached the boundaries of a kind of growth.'[20]

Haque proposes four pillars of 'smart growth', all of which relate to better listening and noticing: Are people healthier, smarter and happier? How can we collaborate? How can we better invest in human capital? How can we focus on being economically 'creative' rather than, simply, productive?

An example of this kind of noticing can be seen in the concept of 'positive deviance': this is where solutions to social problems are found not by looking at the issues of those who are afflicted by any one particular problem – but instead by studying 'positive deviants' – the minority of people who should, in terms of demographics at least, be affected but have managed to function differently.

There seems to be a huge number of organisations looking for creative, social, solutions to our current day problems – in business, economics and society. It's as if, after centuries of adding layers of complexity, and actually moving industrial and civil institutions away from the people that they, ultimately, intend to benefit, we have finally realised that simple, social solutions, such as asking people what they want, can be the most effective.[21] Listening – to popular opinion, to the variegated *long tail*, to the *outliers* – is a skill we could all do well to master. **Social media** gives us the tools, it's up to us to learn how to use them correctly.

The wonderful wisdom of the ping pong ball

It's a Thursday afternoon just before Christmas and I'm drinking tea with cultural theorist Michael Thompson in the RSA's crowded coffee shop. Thompson became interested in **Cultural Theory** in the 1980s when he worked for an East-West think tank in Austria, specialising in risk perception (among other things). **Cultural Theory** argues that social structures create perceptions in individuals that will always reinforce those structures rather than favour the introduction of alternative ones. I ask Thompson if he feels the internet has a part to play in moving us on from this sorry state of affairs.

'The internet is clumsy by design!' says Thompson, enthusiastically.

Coming from Thompson, this is a compliment. In his terminology, 'clumsy' means 'good', even 'best'. Thompson is keen for us to find broad, all embracing, 'clumsy solutions' to cultural problems. He describes these as win-win resolutions where each party gets 'more of what it wants (and less of that which it does not want)'.[22] In essence, all voices are heard, and responded to.

Cultural Theory argues that there are, essentially, four ways of organising things. It describes these four voices or cultural modes as social '**solidarities**'. All too often we focus on just two: the individualistic mode (a free market economy, for example) and the hierarchical mode (for example, a heavily-regulated market). The other voices, which Thompson refers to as fatalistic and egalitarian, are all too often neglected.

Thompson has just finished giving a lunchtime lecture at the RSA, a lecture in which he proposed we can solve the current economic downturn by incorporating egalitarianism (equality with fettered competition) and fatalism (inequality with unfettered competition) more rigorously into future decision-making models. The model aims to be a holistic, 360° one (so inclusive that there is a fifth viewpoint, that of the hermit – who says nothing), so it seems appropriate that Thompson has drawn it on a ping pong ball, which is passed around the room.

The reason the model is on a ping pong ball is that we need three dimensions to represent the four solidarities, each one needs to border on the three others. In this way we see how each solidarity simultaneously depends on all of its neighbours and competes for space with them. The system is inherently dynamic but when one (or even two) colours dominate it is much more unstable. Imagine that intense pressure is generated when one or more of the ball's sections are compressed: if one colour takes over then it expands and is stretched to breaking point – the situation becomes volatile and unpredictable.

Our love of the 'pendulum' model (arguing between one of two extremes) and desire for an 'elegant solution' (using single definitions) leads us to favour a simplistic decision-making process in which alternative voices are excluded; additional viewpoints become 'uncomfortable knowledge' and are often dismissed without serious consideration. This has resulted in a world which is 'effectively one colour' says Thompson – individualistic, market-orientated: representing a 'self interest ideology'. This world has been hit by what Alan Greenspan, the former chairman of the US Federal Reserve, called a 'once in a century credit tsunami'.[23] It seems inevitable that, given our penchant for the pendulum, something 'hierarchical' will happen – and this is what we are seeing now, in the effective nationalisation of many major banks.

Financial institutions are just one example. Thompson opens his lecture with the story of Arsenal Football Club (an individualistic player), who approached Islington Council (hierarchical) to build its £60,000 seat Emirates Stadium. Within days, a third actor appeared – The Highbury Community Association (egalitarian) – and 'all hell broke out'. But all three voices were heard, some under-used land was found, and a 'clumsy' solution emerged. The new stadium was built on time and on budget; all parties were happy.

Another example is that of the Brent Spa storage and tanker-loading buoy which Shell wished to dispose of by sinking it in the Atlantic Ocean in 1995. Shell (the individualistic player) obtained consent from the UK Government (hierarchical). But Greenpeace (egalitarian) heard of the plan and launched a world-wide campaign against this type of disposal. A heated debate ensued and 'new paths were exposed that had been hitherto hidden', according to Thompson. Eventually, Shell agreed to re-purpose much of the original structure.

Thompson argues that the pendulum model reflects Robert Dahl's Classic Pluralist Theory in that it contains just two opposing viewpoints. The best we can hope for is some kind of democratic equilibrium ('pluralist democracy' – high responsiveness/accessibility); at worst, an authoritarian state ('closed hegemony' – nil responsiveness/accessibility). But if we add **Cultural Theory**'s three most active voices (the market, hierarchical and egalitarian voices) to Dahl's axes, the two outcomes are enhanced by a three-by-three grid of *nine* possibilities. Closed hegemony now comes in three forms, depending on which voice is drowning out the other two, while pluralist democracy (which

Thompson renames 'clumsy institution') comes in just one form – with all three voices heard and responded to by the others.[24]

If we stick with the pendulum model, says Thompson, we're going to be confined to just four of the nine provinces in his grid – and those four provinces are 'the most impoverished in terms of deliverable quality'. This impoverishment is demonstrated by adding a third dimension to the grid: now the 'clumsy institution' towers above all others, while closed hegemony 'really is the pits'.

When it comes to influencing the outcome of a system, the number of variables you take into account should match the variety of possible outcomes.[25] This means that to get a good, clumsy solution you should pay attention to at least three or four *solidarities*. For good business leadership, it's not so much a matter of representing all these *solidarities* simultaneously but more about being aware of the different approaches, and looking to facilitate ongoing discussion between them.

Such an approach isn't always going to be workable – clearly it takes time for a business leader to seek out and listen to opinions, especially those that disagree with him/her, but I really like Thompson's metaphor of 'clumsiness'. It ties in with the web's propensity for democracy and its ability to throw up the '*long tail*' of human opinion. We can assume all four *solidarities* would be present at some point in the tail (while some might be under-represented in the short, fat body).

The wrong sort of feedback

In the UK, there's a clutch of jokes that come around perennially when our National Rail services start to blame any delay or cancellation on the unpredictable weather. A favourite is the much-maligned platform announcer who, one year, blamed late-running trains on the 'wrong sort of snow'.[26]

British weather is famously unpredictable and difficult to prepare for. As the UK's rail networks fear the 'wrong sort' of weather, so companies are terrified of the 'wrong sort' of feedback: there's nothing more uncomfortable than being forced to listen to something you really don't want to hear. Praise and benign comments are all very well, but things can go haywire if a customer suggests a solution that doesn't chime with the corporate master-plan.

Salesforce.com has built a reputation on managing customer relationships efficiently. It offers more than 800 different types of software – but these aren't sold in packages to be installed on your desktop, they sit in the **Cloud** – you subscribe to them online, as a service. Salesforce.com's flagship product is a web-based 'sales force automation' service which provides 'streamlined' **Customer Relationship Management**. It's difficult to make automated services exciting, but the simple interface Salesforce.com offers, combined with the speed at which it works and is updated, has caused quite a stir.

The company's headquarters are in San Francisco's Financial District, alongside the banking and corporate offices, and just off the Embarcadero (waterfront), handy for the tasteful market stalls and fashionable shops in the city's renovated ferry terminal. It's in the terminal that Lorna Li, Salesforce.com's Web Marketing Manager (**social media** and **social networking**), arranges to meet me.

We sit down in the ferry terminal wine bar and order some Napa Valley wine and Cowgirl Creamery cheese. Li tells me about her cool job. It seems she gets to spend most of her day surfing around on **social networks**, upping the profile of Salesforce.com and striking up meaningful conversations with as many people as possible. As Salesforce.com is a definitive **Web 2.0** company, there's no limit on the debates she can get involved in or the topics she can address.

Li tells me about Salesforce.com's Ideas platform which was developed to provide a focused conduit for customer suggestions: customers send in ideas, and the customer community votes on the ones they think should be prioritised. Both *MyStarbucksIdea* and Dell's *IdeaStorm* were built on this platform.

Li recalls how some users of *IdeaStorm* started asking for **Linux** on their PCs. Dell, convinced that this was only a minority concern, introduced a 'vote down' button in order that other users might demote the issue; this backfired when users voted down, instead, a whole raft of other topics. Dell then chose to combine the requests for **Linux** with other, similar, suggestions, again causing an indignant reaction: as one **blogger** commented, 'What's the point of seeking ideas and feedback if you're going to delete (or "merge") the ones you don't like?'[27] Eventually Dell relented and installed **Ubuntu**, a **Linux** based operating system, on some of its computers, but the experiment didn't last.

MyStarbucksIdea has proved less controversial: within two weeks of launch, Starbucks had moved to implement the top two customer requests: free coffee for frequent buyers and universal free wifi (hardly contentious issues). Starbucks had very little in terms of **social media** when they launched the site in 2008 – not even a **blog**, and the site was, generally, well-received: 75,000 ideas were submitted within the first six months of launch. 'Whether you love or hate Starbucks, I think they deserve some credit for this relatively bold step,' wrote Eric Suesz, an online community manager and **blogger**.[28]

In 2006, Salesforce.com launched its own branded version on the Ideas platform: *IdeaExchange*. Although not all ideas that come through *IdeaExchange* are popular with Salesforce.com's staff, the company prides itself on the fact it listens. Overall, *IdeaExchange* has vastly improved product development at Salesforce.com: every time Salesforce.com issues a new software release, around half the new features come directly from customer suggestions.[29]

Ultimately, *MyStarbucksidea*, *IdeaStorm* and *IdeaExchange* have proved a great means for their respective companies to grow and nurture an ongoing conversation with their customers. All three have benefited from a better overall picture of their consumer base, in particular the most vocal customers (all too often, running a business can be a bit like sitting behind a two-way mirror). The duty of having to listen to customers may seem onerous to start with but, as Li points out, it's a great way to gain – or maintain – competitive advantage.

An increased commercial sharpness is just one feature to be delivered by these conversational tools. They also help enrich the business ecosystem by bringing in diverse opinions and multiple viewpoints. Again, it's a means of reaching out, connecting, listening and responding to those ideas at the edge of your marketplace.

If any city has a reputation for listening to diverse voices, it's San Francisco. To the West of the financial district, where I meet Li, the boutique-lined streets of Haight Ashbury mark the historic birthplace of the hippie movement. North Beach is famous as the 1950s haunt of the counter-cultural Beat poets. Chinatown plays host to the largest Chinese New Year Parade outside of China. The Castro is the world's best known gay neighbourhood. For the past half century, San Francisco has been a centre of liberal activism, and the Democratic and Green parties dominate local politics. Maybe it's no surprise that so many businesses representing the participative, **Web 2.0** culture have established themselves here.

Local Hero

It's a bright, crisp September morning and I'm still in San Francisco: walking up Cole Street, taking photos and generally killing time before my next appointment. Cole Street runs along the western edge of groovy Haight

Ashbury. The roads are typically steep, the buildings and shop fronts familiarly pastel-coloured.

Half way up the street, on the opposite side, I see a short, slightly portly, man in a grey jacket and beret bend down to offer something edible to a short, slightly portly, dachshund. The dachshund jumps up, politely, as each new treat is offered, her tail wagging. The man is not her owner, but she is clearly pleased to see him.

'There you go, Coco,' says the man.

Although we've never met, the man has certain features which enable me to recognise him as Craig Newmark, founder of the classified ads site, *craigslist*. I step over to say hello. A discussion ensues between Newmark and Coco's owner as to whether or not the little dog is overweight.

Coco looks healthy – glossy, even – and I'm sure Newmark's treats aren't doing too much harm. After all, this is a man who has built his reputation (and modest fortune) on ensuring customer satisfaction.

An hour later, I meet Craig Newmark again – this time for our scheduled chat at his local, The Reverie Café. He's still concerned about the neighbourhood dogs.

'I've run out of treats,' he says, patting his pockets, fruitlessly.

Conversation with Newmark is peppered with asides like this. His attention is easily diverted, sometimes by a *realtime* interruption, sometimes when a pressing thought crosses his mind. He seems curious about each new person who arrives in the café: what they are doing, what they might need, how their lives might work.

You get the impression that Newmark's charming unpredictability was one of the factors which made him decide early on that he wasn't right to run a global business. Since 2000, stewardship of *craigslist* has been in the hands of the current CEO, Jim Buckmeister. The irony is that Newmark is famous for listening: his interest in others is what has made *craigslist* the enormous success it is today.

And, by the way, *craigslist* isn't a typo – Newmark insists it be spelt with a lower case 'c' – the last thing he would want is that anyone sees him as important in all of this. One of the other interviewees for this book warned me (kindly) that Newmark was 'humble to the point of ludicrousness'.

Now we've met, I can see why. In a world of towering egos, Newmark is a refreshing blast of fresh air.

Newmark started *craigslist* back in 1995 when he'd just moved to San Francisco and wanted to create an online listing service for events in the Bay Area. By the end of 1997 the site was getting one million page views per month. By 1999, the service was doing so well, Newmark incorporated it as a business. Today, *craigslist* is a global phenomenon, serving 450 cities in 50 countries. Newmark retains the title of Founder, but spends most of his time working in the area that interests him most – customer services:

> 'Consumers and line workers are the people who know how the business should run. In hierarchies, you have a lot of problems. The people who are good at climbing up the career ladder, their job skill is climbing up the ladder and not anything else. That's why hierarchies tend to get dysfunctional all the time...I guess the approach is to try and stay flat.'

The original *craigslist* office in San Francisco still only employs 25 people. Newmark quickly realised that the best way to manage an online community was to enable it to run itself. *craigslist*'s moderators, content producers and community managers are all volunteers from the user community.

Newmark says that good customer service – and employee/employer relationships – is what keeps his staff, volunteers and customers coming back. He believes that the *craigslist* community shares a 'culture of trust' which means most of its members are incredibly loyal.

> 'The value that generates trust, is the value of treating people how you want to be treated...I am constantly in touch with our community and I'm always learning. I have learnt that there are people that you can't please and some people who are very passionate about helping and you should empower them. On the other hand, there are people who want attention and will do anything to get it. They're the people we call **"trolls"**.'

The term '*troll*' is geek parlance for someone who posts inflammatory or off-topic messages in a community, simply because they want to provoke an emotional response. One way in which Newmark deals with the handful that besiege his network is through public humiliation: he posts their scurrilous comments on his 'You may be a *troll* if...' page.[30]

Much of Newmark's day is spent following up complaints, and checking and re-checking postings, looking for any signs of abuse or scamming. Meanwhile, he does his best to follow up any genuine suggestions from members of the community: in the early days, there was pressure to ban banner ads from the site; Newmark was happy to oblige.

Now Newmark has stepped aside as CEO, he has more time to focus on the things that matter to him. His candid philosophy, combined with the commercial success of *craigslist*, means that he's in constant demand for media interviews, and regularly invited to conferences around the world. Newmark acknowledges that he has a public role to play:

> 'I feel like I'm having an extended 15 minutes of fame. For some reason, people listen to me, so I might as well have something useful to say. There are causes that need people to stand up for them.'

Newmark speaks on behalf of the Iraq and Vietnam War veterans and campaigned for Barack Obama to win the Democratic nomination. He also promotes Spinewatch, a campaign set up by journalist Jay Rosen to encourage the US media to be more critical (where necessary) of the US Government.

The fact that Newmark champions a variety of causes is a further indication of his ability to listen: the causes all represent different groups, but Newmark is clearly just at home chatting with powerful politicians like Obama, as he is speaking to war heroes who have suffered great physical and psychological damage. Newmark has built an impressive, sustainable business in *craigslist*. It comes as no surprise that his network of influential friends is also diverse, rich and robust.

Tracking the influencers

Times have changed: a company's network (i.e. the matrix of relationships between the people it serves and employs, as well as those who, officially, 'govern' it) is now as powerful as – if not stronger than – the traditional hierarchy. In *The Starfish & The Spider*, Brafman and Beckstrom question the whole idea of the pre-eminence of the hierarchy compared to a company's informal networks. According to Brafman and Beckstrom, it's the strength of one-to-one personal networks that actually defines a company's success.

People like Craig Newmark understand this – he has virtually eliminated corporate hierarchy at *craigslist* – but many of us are still addicted to more traditional ways. It's not so much that hierarchies are *wrong*, it's just that they need to be viewed in context – we need to appreciate that there are other ways of doing things (a key tenet of **Cultural Theory**).

In September 2008, Mat Morrison, Global Head of Digital Planning at Porter Novelli (a PR agency), started developing a network analysis tool called **Rufus**. The tool aims to map online 'influencers'. This means that a client can, for example, see who's talking to whom about a certain product – and, more importantly, who's listening.

I meet Morrison one Friday morning at Tuttle Club, where he's showing off **Rufus** to a handful of admirers. What the tool has been great at, says Morrison, is demonstrating how tangential a company's influence can be, particularly where its own products or services are concerned.

Rufus works by processing information freely available on the web. Starting with a keyword (such as diabetes), **Rufus** acts like a smaller version of Google, using a spider to go through the search results looking at links, and reciprocal links. From this, it can see who the key stakeholders in a conversation are, and who's listening to whom.

Rufus is just one of a number of mapping tools that can help organisations learn more about their own internal communications. Any corporate org chart can show who reports to and who oversees whom, but the real power (i.e. influence) often lies outside these lines. Tracking relationships on **social networks** is a great way to learn about these informal structures.

Years ago, when I worked at the satellite television broadcaster BSkyB, I remember that the Facilities Manager, Mandy, had a tremendous amount of control. Partly because she had a gatekeeping role, but also because she had been with Sky Television (BSkyB's predecessor) since day one, had watched everyone else come in, and was acutely aware of who talked to who and what else was happening in the company. If **Facebook** (or an internal version) had existed then, Mandy would have had the most friends.

I'm wondering what different organisational maps might look like. Two of Morrison's **Rufus** maps catch my eye. One shows the conversation flow between educational policy makers, the other represents people discussing research into diabetes. Each data set generates a very different graphic. The map of policy makers contains many small, disparate groups, each of which consists of a series of spokes and nodes radiating out around a key influencer. Some policy makers appear to be completely isolated. Interestingly, the key influencers don't seem to want to communicate with each other. The map of researchers is more networked, with nine or ten people who have circles of smaller nodes attached to them; there is also a degree of communication between each of the key nodes: I would hazard a guess that this is the healthier community.

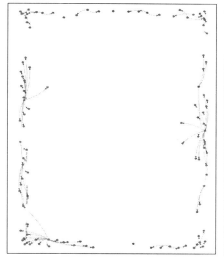

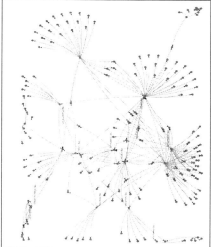

Educational policy network   Diabetes research network

One of the first things Morrison did when he arrived at Porter Novelli was send around an email with a **SurveyMonkey** survey to find out who'd been talking to who about digital in the previous two months. This helped him map out the influencers and get a sense of the network he needed to connect with.

Understanding these informal patterns and identifying key nodes or 'point' people is a great way to start getting things done in your organisation. Which of those two **Rufus** maps do you think your informal network might look like?

Sometimes, truth hurts

To borrow a phrase from George Orwell, it seems all people are networked, but some are more networked than others. Employers who listen best will be ahead of the curve. The critical success factor lies in coaxing the best out of the people you work with and, much like a marriage, knowing when to bite your tongue and accept the other person's view when it matters.

In *The Living Company* Arie de Geus argued that that all decision-making is primarily social: unheroic and unscientific. It should be seen as a learning process, he said, where as many different viewpoints as possible should be encouraged and heard.

This is exactly what Michael Thompson is talking about earlier in the chapter: diverse viewpoints are essential input for any 'clumsy solution' but, all to often, they become 'uncomfortable knowledge,' to be dismissed without serious consideration.

Listening to what employees really want has led to a whole slew of innovations in business in recent years. These often concern strategies that concern every day working conditions. For example, 'duvet days' is a relatively new practice whereby employees are permitted a set number of days to take off annually not because they're sick but because they're hung over, fancy a lie in, or simply can't be bothered to come in. Employers are adopting this policy in an effort to reduce the number of sick days taken each year.[31]

It's no coincidence that prominent PR consultant Julia Hobsbawm has written a book[32] championing flexible working as the most significant workplace trend of the 21st century:

> 'Surely the most important factor is how to be the most productive – both commercially as well as in terms of factors such as motivation? The challenge for all employers is to tune in with the way their current practices can or can't reflect this new priority, to think less in terms of office-based office hours as a culture for achieving productivity and more in terms of highly personalised solutions.'

Hobsbawm believes that real change will take a couple of generations. She thinks that, ultimately, our expectations will alter so much that people who have limited flexibility will be paid more than those who can work with a higher degree of autonomy: in other words, there'll be a reward system for those who experience restrictive working conditions (oil rigs, for example).

Playing politics

I once worked in a TV newsroom where the news editor regularly shouted insults and admonishments at his team. But the wall of his office was heavy with the awards that he'd won for excellence in news production. With tens of other freelancers lined up to take our places, there wasn't really much point in persuading him to 'listen'.

To some extent, CEOs and senior managers can decide how they wish to run their business units. Each individual leader will take a look at the processes and requirements of his/her sector and decide which management practices yield the best results. Certainly in many of the creative environments I've worked in, where deadlines rule and facilities are expensive, the command-and-control style is extremely common. Listening takes time, and time is money.

For democratically-elected politicians, however, good listening is crucial. If a politician doesn't ask his constituents what they want, and make sure he actually hears their answers, and responds appropriately, rather than pay lip service, his position will be up for grabs at the next election.

No politician established a better reputation for listening as quickly as Barack Obama. Since he won the US Presidential election in November 2008 there's been a slew of books about the Obama strategy and consequent lessons for business. Obama's use of **social media** to connect with voters, raise funds and galvanise support was nothing short of phenomenal. And it's true, leaders everywhere have a great deal to learn from this approach.

Listen, don't acquiesce

It's April 2009 and the day before the G20 Summit in London. Democrat campaigner Karin Robinson should be out on the streets, leading the pro-Obama rally she's been promoting. Instead, she's put her back out, so she's confined to her flat, going stir crazy and watching news of various anti G20 demonstrations online. This has given her plenty of time to assess the strategy of the demonstrators. Overall, she's unimpressed.

> 'Let's say they got what they wanted. Let's say Barack Obama woke up this morning and went, "Hey, these protesters are right, I'll do what they want!" Do they even have an agenda? One of the signs said 'Abolish Money'. Are these protestors going to thrive in the new barter economy? Are they farmers, are they shepherds? What's their rationale?'

As a US citizen and fervent supporter of Obama, Robinson knows all about agenda-setting. She worked as a regional field director on Obama's US presidential campaign between July and November 2008. Her remit was to mobilise as many US Democratic voters as possible across the UK, Ireland, Scandinavia and South Africa.

From her base in London, Robinson made daily reports to campaign headquarters in Washington, DC. Every day, she'd get reviewed targets back:

'There was a lot of pressure to reach targets, we were really working our tails off. But it would have been easy to miss the opportunity to capitalise on all those volunteers. There were stories that [Republican candidate John] McCain volunteers were being sent home because the campaign wasn't prepared for them.'

By contrast, the Obama Campaign was meticulously organised at every level:

'In some of our key states we had forty per cent of people having some kind of contact with the campaign. [The campaign organisers] made it clear from the start that they wanted an unprecedented level of contact – face to face contact – the ability to use *social media* to make that happen was a very clever exploitation.'

Robinson goes on to describe how the campaign used sites such as **Facebook** and MeetUp as an adjunct to, and extension of, face-to-face contact.

'We were using [*social networks*] to find people and to communicate and to directly organise...Every single objective [was about] getting people offline. Every **YouTube** video would end with "Go volunteer, go give money, go do this!". One of Obama's signature endings for his stump speech, his generic campaign trail speech, was "So if you'll work with me, come out and vote with me, we'll do this!". The whole tenor of the event was geared towards getting people out.'

This emphasis on calls to action was present at all levels of the campaign. Robinson remembers the Democratic Nomination Convention which took place in a 75,000 seater stadium in Denver in August 2008:

'Under every seat was a piece of paper with a list of names. Before people came out and started doing speeches, the voter registration director asked everyone to take out their mobiles and call four people on their list. We wanted to send a signal at the highest possible level that this was a volunteer-led campaign.'

But the most revolutionary aspect of the Obama Campaign was the fact that it was the first in history to be majority-funded by small donations. The donors were encouraged not only to connect with their regional campaign headquarters, but to connect with each other. The community built quickly, brimming with *social capital*. The very image of Obama himself embodied change, and the campaign was meticulous in repeating that symbol of change everywhere. By the end of the campaign, the official White House website was transformed from an authoritarian, text-heavy front page to a welcoming portal, a smiling Obama beaming from the top right hand corner.

On Obama's *Change* website, Google Moderator is now being used to enable US citizens to vote up issues of importance to them (although the 'Open For Questions' function raised eyebrows earlier this year when marijuana legalisation topped the poll). *MyBarackObama* continues as a thriving community, with the 'Obama For America' campaign now rebranded as 'Organising For America'. Obama's **Twitter** stream, **MySpace**, **Bebo** and **Facebook** profiles all remain active.

Obama also has an offline way of getting a feel for what's bothering people at a grassroots level. Every day, according to Robinson, he asks for a selection of letters from the public to glance through: 'He's really concerned that once you become president you become detached from reality. He's very serious about not losing touch.'

And Robinson adds that despite Obama being a great listener, the world's expectations of him can run impossibly high. We're back to those G20 protestors again, and their unclear agenda: 'Obama really is listening to people but what you've got to remember is he's not just listening to you. People sometimes mistake listening for acquiescence.'

The new zeitgeist

In an article entitled 'Staff Finds White House in the Technological Dark Ages,' Washington Post reporter Anne E. Kornblut talked about the Obama team arriving on their first day in their new office, brimming with iPhones and MacBooks, only to be confronted by reinforced firewalls and ageing Microsoft technology.

When I remind Robinson of this, she laughs at the memory:

> 'It completely rang true for me. A lot of the campaigners, they **Facebook'ed** and they instant messaged and a lot of their tools were blocked in the White House. When they got in there, they couldn't contact anyone. They said "I don't have anyone's phone numbers!"

> 'I do think that a zeitgeist changed. The people who have come into the White House now are accustomed to having **realtime** sharing of their lives. They're constantly **blogging**, they're constantly YouTubing, they're constantly **Facebooking**. Their assumptions about how you interact with the world are different.'

The Bush Administration's lack of familiarity with new media seems an apt metaphor for the way in which it, ultimately, failed to connect with world opinion. It is too early to tell if the Obama Administration will truly fulfil its promise of bringing change to America, but at least the new White House staff is fully wired in and switched on to **social technologies**. We can only presume this means that they are clued up, as well.

Listen well, listen good

Obama's apparent ability to listen is one that will be tested with time and only history will confirm whether or not he is a truly innovative leader. The current US President's humility, his ability to say sorry and his keenness to connect with his constituency are all signs (although not necessarily proof) of at least a *willingness* to cede some control and open up matters of strategy and governance to external review and input, where feasible.

Leaders like Obama and Newmark have shown that its possible to listen to your community – whether it consists of voters or customers. Companies like Salesforce.com and Porter Novelli – along with **Facebook**, **Twitter**, **Huddle** and others – are among those providing the tools.

It's true that, today, many businesses are learning how to listen. They have learnt to monitor what's being said about them, both internally and externally. Most have accepted that **social media** is now a key part of the enterprise landscape. But listening is one thing – true collaboration is more difficult. If we really want to strengthen our organisations and arm ourselves with the diverse viewpoints that enable informed, 360 degree decision-making, then we need to reach out to the influencers and work with them. The possibilities – and challenges – of such collaboration will be discussed in detail in the final chapter.

Notes

1. www.elsua.net/2009/02/02/on-humanising-titans
2. See, for example: *Women Matter: Gender diversity, a corporate performance driver* (McKinsey & Company, 2007) and *The Bottom Line: Corporate Performance and Women's Representation on Boards* (Catalyst, 2007).
3. BBC Radio Four *In Our Time* programme on Darwin, cited in Chapter 3.
4. The term 'ecosystem' has become a business buzzword but I'm using it to signify more than just an 'efficient market' – in the context of this book, the term encompasses the whole environment in which a business operates, and should take as many variables as possible into account, including human and environmental factors.
5. Nassim Nicholas Taleb (2007), *The Black Swan: The Impact of the Highly Improbable*. Random House, p. xix.
6. *ibid*.
7. *ibid*, p. 225-6.

8. Marco Iansiti and Roy Levien (2004), *The Keystone Advantage: What the New Dynamics of Business Ecosystems Mean for Strategy, Innovation, and Sustainability.* Harvard Business School Press.
9. *ibid*, p. 1.
10. blog.twitter.com/2009/04/discovery-engine-is-coming.html
11. This has been observed by a number of mathematicians and is argued particularly strongly by Deborah J. Bennett in her book, *Randomness* (Harvard University Press, 1998).
12. en.wikipedia.org/wiki/Pareto_distribution
13. en.wikipedia.org/wiki/The_Long_Tail
14. Chris Anderson (2006), *The Long Tail: Why The Future of Business is Selling Less of More.* Hyperion.
15. en.wikipedia.org/wiki/Edge_of_chaos
16. Around 200 million years ago, the Earth's land mass was made up of two super-continents, Laurasia and Gondwana. Approximately 60 million years ago, the tectonic plate containing India broke away from Gondwana (the southern super-continent) and began to float north towards the south-east coast of Laurasia; the Himalayas were created around 40-50 million years ago, when the plate containing India finally collided with the plate containing Laurasia.
17. www.stoweboyd.com/message/2006/07/edglings.html
18. *ibid.*
19. www.gapingvoid.com/Moveable_Type/archives/004663.html
20. blogs.harvardbusiness.org/haque/2009/01/davos_discussing_a_depression.html
21. See, for example, the work of the award-winning Thinkpublic: an agency focused on improving service experiences in the public sector (further information at www.thinkpublic.com).
22. Michael Thompson (2008), *Organising & Disorganising.* Triarchy Press, p 4.
23. news.bbc.co.uk/1/hi/business/7687101.stm
24. Michael Thompson (2008), pp. 13-15.
25. This is known as the Requisite Variety Condition, which Thompson discusses in *ibid*, p. 32.
26. *Daily Mail* columnist Harry Phibbs recalled the story: 'In 1991 the trains were halted by some moderate snow fall. British Rail told outraged commuters that the quantity may not have been too severe but that: "It was the wrong sort of snow." That phrase has lived on in infamy as symbolising the defeatist mentality of those who gave up and offered excuses at the first sign of difficulty. The mentality that lost the empire.' (www.dailymail.co.uk/debate/article-1133790/HARRY-PHIBBS-Wheres-true-grit-face-snow-And-did-cancel-ALL-Londons-buses-asking-Boris.html#ixzz0Ss2KvXSh).
27. tech.blorge.com/Structure:%20/2007/03/01/dell-censors-ideastorm-linux-dissent
28. blog.getsatisfaction.com/2008/03/30/mystarbucksideacom-a-half-full-idea
29. Additional information about the *IdeaExchange* platform is from Charlene Li and Josh Bernoff (2008), *Groundswell.* Harvard Business Press, pp. 185-186.
30. www.craigslist.org/about/best/sfo/43786789.html
31. For more information, see: www.duvetday.org
32. Julia Hobsbawm (2009), *The See-saw: 100 Ideas for Work-life Balance.* Atlantic.

Myth: Giving stuff away is commercial suicide

Reality: Collaboration makes you richer

It's March 2009 and I'm sitting in Mark Rock's office near London Bridge. It's been three weeks since the launch of his latest creation, **Audioboo**, and Rock is quietly pleased with progress. This morning the brand new **social network** was name-checked by Chris Moyles on his Radio One show. Tony Blackburn, Stephen Fry and the BBC's Technology correspondent, Rory Cellan-Jones, are all fans. In addition, there have been numerous remarks in the national press and even a leader mention in *The Guardian*.[1]

Audioboo lets people record and upload five minute snatches of audio from anywhere, using a mobile phone (the technology is currently only available on the iPhone, but Rock has plans to make it available on other models soon).

Audioboo is not only dead easy to use – it's virtually free. When Rock's company, Best Before Media, launched **Audioboo** in partnership with Channel 4's 4IP project, they decided to make it a '**freemium**' service. This means that while the majority of users access the software for nothing; a small proportion (currently around 5 per cent) pay a monthly subscription of £2.95 for additional features (e.g. easier uploading, larger photo allowance) and a tiny number of corporate clients (which currently include the British Library and the BBC) pay around £500 a month for **customised** versions.

There are three reasons for launching **Audioboo** in this way, says Rock:

1. It's a **social network** so it doesn't work without content
2. The costs of adding each extra user are minimal
3. It's an innovative product – a relatively new idea

Podcasters love **Audioboo**: earlier this year, Christian Payne (aka Documentally) **audiobooed** the birth of his son. Stephen Fry says it's a great alternative to **Twitter** when he's forgotten his reading glasses. And news journalists are also finding it useful: when BBC reporter Matthew Weaver forgot his digital recorder at the G20 protests in London in March, he used **Audioboo** instead.

This is exactly the market Rock wants to target. He sees his new baby as 'an audio version of **Twitter** or **Flickr**'. Like all true innovators, Rock is carving out a market for something that we don't know we need – until now. He's been thinking a lot about 'sound ecology' (our aural environment) and speaking to people called 'acousticians'. Rock has a winning way of selling his idea:

> 'The real value from **Audioboo** will be in 5 or 10 years time. So when my 3 year old is 13, I've actually got a huge aural record of her life – meta data we can slice and dice and reversion in so many different ways...it's priceless!'

Every profile and **tag** on **Audioboo** has an **RSS feed**. And users can create audio maps featuring any type of sound they like. Soon, Best Before will publish an **API** that'll enable third parties to build applications that expand **Audioboo**'s functionality. It's all very much a work in progress.

> 'It's the "agile" approach. The customer is more important than the business plan. You iterate...you build as you go rather than saying "we'll launch in nine months". [It] really means that you can try stuff and see if it sticks and then continue to do it.'

These are still early days and it will be a while before **Audioboo** starts showing any return on its investment – but Rock is optimistic. He has good reason. Networks such as **Flickr**, **Last.fm** and **Spotify** are all examples of successful social sites that use the **freemium** model. **Flickr** was acquired by Yahoo in 2005 for £22m ($35m), **Last.fm** by CBS for £140 million ($280 million) in 2007 and Swedish start-up **Spotify** received venture capital rumoured to be as much as £31 million ($50 million) in August 2009, giving a significant boost to the company's market value.[2]

Culture clash

The Free, **Open Source** and – latterly – **Creative Commons** movements have been intrinsic to the growth and success of the web. They underpin a whole raft of applications, products and services – from online communities to business models. Rock's **Audioboo** is just one example; **Huddle** and **SocialText**, featured previously, also use a **freemium** model. Google's software is freely available to consumers (albeit with a closed source code). Conversely, there are plenty of applications, such as **Moodle** or **Drupal**, which are free and **open source**.

Books promoting a 'sharing' mentality, such as Don Tapscott's *Wikinomics* (2006), Jeff Howe's *Crowdsourcing* and Charles Leadbeater's *We-think* (both 2008), have become global best-sellers. These books promote different approaches to mass collaboration, which in itself can be broadly divided into two categories: **peer production** (relatively structured, between business partners) and **crowdsourcing** (an open call for ideas and input; often on vast, ambitious projects). **Peer production** has taken place for some decades via **Lotus Notes** and earlier **groupware**, while **crowdsourcing** is relatively new, via the internet.

But for most businesses, the act of giving a service away free or sharing research and data about products, services or even corporate strategy is still fraught with risks. 'Some rights reserved' licensing is generally anathema to the corporate world. Successful business has always been based around the idea of adding value and monetising that value wherever you possibly can. As any *Apprentice* wannabe will know: sell stuff at a higher price than that which you paid for it. Giving anything away seems counter-intuitive.

This practical issue is compounded by a cultural one: sharing needs to be done in a certain spirit, otherwise it's going to be misinterpreted at best; costly and/or destructive at worst. So, we have a situation where a business might (reluctantly) try an **open source** or **creative commons** approach, experience failure, and then reel this 'test case' out at any point in future when a similar project is proposed, as a concrete example of why such a strategy can never succeed. Peter Senge referred to this situation as 'the delusion of learning from experience'.[3]

The underlying motivation for any kind of 'open' strategy – whether it be to give a product or service away for free, to share otherwise privileged information or to publish a creative 'work in progress' – needs to be generous: the strategy should be informed by an honest desire to build social capital and strengthen community rather than generate revenues (at least, in the short term). There may well be a reward, but you might need to be patient. The reward will not necessarily be easy to measure (another hurdle) and it is likely to come, initially at least, in the form of goodwill or an enhanced reputation, rather than direct revenues.

This chapter describes the different free/open/shared strategies in more detail, and explores the nature of the generosity that underlies such approaches. I don't advocate these strategies as the *only* way of working in future, but they are good tools to have in your toolbox. And **social technologies** are enabling them to be increasingly common.

Free love

Open source is a strategic model that (according to **Wikipedia**) 'allows concurrent input of different agendas, approaches and priorities, and differs from the more closed, centralized models of development'.[4] The term has its origins in software development and is usually taken to mean, literally, that the 'source code' (i.e. the collection of human-readable statements that make up a computer program) is made available for public collaboration through an **open source** license.

The Free Software Movement began in 1985 when computer programmer, Richard Stallman, set up the **GNU project**. The movement is built around an **open source** principle but has a broader philosophical approach (considered by pragmatists to be too confrontational), which encompasses 'the users' [complete] freedom to run, copy, distribute, study, change and improve the software.'[5]

Stallman and the GNU project pioneered open source licenses which proved to be very practical: many indispensable tools were developed under them (free compilers such as GCC, for example, without which **Linux** would have been impractical for Torvalds to develop). Today, the GNU General Public License (GPL) is the most widely used free software license on the web. It has been successfully tested in court and it is a great example of viral effects; the license must be copied whenever the software is copied.

Since the mid 1990s, Stallman has spent much of his time campaigning for free software and arguing against software patents and the excessive use of copyright legislation. He is a keen promoter of copyleft, a form of licensing that allows free reproduction, adaption and distribution, and has been crucial to the success of many software projects including **Apache** and **Linux**. The GPL copyleft license pre-dated 'open source' and 'creative commons' licenses by decades, which may account for some of the hostility between the proponents of each movement.[6]

The principles of free software have been around since the 1950s, when IBM released source code to nascent developer communities. The birth of the internet itself in 1969 was due to the collaborative methods used by researchers working with **ARPANET** (the Advanced Research Projects Agency Network), and the construction of the World Wide Web some twenty years later was through a similarly collaborative process.

Robert Cailliau is an ex-employee of **CERN** (the European Centre for Nuclear Research), who worked with Tim Berners-Lee on the development of the

World Wide Web in the early 1990s. Cailliau remembers how the use of **open source** technologies enabled his team to work faster than their competitors:

> 'At that time there were many different people thinking about this idea and ours was the one that took off. If we'd "locked" it up, those other people would have got in on the act.'[7]

But it was only around the turn of this century that **open source** and free models really began to take hold in the software market.

In 1998 Netscape had the innovation of giving away the source code to its early web browser, Navigator, but continuing to publish proprietary work containing that code. By 2005, the idea of giving away the source code was becoming mainstream with projects such as **Linux**, **Apache**, MySQL, PHP, Firefox, and Eclipse all becoming well-established 'brands' in the software sector.

The centre cannot hold

Although free and **open source** methods originated in software, such approaches are now being applied in other areas, e.g. biotechnology and the cultural industries. In recent years, **Creative Commons** and Science Commons licenses have been developed as 'some rights reserved' alternatives to traditional intellectual property laws (copyright, patent and trademark), which are generally considered to be too restrictive for the new digital world.

The **Creative Commons** Foundation was set up by Lawrence Lessig, James Boyle and others in 2001. The Foundation was established as a response to the exponential growth in personal computer ownership and internet use which was enabling the rapid and relatively inexpensive distribution of culture via digital media. The **Creative Commons** founders realised that the existing legal framework did not accommodate this new consumer behaviour.

As we know, the internet enables extremely low-cost, in some cases no-cost, distribution and production. Words, music and movies are easy to circulate in digital format. And the cheap duplication and production doesn't stop there: once 3D printers become mainstream, as Neil Gershenfeld points out in *Fab*, we'll be able to 'print' off virtually anything we want: from clothes and kitchen utensils to torches and alarm clocks.[8]

Today there is virtually no restriction for artists, musicians and writers who want others to see or hear their work, and no limit for those who wish to make and share copies of this work. The boom in **social networking** and trend towards an increasingly participative, 'bottom up' web have only accelerated the blossoming of an **open source** culture. We now live in a world where many people, especially the under 30s, want to access and share digital content wherever and however they wish. Through **social media** like **MySpace**, **YouTube**, **Pirate Bay** and **BitTorrent**, users can listen to whatever they like and watch whatever they want to.

Traditionally, the reaction of business has been to do what it can to halt this cultural tsunami. For example, both the RIAA (Recording Industry Association of America) and the MPAA (Movie Producers Association of America) continue to take an aggressive stance in the US, filing lawsuits against individuals who illegally download music and movie files. This behaviour has probably caused more harm than good to both industries, although its impact is hard to quantify.

In August 2009, the UK's Trade and Industry Secretary, Lord Mandelson, announced proposals to cut off internet access for people who persist in illegal file-sharing. Such legislation is likely to be challenged by privacy groups as they are highly impractical and possibly illegal: a similar law in France was ruled unconstitutional by the country's highest court.[9]

To apply the language of **Cultural Theory**, these are all 'hierarchical' solutions being applied in such a way that they drown out other possibilities. Our fears about some 'blood dimmed tide'[10] of anarchy have created a highly volatile situation. It would be good if an egalitarian approach could be considered. People are using **social media** to organise alternative voices (through e-petitions, for example), but the dominant, decision-making organisations, whether they are industry bodies or government, do not seem to have the right listening mechanisms in place. One thing is for certain: the continuing sea change in cultural expectations, catalysed by the internet and combined with the sheer scale of digital file-sharing, means that business – and governments – need to modify their approach.

Don't worry about Bluebeard

> 'It's not theft, it's copyright violation – it's a different thing completely!
> If I steal your watch it means you don't have it any more and I do.
> Whereas if I infringe your copyright, you still have the thing I've
> infringed. I've taken a copy of it but you've still got it. It's a bit hysterical,
> calling it theft.'

Suw Charman-Anderson smiles sweetly but it's clear she's fed up. We're ensconced on a sofa at One Alfred Place, and Charman-Anderson is explaining the motivations behind the Open Rights Group, the non-profit organisation she set up with fellow web luminaries, Cory Doctorow (**Boing Boing**) and Danny O'Brien (Electronic Frontier Foundation) in 2005.[11]

The ORG champions our digital rights in the UK; it does this by ensuring that traditional civil liberties are extended into the digital world. Reformation of copyright laws is a key objective; Charman-Anderson believes copyright law is so out of step with reality that politicians will eventually have no choice but to change it.

> 'Copyright is becoming an ass. It's technically illegal for you to copy your CD on to your ipod...but for the majority of people, that's not an offence: it's reasonable behaviour and there is no moral or ethical reason why it should be illegal.'

Charman-Anderson feels that the language favoured by the business community, in order to protect its interests, is exaggerated and not legally accurate: 'The very word piracy is loaded with images of Bluebeard and people getting their heads chopped off!'

The situation is more complex and nuanced than people appreciate, says Charman-Anderson. She points to the film industry's use of pressing plants in South-East Asia to manufacture DVDs:

> 'They give permission for say 200,000 copies and the pressing plant says oh my gosh, look at this, we've accidentally pressed an extra 200,000! And they send them to China. In many ways the film and music industry are authors of their own demise because they've shut down pressing plants in the West. Now they've got no jurisdiction in Asia where the real "piracy" goes on.'

A particular problem for the creative industries is that, in recent decades, business models have increasingly focused on identifying and protecting intellectual property. But Charman-Anderson points out that there are many ways in which the sharing of creative work can bring its own dividends: authors are 'natural bloggers', for example, and this can help them build a community of loyal readers who are likely to buy their next book; for musicians, it's the experience of a live gig that their fans want to pay for – giving tracks away over the internet makes good marketing sense.

Increasingly, the very idea of intellectual property is being questioned. Richard Stallman believes that it is little more than a 'seductive mirage'. He argues that intellectual 'objects' are not property in the traditional sense, and the law on copyright and patents is quite different from the law on other crimes against physical property.[12]

Internet-enabled digital filesharing has provoked the intense debate in which figures like Charman-Anderson and Stallman are currently fighting their corner. But the disagreement over the exact nature of intellectual property, and the question over who should be entitled to 'own' it, is part of a wider battle that can be traced back over centuries. Cultural commentators such as Clay Shirky and Howard Rheingold have reminded us that the idea of 'commons' – public goods – dates back to early human history when people shared common grazing land at the centre of their town or village. The concept extends to valuable knowledge in science, technology and the arts. Rheingold sums up the dilemma for business nicely:

> 'Consider the Internet: at its core, it's a public good. Anyone who follows the technical protocols can use it. But it's also a source of commercial innovation and wealth. Tim Berners-Lee did not have to ask permission or pay a fee to launch the World Wide Web. The founders of Amazon and Yahoo! became billionaires through their use of the Internet commons to create new kinds of private property.'[13]

For The Common Good

It's a warm summer's day in Durham, North Carolina and in a few hours, Professor James Boyle will shut up his office at Duke Law School and set off on a family trip to Hawaii. Before he goes, we've a **Skype** chat scheduled, and he just wants to get a few things straight:

> 'We didn't set **creative commons** up as a method for providing a business model for people online and we're not going out and telling the world you should use it. There are some people in the business world who have used it which is great...but that wasn't our goal...no-one is going out and evangelising saying, you should use **creative commons**. I think one of the biggest difficulties is that this debate gets set up as though there were a group of people who were saying, anyone who doesn't use an open licensing strategy is somehow retarded or behind the times and to my knowledge no one is saying that – it's just a kind of silly non-debate.'

A respected legal expert and author with an international reputation, Boyle has always worked on the academic side of the law. He assures me that the ideas underlying **Creative Commons** are equally well-received by practising lawyers, many of whom do pro bono work for the Foundation. But **Creative Commons** suffers from a lot of misleading press. As potential **wiki** users might be turned off collaborative software because they consider **Wikipedia** to be an anarchic, error-ridden sprawl, so others fear **Creative Commons** because they see it as a direct threat to commercial livelihoods.

> 'People...use **creative commons** as a sort of catch-all for meaning vaguely critical ideas about intellectual property ranging from simply using different business methods within the business realm to all the people saying, no, the copyright system is out of whack, the copyright term is too long etcetera. Those are really two different things and I think that people lack the ability to differentiate between them.'

Creative Commons is actually built on one simple, powerful piece of logic: that creators should be entitled to do exactly what they want with their work. And if this desire agrees with the common good, then all the better. Boyle cites the fact that MIT makes some of its courses available under a **creative commons** license so anyone can not only use the materials, they can translate and adapt them in various ways. He also points to Nine Inch Nails getting the number one best selling mp3 of 2008 despite the fact that the track had a **creative commons** license.

Science Commons is a relatively new initiative and one which Boyle has great hopes for. He argues that our economic strength is built on a commons of scientific and technical information, and that society can be greatly enriched if this area is protected:

> 'There are a lot of inefficiencies that have huge human costs. [We could] increase profits and save lives by...adopting "open" approaches.'

Science Commons is aimed at areas where progress is slow and there is an incidence of what Boyle refers to as 'failed sharing' – where people wouldn't mind sharing materials, data or literature but are inhibited from doing so. Science Commons offers concrete suggestions to speed up the research process:

> '[It allows] people to say, for example, [these materials] are available under the universal biological transfer agreement version 1.0. Are you a non-profit institution? Yes? In that case you can buy the plasmid or the reagent for $29.95 from Genes-R-Us.'

Boyle admits this type of strategy may not be embraced by everyone. He believes many people have a genuine cognitive problem in accepting open approaches (as mentioned right back in the Introduction):

> 'We have this sort of cultural agoraphobia. We are very good at seeing the downsides of open systems, their anarchy and the ways that they

might collapse and we're not very good at seeing how they might work and work very well.'

Boyle goes on to explain that open systems do indeed generate a cost in that you cede control but there is also a great benefit; for instance, you can learn from the mistakes of others just as they learn from your mistakes.

Boyle's views – and those of the rest of the **Creative Commons** board – have been buoyed up by the development of various business approaches which place the sharing of information at their core.[14]

Call of the crowd

In 2004, James Surowiecki's *Wisdom of Crowds* argued that large groups of people could be smarter than a handful of experts, as long as a few ground rules were followed. Surowiecki was a staff writer in business at *The New Yorker* and his ideas were informed by changes he was seeing in organisations. Examples he used included: **Linux**, The CIA and Google. Methods addressed in Surowiecki's book centre on **crowdsourcing** and **open innovation**.[15]

But it wasn't until 2006, when *Wired* reporter Jeff Howe coined the term '**crowdsourcing**' in a magazine article,[16] that the idea of harnessing crowd wisdom in collaborative projects began to take hold. Howe was inspired by the growth of websites like istockphoto, which sells photos by amateurs at a fraction of the price professionals would charge. He developed his ideas and published a book on the phenomenon, *Crowdsourcing,* in 2008.[17]

On his website, Howe describes **crowdsourcing** as 'the act of taking a job traditionally performed by a designated agent (usually an employee) and outsourcing it to an undefined, generally large group of people in the form of an open call'.[18]

There is often confusion between a straightforward *open call* – where members of the public are requested to contribute a ready-made idea or solution (for example: 4IP, Procter & Gamble's Connect & Develop, The Longitude Prize) and **crowdsourcing** which involves mass collaboration (see examples below).

Crowdsourcing has come under attack because a crowdsourced project can sometimes end up costing more than a traditionally outsourced project. There are other issues that can cause problems, for example: low quality work, low wages (or no payment at all), lack of written contracts and legal protection for any party. But *crowdsourcing* is interesting because, like all these examples, it describes how technology is changing the way business can operate, and how it really taps into (and, if done well, reinforces) the business community. As Howe says:[19]

> 'It forces companies to approach us [the consumer] as potential partners and that's much more interesting. And much more exciting. We do buy things but we also participate meaningfully in the process by which those products are created. What we see with these successful forms of collaborative development is that they came up organically from the people formerly known as customers, the people formerly known as the audience.

> 'I like to think about the online community as kind of a building block of *crowdsourcing*. It's what the corporation is to the industrial era. It showed that people could come together and self-organise into productive units. What once took managers and a corporate hierarchy can now be done in the context of the community.'

The ways in which people can now self-organise to conduct business was discussed in detail in Chapter 1. The *crowdsourcing* process takes this propensity for self-organisation one step further – it throws an active project (or mission) into the mix. Where a vibrant community already exists, *crowdsourcing* can work in a number of ways.

For example, Mark Rock decided to crowdsource funding for **Audioboo**, inspired by the growth and commitment of the user community. He made plans to sell off 20 percent of the equity in one percent packages – for £10,000 each. His hope was that established media organisations – especially those who already use **Audioboo** – would be among the public buyers.[20]

Crowdsourcing seems to work particularly well when it involves grand projects that affect society as a whole. Examples include NASA's 'clickworkers' initiative, where volunteers were asked to identify un-catalogued craters on the surface of Mars, and Galaxy Zoo, where a quarter of a million galaxies were classified by 150,000 volunteers, with the results published in respected journals (the same model is now being applied to finding supernovae). Another example is the Groklaw website – a sort of Wikipedia for internet law, written by developers and lawyers in the free/open source community.[21]

Crowdsourcing is often about grand scale, big ideas, which are, inevitably, hard to pin down. The lack of definition means it is difficult to manage expectations and define roles. In a business context, this can cause problems. In addition, when the project is specifically for the greater 'good' (that is, working for a non-commercial organisation), participants are unlikely to be concerned about any share of profit or intellectual property. Business projects don't tend to fall into this category.

The fail whale[22]

In January 2007, *The Economist* magazine launched Project Red Stripe, an ambitious venture which aimed to create 'an innovative and web-based product, service or business model,'[23] using **crowdsourcing** (among other approaches). The project was scheduled to run for six months; it was given a budget of £100,000 and six hand-picked members of staff working full time. But the team failed to deliver. Andrew Carey was an observer on the project throughout:

> 'To me it seems that this whale-of-an-idea was sometimes too much for the team. Too much for any team. They tried to bring it back down to size by playing with it: "Let's divert the Thames through Lichfield", "Let's make the world square". But still it became the elephant in the room, to mix gargantuan mammal metaphors. And the team found themselves becoming-whale-of-an-idea-in-the-room. Then they had two ideas. Which one should they choose? Had they chosen the right idea? Then the idea was altered. Was it still good enough? Then it was changed altogether. As time ran out there was an awful dread that they had missed their chance. And, from the moment that they decided to look externally for their idea, there was a pervading sense that the idea lived "out there". Which meant, in turn, that the team would not be the authors or creators or owners of the idea.'[24]

There were also practical problems:

> '[The team] caused a rumpus by offering readers who submitted an idea a year's subscription to the magazine (rather than a share in a potentially huge business) [and] they had to walk a fine line between openly sharing those ideas that were submitted and keeping their development plans under wraps while they were commercially sensitive.'[25]

Project Red Stripe lasted for just six months during which the team was overwhelmed by the vast complexity of the problems they were trying to address. One specific proposal did emerge, but senior management at *The Economist* didn't like it. The brief was so open that permission to go live wasn't necessary, but the team was fearful of creating bad publicity.

Ultimately, there was a lack of genuine engagement with the outside world. In cases like this, a robust third party mediator can be a great asset.

Ways and means

At Nesta Connect, the public-funded programme for collaborative innovation, Roland Harwood enables large multinationals such as Procter & Gamble, Oracle and Virgin to connect with the small innovative companies – and individuals – that can help them. A central aspect of Harwood's research is the question of how big companies can organise themselves more effectively in today's fluid economic, technological and social environments.

The assignment of intellectual property rights is key in these relationships. Small players are fearful of being taken advantage of, while larger businesses are increasingly sensitive to accusations of greed or exploitation: for example, the big player may develop a product independently that turns out to be very similar to an idea that has been sent in by a potential (smaller) collaborator. Because of this issue, in particular, it is common for large businesses to have a policy of refusing to sign non-disclosure agreements. This means that, ideally, potential collaborators will have a patent in place if they want to talk. But securing a patent is expensive and can take years so potential partners are often excluded.

Procter & Gamble has a long history of collaboration but it wasn't until the company experienced a share price collapse in 2000 that Connect & Develop was created – an *open innovation*[26] programme specifically aimed at attracting outside collaborators. Through this initiative, Procter & Gamble actively shares its problems with the outside world. The Connect & Develop portal contains a list of around one hundred 'live' concerns including finding a solution to keep probiotics alive in dry food, or the need for ideas for whitening products that are non-peroxide and non-abrasive. The programme is an open call: absolutely anyone can send in a well-developed idea.

While Procter & Gamble's strategy is to increase the percentage of products which involve an external collaborator, the need for patents creates a barrier. Harwood describes how his team stepped in as a 'trust broker' between Procter & Gamble and its potential collaborators:

> 'We were trying to open up the dialogue between Procter & Gamble and small innovative companies. We formed what was essentially an "air lock" between Nesta, Procter & Gamble and the smaller players. The big learning from that whole project was that if you want large and

small companies to communicate you need to build trust, and involving a neutral third party can be a good way of doing that.'

The issue faced by Procter & Gamble exposes a tension often found in collaborative projects: the problem of operating commercially in an environment where there is a strong, committed, but independent, community. The market will wish to exploit common goods to maximise profits but the people who generated those goods may not be too happy.

Cultural Theorist Michael Thompson gives a good example of this tension when he relates the story of Coca-Cola in India: the soft drinks giant ran into trouble over its use of local water in soft drinks production – it was accused of making a private good of something which was considered to be a community resource. If the egalitarian view (as expressed by the local villagers) had been accommodated into the planning process (for example, by Coca-Cola agreeing to offer some kind of compensation), community anger might have been assuaged, and the negative publicity about the affair might never have surfaced.[27]

All for one, one for all

In 2002, Harvard academic Yochai Benkler coined the term 'commons-based **peer production**' in a paper for the *Yale Law Journal*.[28] The term was used to describe any collaborative project based on the sharing of information – Benkler used the **open source** operating system **Linux** as an example. Benkler went on to argue that a society where information was shared freely might prove more economically efficient than one where innovation was held back by patent or copyright law.[29]

In *Wikinomics*, consultants Don Tapscott and Anthony D. Williams develop Benkler's ideas further.[30] They argue that **peer production** is transforming the world of business. This type of collaborative work involves the sharing of otherwise privileged information. It is a higher risk for a company to adopt such a strategy, but the potential rewards are greater. Tapscott and Williams see it like this:

'As a growing number of firms see the benefits of mass collaboration, this new way of organising will eventually displace the traditional corporate structures as the economy's primary engine of wealth creation.'[31]

While Tapscott and Williams' bold prediction is unlikely to come true in the near future, it is clear that collaborative approaches have the potential to change the shape of certain sectors, especially the ones that are finding themselves most under treat from new technologies, like print journalism.

The journalist and academic, Jeff Jarvis, has talked about a new approach to community journalism at the *New York Times*. The paper dispatched two of its correspondents to communities in New Jersey and Brooklyn. The job of the reporters was not so much to break stories as to build relationships, working with community leaders at grassroots level, as well as local *blogging* sites:

> 'All these parties must collaborate, not compete. They must create complementary content that fills out their local news worlds so that each of them adds value and stands out for it [...] The days of one news organisation owning a town and its news are over; no one can afford to do that any more. Instead, if these experiments succeed, they will do so by collaborating to create a new network – a new ecosystem – of local news.'[32]

This approach is part of the new '*long tail*' trend of 'hyperlocal' (which Jarvis describes as 'the ability to serve readers and small advertisers in highly targeted geographic niches'). And here's the 'ecosystem' motif again. The assumption is that stakeholders within these niches are dependent on each other for survival and therefore co-operation is essential. As Tapscott and Williams argue, this hypothesis is now being put to the test not just at a local level and within communities of interest but also within markets.

Tagging the future

The world headquarters of Arup (although few in the company like to refer to them as such: they call it 'the London office'), consists of three shiny buildings on Fitzroy Street, on the northern edge of London's West End. Two of the buildings have been gutted and re-furbished, while the third, newly re-opened, was razed to the ground and completely rebuilt. At first glance, the buildings don't look very dissimilar to the ordinary office blocks in that part of town. But then you look a bit more closely and notice a flourish here, a serpentine line there.

The Arup signature graces landmarks as diverse as The Sydney Opera House, The London Gherkin, The Scottish Parliament Building in Edinburgh and Beijing's Bird's Nest Stadium. The 60 year old multinational is a hybrid firm of engineers and architects, and has been at the top of its game now for over half a century.

Arup is tuned into the **Web 2.0** world – its employees (or, rather, partners) have had invitations to Tim O'Reilly's exclusive Foo camps and the equally exclusive **Pop!Tech** and **TED**; the company attends digital media conferences around the globe. Arup is a darling of the **social media** scene because much of what it does has collaboration and sharing at the core.

As an indication of Arup's desire to be 'open', a section of the ground floor of 13 Fitzroy Street has been turned into a public exhibition space. It's here that Arup 'futurist', Duncan Wilson, meets me. He shows me round the current display, which focuses on Arup's extensive work in China. It's all nicely timed: this is August 2008 and the Beijing Olympics are taking place as we chat.

Wilson's job, as one of the eight-strong 'Foresight' team, is to run 'thought-leadership-type' events and workshops, and create content for the ongoing 'Drivers of Change' project, which publishes books and sets of flashcards on future trends – for both in-house and public consumption.

In the first 18 months of the project, Wilson and his team had garnered opinion from 'about 10,000 people worldwide', most of them from within the construction industry. This information was gathered partly through the events Wilson organises in collaboration with Arup's diverse clients and suppliers, such as Marriott Hotels or DuPont Chemicals, and partly through international conferences. As a means of turning the Drivers of Change research into something that could be experienced live, the Foresight team built a **tag cloud** application.

> 'We wanted to create an application that could be used before an event, to say here, look, here is our base set of 50 issues, they are 50 drivers of change, you can go in and vote on the issues that you think are important or not… and of course with a **tag cloud** you can also submit your own ideas, you're not constrained by the **taxonomy** that somebody else has defined.'

The **tag cloud** was showcased at the National Retail Federation Conference in New York in January 2007 (where ageing population was voted as the top driver of change), and then presented at the **Pop!Tech** conference in Maine in October (peak oil). At the World Economic Forum on Africa 2008 (empowerment of women and youth), the cloud was used to help set the Forum agenda.

Wilson and his team report directly to Arup's chairman. What is the attitude of the senior management at Arup towards this sharing of development with associates and competitors? Wilson admits that most of his work, including the drivers of change research, is 'pretty much under the radar'. But he adds that the pervading culture at Arup allows people to work autonomously: 'we do it and then seek forgiveness afterwards'.

Wilson points out that Arup has always fostered this type of innovation. From the day that Anglo-Danish engineer Ove Arup founded the business back in 1946, the company has always fostered collaboration:

> 'If you go back to Arup himself, his whole approach was that design should be holistic. In the 1960s and 70s, that was highly unusual. That collaborative approach (engineers working in conjunction with architects) is embedded in the culture here. There's a "de facto" sharing nature. People expect [openness] of Arup.'

From Soy Sauce to Open Source

I'm sitting in a Vietnamese café in London's Kingsland Road with RedMonk founder James Governor. We're watching the owner's two daughters run, play and generally get in the way of the ever-smiling kitchen staff as they try to prepare food. It's been a long morning and we're both starving. After what seems like an eternity, the waitress arrives with plates of steaming Cha Nem Chay (spring rolls) and Pho Xao Dau Rau (stir fried tofu).

Over lunch, we get to discuss the merits of what Governor likes to call '**open source** business'.

RedMonk, the software analysis business Governor co-founded in 2002, operates on what might be described as a **freemium** model. The company publishes research papers for free and is 100 per cent funded by 'supporters', 'sponsors' and 'patrons' who pay subscriptions for additional service packages – an entirely different model to most other research businesses.

When I ask Governor if I can use the term **freemium**, he demurs:

> 'That would be fine. But OSS [open source software] is more than a marketing term. We rely on OSS infrastructure...we use **WordPress**... [we] sponsored an open source plug in for permissive content licensing using creative commons...'

It's true, RedMonk does its best to live and breathe an '*open source*' philosophy in all possible ways. Not only are the company's servers and website built on *open source*, RedMonk has spent many years fostering its community and now works closely with that community – engineers, software developers and information architects – to develop its ideas.

> 'The *open source* model came out of our frustrations with editing each other's work. We just started *blogging* and thought, let the Internet be the editor. We don't agree with companies writing white papers for vendors. You can't claim independence when you're really a PR man. *Blogging* became a much more natural way of developing our content.'

Governor thinks internet based *peer production*, has 'significant value'. He and his founding partner Stephen O'Grady have always done their best to support this type of work. In 2004 he and O'Grady wrote a paper on compliance and published it under a *creative commons* license. EMC, a large, established IT company, took RedMonk's paper, added to it, and circulated it among its customers. Governor and O'Grady didn't receive a penny, but a couple of years later, Thomas Otter [now Gartner Group, then SAP] got in touch after seeing their paper – this led to SAP becoming a client.

Governor's patience had paid off: 'When you're open in this way, other people become your evangelists. You don't need a huge sales and marketing team.'

RedMonk is a bit like marmite to the IT industry – people either love it or hate it. But Governor's open strategy has proved successful. From the start, he wasn't interested in courting any one particular client, instead, he wanted to specialise in 'ecosystem coverage' and set out to build a comprehensive view of the whole industry. Now Microsoft, IBM and most of the industry's major players are clients.

For Governor, the recipe is simple:

> 'We don't sell content – at least, not white papers – but we sell services around that research. It's all free, but when people want to take it somewhere else, then they have to pay. We're out in these networks, without any groupthink, and that's increasingly valuable.'

As we saw in Chapter 3, today's smart businesses are not so much about creating and owning knowledge as about applying and learning from it. If RedMonk's *blog* posts and research papers are freely available, to be used, re-mixed, mashed up and built upon, that's fine: the core competence of RedMonk's business lies in the minds and knowhow of its consultants. And Governor is confident enough to know that that can never be emulated.

Always in beta

Twenty years on from the inception of the World Wide Web, the propensity for online collaboration is being explored, at least, if not fully realised, across a whole variety of sectors. We are seeing a genuine 'opening up' across the board as **social technologies** allow us to do business in brand new ways.

As Arup and RedMonk have shown, the creative process can benefit greatly from outside input. Arup's Drivers of Change and RedMonk's white papers are peer-produced projects which mean more to the communities who helped create them because those communities have been engaged from the start. This involvement works on two levels: it enriches the project, clearly, but it also gives the community a sense of ownership and raises brand awareness, which is fantastic for marketing.

The artistic community, in particular, has seized on the fact that, today, anyone can get their creative work 'out there' – there is no need to go through a gatekeeper. Musicians post snatches of music or song lyrics on their **MySpace** page in order to gauge their impact, or upload low budget pop videos as a way of testing out a storyline; writers use **blogs** as a sort of public notebook through which to get feedback on ideas. And if an artist needs genuine collaborators, where better than the web to recruit them? In Summer 2009, sculptor Antony Gormley invited members of the British public to apply to be a part of 'One and Other' – a conceptual work in which individuals were able to occupy the vacant Fourth Plinth in London's Trafalgar Square for an hour at a time: participants were recruited through the project website[33] and the invitation spread virally through **social media**.

'Obscurity is a far greater threat to authors and creative artists than piracy' wrote Tim O'Reilly in 2002[34] – and the web is a great way to involve others in your embryonic projects. Of course you can share completed work – but an unfinished product is so much better, because it lends itself to conversation.

For technology companies, iteration has become a key part of the development process. Today, many software products are released to the public for software testing prior to official release. These products are said to be 'in beta', which means that bugs may be encountered, and new features are regularly added without full testing. The advantage to the user is that this type of software does not only provide a preview of a new, exciting technology, it also tends to be lighter and more agile to use than officially released versions. The **Web 2.0** era has seen a proliferation of **perpetual beta** business models – products which remain 'in beta' for a lengthy or even indefinite period of time. Examples include Google Apps, *Flickr*, *Delicious* and *Audioboo*.

Today, we are so used to seeing 'in beta' sites that we give little thought to the impact our feedback may have. But when beta access is marked as a privilege, it's interesting to see how quickly word spreads. When Google released *Google Wave* as a invite-only preview in September 2009, *social networks* like *Twitter* were abuzz with people talking about Wave and clamouring for invites.

The tech community is not the only one known to be passionate about new stuff, the gaming community is also brimming with early adopters – and a great way to impress them is to engage them in beta development, designing and shaping the games they love.

Intensely social

You may know that *Call of Duty 4* was the third best-selling video game from 2008. I'm not a gamer, so it's news to me. Apparently, *Call of Duty 4* had the misfortune to be competing head on with *Halo3*, which netted the biggest single first day revenues in the history of entertainment. In a crowded, competitive marketplace, *Call of Duty 4* needed something special to make it stand out.

I'm on the phone to John Horniblow, Head of *Social Media* at the Geneva-based marketing company, LABEL. Horniblow has been working closely with *Call of Duty 4* distributor Activision over the past few years, and he's telling me what makes gamers happy.

Gamers are, by nature, technically aware. Because of their worldwide gaming networks, they're big users of *social technologies*. Many run their own notice boards and set up their own fan communities. They're passionate: they'll queue up outside a store at midnight simply to be the first to get their hands on a game.

For the launch of *Call of Duty 4*, Horniblow's team decided their only option was to target the influencers – the most vocal and social fans. They wanted to give these influencers something big to talk about in their communities. Horniblow's team set up a vanity *URL* called charlieoscardelta (phonetics for C, O and D) which wasn't part of the main brand site. Activision announced the launch of this sister site on network television in the US on the first weekend of the football season, knowing that its core target audience of male 17-30 year olds would be watching.

As the ad ran, the High Definition game format was released online simultaneously. Due to a coding slip on the charlieoscardelta site, the **URL** of where people could get the HD trailers from was accidentally disclosed. The real *fanboys* picked up on this and the 'sneak preview' soon became a hot topic on message boards around the world.

Within five days, Horniblow recalls, the trailer had had hundreds of thousands of views. It became viral: people downloaded the video, re-encoded it and put it on sites like **Facebook**.

> 'Come Monday the PR guys were jumping up and down. They were saying, well that shouldn't have happened, we needed to control that a lot more...And I was like, I think you've got the message completely wrong...these guys have done your job for you.'

Activision's PR team relented and, because the online community, charlieoscardelta, was growing so quickly, they agreed to use it to recruit beta testers for the game. When this was announced, the site crashed immediately under sheer weight of traffic.

The beta test was done online in a closed environment, to an invited set of people. Testers were asked to say what they liked, what they disliked, what they wanted more of and what didn't work properly. Comments and suggestions were incorporated into the final release of the product. For Horniblow, the whole process was marketing nirvana:

> '[We] suddenly had 750,000 avid keen supporters. It built upon itself. A beta like that and it's a first play and suddenly people are talking about it. It builds more buzz. So that you are perpetuating the cycle.'

Horniblow is still debating strategy with Activision's PR team, who have always been used to giving game previews to journalists. His argument now is that traditional media should be completely bypassed in favour of the fans – because they are the ones who really value the gift of exclusivity.

Like bees to honey...

Initially, Activision was reluctant to trust the hardcore fans of *Call of Duty 4*, but when it willingly opened up its development process, the gamers proved their loyalty – no doubt saving Activision thousands of pounds in marketing spend in the process.

If businesses are communities, we need to nurture *all* the stakeholders. And for too long businesses have envisioned a kind of 'them' and 'us' environment: customers have been treated as outsiders, when they are, in many ways, a company's most valuable asset. Engaging with this group is essential, especially now that **social technologies** are giving it a cohesive voice.

> 'People aren't stupid and they'll do stuff if it's in their own interest, in general,' says Mint Digital's Andy Bell. 'There's a kind of ecosystem in a community. When you're trying to create stuff, that's a good way of thinking about things: how can we be generous – what can we give away?'

> 'We need to put a lot of stuff in as creators,' says musician and writer Pat Kane. 'As a gift, to enrich the community. It's a lot of work for us. The community is more like a public library or a community arts centre than it is a marketplace – but it generates such goodwill!'

Luckily, there are many online examples of hard-working, collaborative networks which have been built on a sharing philosophy. We already know about Craig Newmark and the trust he places in the users who run **craigslist**: Newmark was more than happy to cede control of his baby, and the volunteers repay him with dedication and vigilance. Richard Stallman and Linus Torvalds had a similar approach when they wrote the source code for GNU and **Linux** respectively: the code was opened and given up to the developer community; now the community has helped create two products which are widely used around the world, forming a respected and viable alternative to commercial software.

The Economist ran into trouble with Project Red Stripe, Microsoft ran aground with Encarta. Jimmy Wales and Larry Sanger failed with Nupedia (the precursor to **Wikipedia**). The common factor in the failure of all these ambitious, collaborative projects was too much control from the centre.

The communities that drive GNU, **Linux** and **craigslist** are dedicated and passionate. But, most of all, they have been given great freedom. They are relatively flat and highly interconnected. Their members are like worker bees with a great deal of honey to make. Or worker ants with a queen to feed. They have been given a gift: a vision, a product, an idea. And the community builds out around that; the leader's job is to ensure that the community is happy.

What gift will you give?

Collaborative innovation isn't easy. There are issues around security and ownership, there are challenges in the sheer scale of project management and the complexity of different ideas. There will be **trolls** and hackers, there may be people you want to reach who don't even have access to the web. But, as *Wikinomics* author Don Tapscott pointed out in the documentary, *Us Now*: 'These are all in the category of implementation challenges, they're not in the category of reasons not to do it.'

In the past few years, leaders from all walks of life have shown that they are willing to learn a new language, one which enables them to treat people as peers (rather than subordinates). In this new environment, trust becomes a currency, and respect is in vogue. As if to symbolise this, we have had a surge in grand confessions: Chef Heston Blumenthal has apologised for food poisonings at his Michelin starred restaurant, The Fat Duck,[35] Australian Prime Minister Kevin Rudd has said sorry to the 'stolen generation' of Aboriginals,[36] Rapper Kanye West asked singer Taylor Swift for forgiveness after he interrupted her at the MTV Music Awards[37]...and the list goes on.

> 'Old-style leaders hoarded their resources,' observed American publisher and **blogger**, Michael Hyatt. 'They played a zero-sum game. They didn't believe they could be generous without depleting their own pile of stuff. New-style leaders are just the opposite. They have an abundance-mentality. They freely share.'[38]

While Blumenthal, Rudd or West may not rank among the humblest of leaders, their public displays of humility show how social expectations are changing. We are beginning to realise the inter-relatedness of things: instead of silos, the future is hybrid: it make sense to cultivate your connections. We are in an age when we worry a great deal about loss – we fear that we are approaching (or have passed) the peak supply of many things (oil, water, bees...), yet knowledge is a growing commodity. In wisdom, at least, we can afford to have a sense of abundance – and a mindset of generosity.

Notes

1. www.guardian.co.uk/commentisfree/2009/may/25/editorial-twitter-social-networks
2. 'Music Service Spotify wins high-profile backing', *FT online*, 3 August 2009 (www.ft.com/cms/s/0/d890cbea-8066-11de-bf04-00144feabdc0.html?nclick_check=1).

3. Peter M. Senge (1990), *The Fifth Discipline: The Art & Practice of the Learning Organisation*. Random House, p. 23.
4. en.wikipedia.org/wiki/Open_source
5. www.gnu.org/philosophy/free-sw.html
6. Most of the information on Stallman was provided by this book's editor, Matthew Fairtlough, with additional material from en.wikipedia.org/wiki/Richard_Stallman
7. Robert Cailliau speaking at Media Futures 2008, Alexandra Palace, London, 20 June 2008.
8. Neil Gershenfeld (2005), *FAB: The Coming Revolution on Your Desktop: From Personal Computers to Personal Fabrication*. Basic Books.
9. www.guardian.co.uk/technology/2009/aug/25/file-sharing-internet
10. Both 'blood-dimmed tide' and this section's subtitle ('The centre cannot hold') are from William Butler Yeats' poem, *The Second Coming* (first published 1920); the first verse seems a good analogy for the fears some have of the internet.
11. Suw Charman-Anderson was Executive Director of the Open Rights Group between July 2005 and January 2007; she now works as a freelance *social media* consultant and *blogger*.
12. Richard Stallman, 'Did you say "Intellectual Property"? It's a seductive mirage', GNU website, 2004 (www.gnu.org/philosophy/not-ipr.html).
13. Howard Rheingold (2004), 'Culture: The Battle For The Commons', Institute of the Future, p. 1.
14. My editor points out that this kind of sharing is not necessarily new; Ginsparg's arXiv was established 18 years ago and houses over 500,000 pre-prints predominantly in the mathematics and the physical sciences.
15. James Surowiecki (2004), *Wisdom of Crowds*. Doubleday.
16. Jeff Howe, 'The Rise of Crowdsourcing', *Wired Magazine*, June 2006 (www.wired.com/wired/archive/14.06/crowds.html).
17. Jeff Howe (2008), *Crowdsourcing: why the power of the crowd is driving the future of business*. Random House.
18. crowdsourcing.typepad.com
19. Both these quotes are from 'Crowdsourcing: The Trailer', 28 July 2008: www.youtube.com/watch?v=F0-UtNg3ots
20. www.guardian.co.uk/media/pda/2009/jun/15/audioboo-iphone
21. Groklaw has had a number of scoops including exposing the long-running legal action by SCO against the *Linux* open source community. It went on to become the most comprehensive and reliable repository of information on the SCO actions and was instrumental in the SCO's failure to win any of them; a failure which resulted in SCO filing for Chapter 11 bankruptcy (groklaw.net).
22. The 'fail whale' is a graphic of a whale held up by a flock of birds illustrated by designer Yiying Lu; this graphic appears on *Twitter* when the network experiences an outage (due to too many users sending *Tweets* at any one time); it also seemed like a nice metaphor for the Red Stripe Project.
23. projectredstripe.com/blog/about
24. Andrew Carey (2008), *Inside Project Red Stripe*. Triarchy Press, p. 2.
25. Andrew Carey, in email to Jemima Gibbons, 16 September 2009.
26. The Berkeley academic Henry Chesbrough defined *open innovation* as: 'a paradigm that assumes that firms can and should use external ideas as well as internal ideas, and internal and external paths to market, as the firms look to advance their technology.' (H. W. Chesbrough, *Open Innovation: The new imperative for creating and profiting from technology*, Harvard Business School Press, 2003, p. xxiv).
27. Michael Thompson, lecture to the RSA, 4 December 2008.
28. Yochai Benkler (2002), 'Coase's Penguin, or, *Linux* and the Nature of the Firm.' *The Yale Law Journal 112(3)*.
29. This is a key thread in Yochai Benkler (2006), *The Wealth of Networks: How Social Production Transforms Markets and Freedom*. Yale University Press.

30. Don Tapscott and Antony D. Williams (2006), *Wikinomics.* Portfolio.
31. *ibid*, p. 2.
32. www.guardian.co.uk/media/2009/mar/16/digital-media-new-york-times
33. www.oneandother.co.uk
34. 'Piracy is Progressive Taxation, and Other Thoughts on the Evolution of Online Distribution' by Tim O'Reilly, 11 Dec 2002 (article for p2p.com).
35. www.guardian.co.uk/lifeandstyle/2009/sep/25/report-blumenthal-restaurant-poisoning
36. www.youtube.com/watch?v=B1jeWeDpc68
37. news.bbc.co.uk/1/hi/entertainment/8253909.stm
38. 209.85.229.132/search?q=cache:Z2WQ18Fcp0IJ:michaelhyatt.com/2009/05/leadership-20

Conclusion

This book is a little different from the one I set out to write. Back in 2005, I was interested in the web's relationship to management and business leadership. As the project grew, it became clear that you can't look at leaders without followers, and you need to explore the processes that connect them, and the environment in which they operate – over time, the entire workplace became the focus. Now, with the increased spread of work into home and social life, the wiry ball of issues I was dealing with became ever larger and more entangled. This is not just about management, it's not even just about work and technology: politics, religion, science, ethics, society and the environment all enter the fray. Everything is interconnected – and it's this vast interdependence that is the real story. And as **Web 2.0** evolves into the **realtime** web, the **semantic web** and no doubt other incarnations to come, we all have a part to play in shaping it.

Whatever type of business you're in: small or large, start-up or market leader, distributed or centralised, chances are that you're already on the World Wide Web – enmeshed in a mercurial network which can provide you with all the knowledge and ideas you'll ever need – or cause your strategies to unravel. We can work with this network or we can fight against it; one thing is for sure – we can't outwit it.

Brand advisors may tell you that the corporate message can still be controlled in some way. This might be true in some cases inside a company, but as there is now so little distinction between inside and out, that small area where you are actually 'in charge' becomes irrelevant. Once the message has been released, you have to let it go. The message becomes incorrigible: there are no absolutes, only iterations. Your message will be repeated, duplicated, distributed, pummelled, mashed-up and fed back to you in ways that you never expected. It will be passed to and fro between your employees, your colleagues, your customers, your partners and your competitors. Ultimately, it will not be your message, but your reaction to the world's treatment of your message that defines you.

The social, business and technological worlds are clashing in some places, converging in others. No one knows what the work landscapes of the future will look like. We can only prepare ourselves for a vast number of possible outcomes. The infinite monkey theorem tells us that anything can happen.

This book was never intended to be a didactic treatise: it's a lovingly gathered collection of observations and ideas that you should find accessible and inspiring. How you use the material is, of course, up to you. But bear the underlying framework in mind. The chapter breakdown is the result of much fevered planning and discussion: co-creation, passion, learning, openness, listening and generosity are crucial qualities (critical success factors, if you like). If you can tweak your business approaches to assimilate these, you'll be making your company cooperative, collaborative and robust – and giving it the greatest chance of success. You'll be doing what Arie de Geus recommended in *The Living Company*: adjusting your internal environment to better reflect the world outside. Because, of course, everything is interrelated.

If you're motivated and keen to get started, here's a review of the key points from each chapter, with short suggested 'to do' lists. If I were to start my own business tomorrow, this is the template I'd follow – let's call it a social strategy. These quick fixes will cost you little or nothing at all, and you can do them all online in minutes. Pick and choose whichever ones appeal. Good luck!

30 ways to get social

1. Co-create. Don't worry about processes, the big idea or 'doing it all'. *Social media* gives people the tools to self-organise, so you can take a step back. Keep structures as simple as possible. Cut red tape: enable. When Lloyd Davis set up Tuttle, he kept his overheads minimal (so that the project could continue indefinitely with limited funds) and made the space welcoming and inclusive. When Steve Moore started 2gether, he ensured it had a friendly, relaxed, festival vibe. As for the *BarCamps*, they use a formula so endearingly simple that has been adapted and built upon by thousands of people around the world.

- **Go to an *unconference/BarCamp*-style event** and see for yourself how the format works: Tuttle, 2gether, Amplified and Creative Coffee Club are just some of the organisations running events across the UK. Check the listings sites Eventbrite, *Upcoming* or Meetup for events of interest near you.
- Better still, **organise your own event**: barcamp.org/OrganizeALocalBarCamp And then encourage people to take photos, upload videos and report back – in that way the occasion becomes a launchpad for further discussion and engagement.
- Ask lots of questions: if you're fazed by an aspect of social media, **type any question into Google** (or any other search engine) and you'll get a whole list of answers. Or for a more focused response, crowdsource an answer from Vark.com, or *Twitter*.

- Be informed: **set yourself up with an *RSS reader*** (e.g. Bloglines, *Google Reader* or *Netvibes*) and add any *feeds* you think are relevant. (I never get round to reading all mine but love the fact they're there in the right place when I want them). Start with news *feeds* from the BBC and your daily paper of choice. **Add a good generalist technology *blog*** like *Techcrunch UK* or *Mashable!* Don't restrict yourself to work-based topics: try *The Hype Machine* (music), *The Onion Bag* (football), *Popbitch* (celebrity gossip) or *SHOWstudio* (fashion). **Use *Technorati* to find specialist *blogs*** in areas that interest you.

- Once you've got your *RSS reader* up and running, **sign up to *Delicious*** (or any other free *bookmarking* service) so that you can *bookmark* anything you read that's of interest. Share relevant *bookmarks* with your colleagues by setting up special interest groups (e.g. by creating a dedicated list on *Twitter*).

2. Be passionate. Businesses are communities, and *social tools* are a great way of building goodwill and social capital within your business community. The more networked your business, the denser the relationships, the better. Small tech companies like 37signals, *Huddle* and Mint Digital make sure that enthusiasm and excitement drive their work, and that the values that underpin their companies are cohesive and genuine. Focus on intrinsic motivators rather than extrinsic motivators.

- **Pick a handful of *social networks* that you like** and play around with them: get to know them inside out. On *LinkedIn*, for example, you can search for contacts, join groups, sign up for events, set up your own group, comment on other people's statuses and manage projects (using *Huddle* workspaces). If you can't bear the idea of a photo, grab a free avatar from MyWebFace or DoppelMe. If you really don't like the thought of being discovered online, use a pseudonym. You cant understand *social media* if you're not involved. Have fun, concentrate on what you enjoy and you'll soon find your natural collaborators.

- **Experience *the butterfly effect*** for yourself: *Twitter* is probably the best network for seeing the reach (and *realtime* capabilities) of *social media*.[1] **Learn how to use *hashtags* and replies to get the most from *Twitter*.**

- Take an hour to **watch the documentary UsNow** (`watch.usnowfilm.com`) and be inspired! Then **use UsNow as a *social media* ice breaker** for any of your colleagues: organise a screening at work and encourage people to discuss how the issues impact on your business.

- **Don't waste money on building your own *social network***: If you're a small or medium-sized organisation, you can set up your own networks for free on ***Ning**, **Facebook** or **LinkedIn***. If you're a large company you may well need your own in-house community, but it doesn't need to cost the earth. Gary Koelling and Steve Bendt are the two marketing guys at Best Buy who launched their successful online network, *BlueShirtNation*, for under £100.[2]
- **Hire (or designate) champions, moderators and community builders** to ensure everyone gets on board. If you have people around you who love ***Facebook** or **YouTube***, get them involved. If you do set up a work-related group, whether it be on a ***social network***, forum (like ***Google groups*** or Yahoo Groups) or ***wiki***, you'll need engaging content that keeps people coming back for more. Keep the group well moderated and ensure that new points for discussion are planted all the time.

3. Become a learning organisation. The future of the web is semantic. Social ***bookmarking***, ***tagging*** and ***wikis*** alleviate the need for micromanagement. ***Social tools*** will help disseminate information, ease up the bottlenecks and tighten the gaps. As a manager, be aware of espoused theory and theory in practice: keep limiting 'mental models' in check. Catalysts are essential: Gina Poole (IBM) and JP Rangaswami (Dresdner Kleinwort) planted the seed of a new idea within their respective business communities and took a step back, allowing others to develop.

- **Cut back on email**: ask that specific tasks and requests be addressed to one dedicated person rather than a group (so responsibility is taken), even when the email is sent to many people; discourage cc-ing and bcc-ing; ask which conversations might work better if moved into a ***wiki*** or workgroup.
- **Listen to Luis Suarez's *podcast***: Suarez talks about how he swapped email for social software: www.cbc.ca/spark/2009/09/full-interview-luis-suarez-explains-how-to-quit-email
- **Start using collaborative software**: Look at your working processes and ask where ***social tools*** could make a difference; sign up for a free ***wiki*** from wikispaces, wikidot or ***SocialText*** free 50 (for up to 50 people) and start playing. MyOffice, ***Huddle***, Basecamp and Central Desktop also offer free ***wikis***. Ideally, begin with a pilot project that has a small team of people who are enthusiastic about the idea: they can become champions and spread the word to other employees.

- **Learn to play *tag*.** Make information as semantic as possible: ***tag*** stuff, annotate stuff, enrich it. Start by ***tagging*** your ***blog*** posts, ***bookmark***s or photos. Don't worry too much about using the 'right' ***tag***, use as many ***tags*** as you can think of to get a feel for it. You'll soon see your company's unique ***taxonomy*** emerging as the most popular words rise to the top (use search results, or ***tag clouds*** to identify these: for example, one way would be to encourage everyone to contribute to the corporate ***blog*** and then ***tag*** their posts: this is straightforward to do in tools such as ***Drupal*** and ***Wordpress***) .
- **Set up a *reverse mentoring* programme** so digital natives can educate the older generation and vice versa (more experienced staff can hand down knowledge about the organisation, its people and working processes).

4. Open up. Social convergence means the boundaries between public and private identities are becoming blurred. We need to be aware of the type of space we are in: whether we are talking among friends on ***Facebook***, or publishing something to the world on ***YouTube***. Consumers expect genuine social responsibility to be embedded throughout corporate processes, rather than just at the level of public relations (re)positioning. Companies still tend to adopt a broadcast approach when speaking to customers, rather than show nuanced sensitivity. The transparency of ***social media*** is such that you need to tell your story consistently or not at all: honesty is the best policy. ***Bloggers*** like Scott Monty at Ford and Richard Sambrook at the BBC are experimenting with openness: Monty is enabling Ford to become more transparent; Sambrook has changed expectations in the relationship between a senior executive and his staff.

- **Start your own *blog*.** If you're the CEO, fantastic (if not, **get your CEO to start *blogging,*** too). There are plenty of free ***blogging*** tools out there: try ***Blogger***, Typepad or ***Wordpress***. Your ***blog*** doesn't have to be a corporate one, it could be about anything of interest to you: a hobby, obsession or personal crusade. Be aware of any ramifications your comments may have. See Fake Steve Jobs[3] for a great example of how a CEO *shouldn't **blog***.
- **Don't forget face-to-face contact.** This feeds into and reinforces the online network.
- Think about ways to **make your company's governance more transparent**. Most businesses are, by nature, closed, but you can work on having a semi permeable membrane: make yourself more accessible, open up where you can. If ***blogging*** isn't your style, ensure that you have other conversational channels in place:

regular 'open' sessions with a management Q&A, for example. Videostreaming (using Qik or Vimeo) and liveblogging are going to become bigger as the web moves into *realtime*.

- Instead of trying to prevent information flowing out of your company, try to anticipate what sensitive information may get out, and **learn to respond effectively and proportionately**. Sign up to a good *blog* offering advice on managing your brand & reputation online. Scott Monty's personal *blog* is good, or the internal communications experts, Melcrum; Garlik's *blog* is great for personal identity management.[4]

- **Become a content producer:** create photos, video, and *blog* posts around events, products and issues that are central to your business; invite others to create their own material. Let people know the content is there; encourage them to comment and get involved. It's easy to upload videos to Vimeo, *YouTube* or blip.tv, then embed them into your *blog* or website.

5. Learn to listen. Your business operates within an ecosystem where everything is interrelated. Diversity within your organisation is important because it helps you deal with complexity in the outside world. Solutions to intransigent problems can often be found on the edges (or in the '*long tail*') – because edges are the emergent beginning of something else. Rather than worry about reaching an 'elegant' solution, aspire to 'clumsy' ones where three or more alternative views are considered. Listening to your employees is as important as listening to your customers – so the co-creative processes discussed in Chapter 1 are good to apply here. Barack Obama's presidential campaign and Craig Newmark's stewardship of *craigslist* are textbook cases in listening.

- **Give your business community a focal point** by setting up a fan page on *Facebook*, a company page on *LinkedIn* and/or starting one or more *Twitter* accounts. Remember that, as with internal communities, you'll need someone dedicated to building and moderating these groups. Look at the way in which companies like Zappos (@zappos) and Netflix (@netflix) in the US or Moo in the UK (@overheardatmoo) engage and interact with their customers. But remember the lessons from Cillit Bang, Habitat and Nestlé.

- **Listen to what's being said in** *the Long Tail*: set up Google Alerts to track key words (such as your company name or product name) – Google will email you every time it finds a new mention. Then show you're taking feedback on board by posting a comment on any *blog* that mentions you, or by directly contacting – and apologising to – any customer who's been upset.

- Tracking relationships on *social networks* is a great way to learn about your informal patterns of influence. **Map your networks** with a free *social media* mapping tool like NetDraw. *Twitter* has a range of free analytics tools for analysing relationships, such as Twitt(url)y or TweetStats. Use Mybloglog or Google Analytics to tell you which of your referring sites brings the most traffic.
- **Nurture your wider business ecosystem**: comment on other people's *blogs*; start conversations on other networks as well as your own; build your public profile.
- **Establish an environment where it's safe to express dissent**. Remember the Blue Shirt Nation example from Chapter 4? Corporate *blogs*, *wikis* and online communities can be good places for people to air their grievances without fearing repercussions.

6. Be generous. Collaborative innovation techniques like *crowdsourcing* and *peer production* depend on the sharing of ideas and (often) commercially sensitive information with business partners and competitors. But the internet and World Wide Web were built on *open source* and free software, and *creative commons* – where better to go for inspiration? Procter & Gamble's Connect & Develop, Arup's Seeds of Change and RedMonk's white papers are three examples of how business can successfully incorporate *crowdsourcing* and *open source*. The closed beta-release for *Call of Duty 4* is an example of brand-consumer co-creation. New ways of working require new ways of thinking: cultivate an open mind.

- **Sign up to *open source* and free software**: If you're part of a large organisation, it might be best to use a content management system like *Drupal* or *Moodle* and get your IT team to turn that into a collaborative space. *Huddle* and Basecamp offer free project management tools which work well for smaller companies (but you'll find the free version limiting if, for example, you want more than a certain number of people to access a project). Many of the smaller companies I spoke to run all their internal communications on free tools (Mint Digital, for example, uses simply *Skype*, Google Docs and FogBugz).
- Having said that, **beware of beta:** remember that *social tools* are not the be all and end all when it comes to collaboration – especially when the technology's still in development. At Triarchy, we started out using Google Docs to edit this book, but lost chunks of material. We reverted to good old Microsoft Word (shared via *Huddle*). Use whatever works for you, but be wary of un-tested technologies for critical or unwieldy projects.

- Liven up your next presentation or workshop: **use some beautiful, free images from *Flickr***: the photo sharing website has more than a billion photos available under ***creative commons*** licensing (check the exact terms of each license). Then upload your presentation to SlideShare and ***tag*** it in order to share your ideas with the world (and get feedback).
- **Ask yourself what gift(s) you can give to your community**: A restaurant can offer recipes, a band exclusive music tracks, a game distributor the option to help develop the next version (like *Call of Duty 4*), or a chance to visit the design studio, an author can offer a chapter of their book for free (now, there's a thought...). Every business should have some ***IP*** that can be opened up without harming its core competences.
- **Download the *creative commons* versions of Social by Social**: read the 'how to' sections – step by step guides on everything from setting up an ***RSS reader*** to dealing with bad press. **Look for other books available under a *creative commons* license** (for example, Charles Leadbeater's *We Think* and James Boyle's *The Public Domain*).

Wise monkeys

Social media is not about technology. It's about people, relationships and conversations. The web is the enabler. If you can engage with and value this network, and incorporate its collaborative properties into your workplace, then you're one step closer to business zen: an intuitive, harmonious and *enlightened* working environment.

Change is an iterative process. The important thing is to keep trying. If enough people believe in the change, it will happen, and ***social media*** is all about leading by example. I'm working with the RSA, which is trying to become a more dynamic, modular and networked organisation. As a relatively new member I shouldn't have stood much chance standing for election to the new Fellows' Council, but it's a testament to the power of ***social media*** that I got there. Nominees could canvas on ***Twitter***, Facebook and ***LinkedIn***, post their profiles to the RSA's Ning networks, and contribute to online discussions. Now I'm fascinated to see how things progress. I'll be live-blogging meetings, and keeping an open diary of the experience on the *Monkeys With Typewriters* website.

In 1941, Jorge Luis Borges imagined a 'Total Library' of 'dizzying shelves – shelves that obliterate the day and on which chaos lies' which would be created at the end of time if one immortal monkey succeeded in reproducing all human literature. Since then, there have been many experiments testing out the infinite monkey theorem. In 2003, a group of students from the University of Plymouth ran a project involving six Celebes Crested Macaques: the monkeys were given a computer keyboard to play with. Over the course of a month, the primates produced just five pages, mainly containing the letter 'S'. Luckily, we have the ability to do far better than our distant cousins: with two billion of us across the world[5] hitting our keyboards, the web is, undoubtedly, one of the greatest experiments yet.

Notes

1. Danish entrepreneur Natasha Saxberg has written a book on using **Twitter**: the book's in Danish but here are her top tips for corporate **Twitterers**: (1) People relate to people not organisations so make your profile as natural as possible (2) Be confident. Remember the format for **Twitter** is simple: everyone has something to contribute (3) Be completely aware of your reasons for using **Twitter**: is it to listen or to learn? (4) Find role models. Search key words in order to find people who share your interests – and follow them. Ask yourself what it is about their updates that makes them interesting (5) Choose a handful of subjects you really care about and focus on them – that way you'll sound more passionate and others will connect with you more.
2. Gary Koelling and Steve Bendt tell how they built BlueshirtNation from scratch: www.garykoelling.com/?q=node/370
3. www.fakesteve.net/
4. See www.scottmonty.com; www.melcrum.com; www.garlik.com/blog
5. According to Forrester Research, the global internet population will reach 2.2 billion people by 2013 (Zia Daniell Wigder, *Global Online Population Forecast, 2008 to 2013*, Forrrester Research, 21 July 2009).

Glossary

AdSense
See **Google AdSense**

AdWords
See **Google AdWords**

Aggregator
A website that compiles or lists content from a number of other websites; examples include **Digg** (a news aggregator) and **Technorati** (a **blog** aggregator).

Apache
Short for the Apache **HTTP** server – an **open source**, web server (i.e. a computer program that 'serves' or publishes web pages to the web).

API
Application Programming Interface – an interlinking technology (or piece of code) that enables different websites to interact with each other. Open APIs enable collaboration without either website publisher having to reveal their source code.

ARPANET
The Advanced Research Projects Agency Network; created by the United States Department of Defense in 1969 – the world's first computer network and precursor to the internet.

Attention economy, the
An idealised marketplace which revolves around the principle that attention is a scarce resource: consumers are happier because they are shown information which is relevant to them; sellers are happier because their ads are targeted.

AudioBoo
A free audio **blogging** service and **social network**: AudioBoo enables you to record short bursts of audio on an iPhone (up to five minutes) and upload them to the web.

BarCamp

A loosely-structured conference where delegates set their own agenda, usually taking place over a weekend (hence 'Camp'); the first syllable, 'Bar' comes from the geek term, foobar, used in computing to denote an unknown value.

Bebo

An online **social network** aimed at teens and young adults, launched by Michael and Xochi Birch in 2005. 24 million unique visitors per month.[1]

Bing

See **Microsoft Bing**.

BitTorrent

A free, **open source** file-sharing application for distributing large software and media files; the BitTorrent protocol was developed by Bram Cohen in 2001 and enables even small computers to download large files by harnessing the processing power of other computers in the BitTorrent network.

Blog

An online journal or opinion column; the word 'blog' is short for 'web log'.

Blogger

Someone who regularly publishes stories to one or more **blogs**.

Blogosphere

The entire online community of **bloggers**.

Boing Boing

Originally an underground cyberpunk magazine, Boing Boing became a website in 1995 and relaunched as a **blog** in 2000; it is one of the web's oldest and most respected **blogs**, covering technology, science, entertainment and culture.

Bookmark/ing

A way of storing the **url** for a web page or article you like or find interesting, in order that you can return to it at a later date; most web browsers have a **bookmarking** or 'favourites' function, or you can store your bookmarks online using a tool such as **Delicious**.

Butterfly effect, the

A metaphor used by scientist Edward Lorenz (1917-2008) to illustrate the sensitivity of a dynamical system – such as the weather – to slightly varying initial conditions. Lorenz used the image of a butterfly flapping its wings in Brazil having the potential to influence the course of a tornado in a far distant place.

CERN

The European Organisation for Nuclear Research, formerly known as The European Council for Nuclear Research (Conseil Européen pour la Recherche Nucléaire), based in Geneva, Switzerland; Tim Berners-Lee and Robert Cailliau developed the World Wide Web at CERN in 1991, as a way to enable researchers to share information.

Cloud

A metaphor for the internet, most often used in the term *Cloud computing*.

Cloud computing

Using services provided over the internet (in the *Cloud*) to provide software and/or store information, rather than keeping everything on your personal computer: for example, writing documents on Googledocs instead of Microsoft Word, or *bookmarking* through *Delicious* rather than Internet Explorer.

Collaborative remixability

A quality attributed to the web by journalist Barb Dybwad, describing the loosely-structured way in which the web is assembled: a structure which enables constant and continuous re-organisation.

Complexity theory

Complexity Theory originated in Chaos Theory in the early 20th century. The majority of development has taken place in the last 30 years, with the dawn of computers, and the founding of the Santa Fe Institute in 1984, which remains at the forefront of complexity research. Complexity theory tries to identify simple behavourial patterns in highly complex systems.

Cookie

A tiny bit of text stored on your computer by your web browser, so that, for example, the next time you visit a website it appears to 'remember' your password, or what you had in your shopping trolley.

CouchSurfing

A volunteer-run *social network* where travellers can find free accommodation on other travellers's sofas (or spare bed).

craigslist

A free classified advertising site, run mainly by volunteers, launched in San Francisco in 1995 and now with local versions in more than 500 cities around the world; the sole source of revenue is paid job ads for a handful of US cities and paid ads for agency-rented apartments in New York; always spelt with a small 'c' at the behest of founder, Craig Newmark.

Creative Commons

A form of licensing which enables content creators to specify exactly how they want their work to be treated: others can copy, use and distribute individual pieces of work as long as the creators' wishes are respected – some may forbid commercial use of their work, for example. A full list of the Creative Commons licenses currently available can be found at `creativecommons.org/about/licenses`

Crowdsourcing

An open call for ideas and input, often on vast, ambitious projects, usually over the internet.

Cultural Theory

An empirical scheme that identifies four distinct organisational modes or *solidarities*, and links these to universal myths of nature that support and are supported by them; originated in the work of anthropologist Mary Douglas (1921-2007) in the 1950s and '60s. Otherwise known as Grid-Group Cultural Theory.

Customer Relationship Management

An umbrella term for the ways in which companies communicate with customers, and the tools that are used to facilitate these relationships; known as CRM for short.

Customisation

The ability to make or alter something to individual tastes and/or specifications.

Delicious

A free online *bookmarking* application, enabling users to store, share and search for *bookmarks*.

Developer Platform Evangelist

A marketing role within large technology companies – the central aim of the DPE is to encourage developers to use that company's technology platform.

Digg

A free news aggregation website; news stories are posted and then voted up or down by members of the Digg community.

Digital footprint

The record of everything you have ever done that has been captured digitally; can include anything from email messages to online purchases to CCTV camera footage.

Digital Shadow

The 'passive' side of your *digital footprint* – data that you didn't activate or create yourself; *cookies* and CCTV footage are good examples.

DIY

Web content which you can mix and match to suit your purposes: for example, *social networks* increasingly offer users the option to *customise* profile pages, while syndication tools like *RSS*, widgets and badges mean you can publish chunks of other people's content on your own website; DIY is synonymous with *Web 2.0* and the 'Read/Write Web'.

Dopplr

A *social network* for sharing travel plans privately with people you trust; popular with frequent business travellers.

Drupal

A free, *open source*, content management system which allows users to publish, manage and organise various types of content on a dedicated website.

E-learning

Electronic learning, most frequently used for web-based and distance learning.

Eventful

A free events *aggregator* and *social network*; you can join the community of users to discover, promote and/or create events in your area.

Experience economy

An economy in which businesses create memorable events for consumers, and the memory of that event – or the 'experience' becomes the product; a term first described by B. Joseph Pine II and James H. Gilmore in their 1999 book, *The Experience Economy*.

Facebook

The world's number one *social network* and the most popular way to be kept updated with news and photos from friends and family; started in 2004 by Harvard undergrad Mark Zuckerberg as an online year book for Ivy League Universities; opened to general public in 2006; reached 300 million users in September 2009.[2]

Feed

See *Web Feed*.

Flickr

An online *social network* for storing and sharing photos; uses a *freemium* business model.

Folksonomy

A bottom-up system of classification using *tags* (and an organisational structure) generated and rated by members of a community.

Fordism

A term encompassing the range of production and marketing techniques developed by Henry Ford, founder of the Ford Motor Company, at his Detroit factory in the early 1900s: Ford wanted a car that was affordable to the masses so he designed the Model T, a car that was relatively lightweight, compact and easy to manufacture. Ford developed ways of streamlining production and reducing costs, such as strict division of labour and the standardisation of functions; Fordism enabled the transition from craft production to mass production in the United States.

Freemium

A business model where users pay nothing for a basic service but are charged for additional features and/or usability.

Friendster

An early online *social network*, founded by Jonathan Abrams in 2002; Friendster is still popular in Asia and has around 90 million registered users worldwide.[3]

Generation Y
See *Millennial Generation*.

GNU project
GNU stands for 'GNU's Not *Unix*!' and was intended to be the first free, *open source*, computer operating system; development started when Richard Stallman launched the GNU Project in 1984; although nearly all GNU's components were completed in the 1990s, GNU's kernel isn't finished, so the GNU system tools require an operating system kernel such as *Linux*.

Google AdSense
A free tool which enables you to publish relevant Google ads on your website; you get paid a small fee whenever visitors click on the ads (or simply view them, in some cases); the ads are targeted and generated by an algorithm that interprets what content might be of interest to your readers.

Google AdWords
An advertising service: when a user enters a key word to search using Google's search engine, text-based ads for relevant products and services appear as 'sponsored links' on the right side of the screen or above the main search results. The order of these ads depends on how much each advertiser has paid (or 'bid') for the key word(s).

Google for Good
A new, volunteer-run project that uses Google's search and advertising engine to research solutions to big global problems such as global warming, decreasing biodiversity and famine.

Google Groups
A free, *wiki*-like service where you can set up and manage discussion groups on any topic or around any community of interest.

Google Reader
A free *RSS reader*.

Google Suggest
A service automatically offered every time you start to type a search term into Google's search box: Google Suggest offers ways to complete your search term; one factor determining results is the *realtime* popularity of searches by other users – so

if you type in 'London fire' for example, around November 5th, you might get a list that contains 'London fireworks' and 'London firework displays'.

Google Wave

A *realtime* communication tool launched as a preview by Google in September 2009; the tool combines email-, instant messaging- and *wiki*-like functions and enables collaboration and file-sharing; Google plans to release most of the source code as *open source* and allows third-parties to build their own Wave services quickly because it wants Wave to replace email as the dominant form of internet communication.

Groupware

Groupware is another name for collaborative software. The name originated in the 1980s when the software was developed as an aid to what was then known as computer supported co-operative work (CSCW). *Lotus Notes* is an example.

Hashtag

A community-generated word or phrase prefixed by the hash symbol (#); similar to *tags* on photos or *bookmarks*, but added 'inline' – that is, within your text message or status update (on *Twitter*, for example); you can make up your own hashtag, use someone else's, or go to hashtags.org/tags for a full list – a great way to add context and metadata to your conversations.

Horsesmouth

An online coaching and mentoring network; social enterprise launched by advertising guru M.T.Rainey in January 2008.

HTML

HyperText Markup Language – a web standard for creating web pages; text or copy is annotated using HTML *tags*, these enable web browsers to 'read' web pages properly.

HTTP

HyperText Transfer Protocol – a standard method for transferring hypertext documents (or web pages) across the internet.

Huddle

A secure network of online workspaces that offers project management and other collaboration tools; an easy way to work on projects collaboratively with remote partners. Only the most basic level is free.

Information Asymmetry

A term used in economics to refer to a transaction where one party has more information than the other; usually describing situations in which a seller has more information than a buyer (that the MOT on a used car is out of date, for example).

Intranet

A computer network within an organisation that uses Internet Protocol technologies to share information and/or operational systems.

IP

Internet Protocol – the core communications protocol that supports nearly every internet message.

Jaiku

A *social network/microblogging* service where users post status updates from the web, mobile phone or desktop clients; similar to *Twitter* but with more functionality; founded in 2006 by Jyri Engeström and Petteri Koponen; acquired by Google in 2007.

KateModern

An interactive drama series about a London-based video *blogger*; KateModern ran on the *social network*, *Bebo*, between July 2007 and June 2008.

Last.fm

A free music streaming service which recommends tracks you might like to listen to, based on the choices of other users with similar tastes.

LinkedIn

A *social network* aimed at the business community; users create online resumes, set up discussions and groups, and link to colleagues, employees and other work-related contacts; 50 million users worldwide.[4]

Linux

A free *open source* operating system (OS) built by a large community of developers and initiated by computing student Linus Torvalds in 1991; Torvalds was a great fan of the *GNU Project* but had grown impatient waiting for the GNU kernel to be built, so decided to start building his own OS kernel.

Long Tail, the

In a free market: consumers tend to favour 20 per cent of products over the other 80 per cent; in his 2004 book, Wired editor Chris Anderson identified economic value in this 'long tail', arguing that while businesses had traditionally focused on the top 20 per cent, they could just as easily profit from selling a larger number of niche items (the bottom 80 per cent): the internet enables such niche marketing; companies like Amazon have built their business models on the 'long tail' concept.

Lotus Connections

A proprietary suite of social software tools, owned by IBM; the suite includes community management, *blogging*, *bookmarking* and *wikis*.

Lotus Notes

A desktop client for accessing e-mail, calendars and other applications (including *blogs*, *wikis* and *RSS readers*); an early example of collaborative software, the first version was launched in 1989; IBM acquired Lotus in 1995.

Mashup

A hybrid website or application that combines data or functionality from two or more sources; for example, MapMyEvent uses data from *Upcoming*, *Eventful*, *Zvents* and *Yelp* to populate a Google Map of your local area.

Maslovian

Based on, or inspired by, the thinking behind Abraham Maslow's hierarchy of needs (1943) – the belief that people are motivated by values and ideals rather than simply money.

MetaFilter

A *blogger* community website.

Metanoia

Used by management consultant Peter Senge to signify the elevated level of innovation and creativity that is possible in highly charged, well-functioning business environments; the word means, literally, higher-mindedness, or shift of mind.

Microblogging

A form of *blogging* which consists solely of short text updates or micromedia such as photos or video/audio clips; *Twitter*, *Jaiku* and *AudioBoo* are all microblogging services.

Microsoft Bing

An intuitive, *realtime* search engine, which Microsoft likes to call a 'decision engine'; originally Windows Live Search; relaunched as 'Bing' in June 2009.

Microsoft SharePoint

is a system for collaborative working on documents.

Millennial Generation

The demographic cohort following Generation X, also known as Millennials, *Generation Y* or the Net Generation; in their book, 'Millennials Rising', authors William Strauss and Neil Howe argued that the high school graduates who reached 18 in the year 2000 felt a distinct break with the past; Strauss and Howe identified the start year of this generation as 1982 and end year as 2001; Millennials are typified by liberal ideals, civic-mindedness and a high level of digital literacy.

Modularity

Designed with standardised units, dimensions and/or interfaces, components should be able to connect and interact with each other in a number of different ways.

Moodle

A free, *open source*, *e-learning* management system; used by the Open University, among others.

MySpace

A *social network* popular for sharing music, video clips and other items, appealing to a younger demographic than *Facebook* (core audience is 17-19 years old); launched in 2003 and acquired by Rupert Murdoch's News Corporation in 2005; MySpace was once the world's largest *social network* but overtaken by *Facebook* in May 2009; around 100 million users worldwide as of October 2009.

Netvibes

A free *RSS reader* with various additional features including webmail, calendar, to do lists and *bookmarking*.

Network effects

A concept popularised by Robert Metcalfe, founder of Ethernet, in the 1980s; 'Metcalfe's law' is a heuristic which states that the more people use a network, the more valuable it becomes. Its value scales with the number of point-to-point connections rather than with the number of network nodes (so the value is proportional to the square of the number of nodes).

Ning
A free online service/platform where people can create their own *social networks*, launched in October 2005 by Marc Andreessen and Gina Bianchini.

Open innovation
A form of collaborative innovation, defined by Berkeley academic Henry Chesbrough as 'a paradigm that assumes that firms can and should use external ideas as well as internal ideas, and internal and external paths to market, as the firms look to advance their technology'.[5]

Open source
Source code that is freely open and accessible to all; generally refers to software but can also be used to describe a business approach.

Orkut
A free online *social network* owned by Google; launched in 2004 and popular in Brazil and India.

Outliers
In statistics, an outlier is a piece of data which is numerically distant from the rest of the data; in his 2008 book, journalist Malcolm Gladwell defined 'Outliers' as 'people who don't fit into our normal understanding of achievement...exceptional people'.[6]

Peer production
A form of mass collaboration where a pre-defined project is managed/shared between two or more business partners.

Peer-to-peer
Usually abbreviated to 'P2P'; specifically, a computer network architecture where each participant contributes processing power, storage space and/or bandwidth – thereby enabling the network to function without the need for central co-ordination (e.g. from a server); in more general terms, peer-to-peer can apply to any decentralised, grassroots network where each node is considered to have equal status.

Perpetual beta

A business strategy, used primarily for software, whereby the product stays 'in development' (that is, at the beta – 'pre-release' stage) for a long period or even indefinitely: this means that user feedback is constantly being incorporated into the production process.

Pirate Bay, the

A *social network* which tracks and indexes *BitTorrent* files, enabling users to download movies and music free of charge; The Pirate Bay, founded in 2003 by a Swedish anti-copyright organisation, is 'one of the world's largest facilitators of illegal downloading' according to the Los Angeles Times; in April 2009, the site's three founders were found guilty of assistance to copyright infringement, sentenced to one year in prison and fined £2.4 million; The Pirate Bay is widely supported by internet users around the world.[7]

Podcast

A portmanteau of 'Pod' (from the Apple iPod) and 'broadcast', a podcast differs from a straightforward media download because it is episodic; a comprehensive definition comes from researchers at the University of Texas at Austin: 'a digital audio or video file that is episodic; downloadable, program-driven, mainly with a host and/or theme; and convenient, usually via an automated *feed*'; you need a specialist software application (or podcatcher) to detect and download podcasts: e.g. iTunes.

Poke

A feature on *Facebook*; a way for users to 'nudge' their friends in order to attract attention.

Pop!Tech

An annual invite-only conference held in Camden, Maine, USA; Pop!Tech's mission is to 'accelerate the positive impact of world changing people, projects and ideas'; the conference aims to create ground-breaking, inter-disciplinary collaborations that solve world problems.[8]

Presencing

A portmanteau of 'presence' and 'sensing' – a term created by MIT academic Otto Scharmer to refer to 'the ability to sense and bring into the present one's highest future potential – as an individual and as a group'.[9]

Realtime

The attribute of responding to events as they occur: A search on **Twitter**, for example, will happen in 'realtime', giving you an up-to-the-minute snapshot; a Google search, in contrast, will not necessarily give you a realtime result.

Reverse mentoring

A process where older employees are teamed with younger colleagues in order to learn more about using digital communications tools; a practice popular with Stewart Mader (Future Changes) and Luis Suarez (IBM).

Rhetorically replayable present

A powerful narrative or story which will continue to resonate and spread long after it has occurred; a term used by Oxford scholar Keith Grint when he noted how the various accounts (journalistic, verbal etc.) of Florence Nightingale's nursing during the Crimean War (1853-56) had 'locked the past into a rhetorically replayable present'.[10]

Rich connection

A personal or business relationship (online and/or offline) which is strong and robust due to a number of mutual interests and points of understanding.

RSS

A format for publishing **web feeds** so that they can be automatically syndicated (easily distributed to a number of outlets); RSS stands for 'Really Simple Syndication'.

RSS reader

An automated tool which checks **RSS feeds** and updates you with any new material; popular **RSS** readers include **Netvibes** and **Google Reader**.

Rufus

A network analysis tool being developed at global PR company, Porter Novelli.

SaaS

'Software as a Service': a way of licensing software as an on-demand service, accessed via the internet, rather than a one-off desktop product.

SAT

A standardised test for college admissions in the United States (not to be confused with the standard assessment tests used for primary school children in the UK).

Scaleable vector graphics

A family of specifications for describing 2D *vector graphics*, usually interactive and/or animated.

Semantic Web

A World Wide Web in which the meaning of information and data is explicitly defined; making it possible for websites to fulfil users' needs more intuitively; the web is already evolving in this direction.

SharePoint

See *Microsoft SharePoint*.

Skype

A free tool for instant messaging and making telephone calls and using VoIP (voice over *IP*) technology. *IP* (Internet Protocol) is the core protocol underlying nearly all of the internet.

Social graph

A term used by *Facebook* founder Mark Zuckerberg in 2007 to describe *Facebook*'s primary function – to be a global graph of connections and relationships between people.

Social innovation

New strategies, concepts and business models which aim to address or solve social problems.

Social capital

The willingness of people within any given community to co-operate with other members of the community and do things that will benefit the others without expecting anything in return.

Social innovator

See '*social innovation*'.

Social media

Any content (articles, *blog* posts, video, photos etc) that is produced and distributed by individuals free of charge and for primarily social purposes as opposed to content created by professionals such as journalists or film makers primarily for economic purposes.

Social network/ing

A community of people who are inter-connected through relationships and/or shared interests; in this book the term usually refers to an online social network.

Social tools/technologies

Applications and services which enable participative, **peer-to-peer**, communication.

SocialText

A commercial collaboration platform offering **social networking**, **blogging** and **wiki**-building tools.

Software as a service

See '**SaaS**'.

Solidarities

The four voices or cultural 'modes' described in **Cultural Theory**: these prescribe that any argument or viewpoint will inevitably fall into one of four categories – individualistic, hierarchical, fatalistic or egalitarian (there is also a fifth mode, that of the hermit, which remains withdrawn and unengaged).

SoundCloud

A free **social network** for artists and record labels, built around an agile platform for receiving, sending and distributing music.

Sousveillance

A term coined by computing academic, Steve Mann, in the 1980s, meaning, literally, 'watching from below'; more recently, the futurist Jamais Cascio used sousveillance in his concept of a 'participatory panopticon' where ordinary citizens are empowered through digital technologies (e.g. cameras and mobile phones) to record and broadcast the activities of police, politicians and others in authority.

SpinVox

A service which converts voicemail messages to text.

Spotify

A **peer-to-peer** music streaming service, funded by paid subscriptions and advertising.

SurveyMonkey

A free service that enables users to create and run their own online surveys and analyse the results.

Switching costs

The costs incurred when a customer changes from one service or product to another; for example, a change in mobile telephony provider might incur a penalty for breaking a contract and/or an outlay of time and effort in ensuring friends and colleagues have your new number.

Syndicated feed

See **Web Feed**.

Tag cloud

A visual representation of key topics, often used to describe the content of a particular website; the *tags* used by contributors (on *blog* posts, for example) are listed alphabetically in a 'cloud' shaped list, with the most popular ones shown in larger font sizes and/or different colours.

Tag/ging

A keyword or term assigned to a piece of information (for example, a **bookmark**, photo or document), either by the item's creator(s) or by other users/viewers; tags are metadata which helps to describe items and make them more searchable.

Taxonomy

A formal system of classification and naming; Clay Shirky argued that taxonomies could be biased and rigid, while user **tagging** (**folksonomies**) have the potential to be more democratic and self-regulating.

Taylorism

Frederick Winslow Taylor (1856–1915) was an American mechanical engineer who saw the industrial management of his day as amateurish and devoted his life to improving industrial efficiency; in his 1911 book, *The Principles of Scientific Management*, Taylor identified four principles which came to describe what was later known as 'Taylorism':

1. Replace heuristic work methods with methods based on a scientific study of the tasks involved.
2. Select, train and develop each employee 'scientifically' rather than leave them to train themselves.

3. Provide detailed instruction and supervision of each worker in the performance of discrete tasks.
4. Divide work equally between managers and workers: managers apply scientific management principles & planning while workers actually perform the tasks.'[11]

Technorati

A *realtime* search engine to find *blogs* on specific topics, using *tags* or keywords; also a content *aggregator* with popularity indexes rating *blogs*.

TED

An annual closed-invite conference held in Palm Springs, California; TED stands for 'technology, entertainment, design' but the focus of the conference (launched in 1984) is now much broader: high class speakers give short lectures on virtually any subject; although TED conferences are invite-only, TED talks can be viewed by anyone on the TED website, free of charge.[12]

Telnet

One of the earliest Internet Protocols, developed in 1969: Telnet is unencrypted and, while sufficient for connecting remote computers in the days when the internet was solely the province of researchers and academics, has been largely replaced by more secure technologies.

Theory U

A practical theory for personal and organisational development created by MIT academic Otto Scharmer: 'a set of principles and practices for collectively creating the future that wants to emerge.'[13]

Trillian

A proprietary instant messaging application for Windows which can connect to multiple IM services (such as AIM, ICQ, Yahoo! Messenger and *Skype*).

Troll

A geek term for someone who posts inflammatory or off-topic messages in a community simply because they want to provoke an emotional response; according to *Wikipedia*, the original phrase was 'trolling for suckers' and derives from a fishing technique known as trolling – where bait is slowly dragged through water.[14]

Tweet

A *microblog* post (of up to 140 characters) on *Twitter*; Tweets consist of text and can be sent via the web, a text message or desktop/mobile phone client such as *Tweetdeck* or Tweetie; a Tweet can be a straightforward status update, or a reply to someone else, in which case the '@' sign is inserted immediately before that person's name or '*Twitter* handle' in order to attract their attention and create a link to their profile for the benefit of other users); more generally, Tweets can contain *hashtags* in order to link them to wider conversations already taking place; Tweets can be put together manually or generated automatically by applications such as Twitterfeed (which can be formatted to send out a new tweet every time you create a new *bookmark* or *blog* post, for example).

Tweetdeck

A desktop or mobile phone based application for reading, writing and managing *Tweets*.

Twitter

A *social network* and *microblogging* site; a reference tool for finding out what people are talking about in *realtime* and a great way to start conversations with people who share your interests but aren't necessarily a part of your existing network; 44.5 million unique visitors worldwide in June 2009.[15]

Ubuntu

A free, *open source*, *Linux*-based operating system that contains various applications including a web browser, instant messaging and presentation, document and spreadsheet software.

Unconference

A geek term for a gathering with no designated speakers or detailed agenda; the idea being that true collaboration is enabled by avoiding high admission fees and sales-orientated presentations.

Unix

A computer operating system developed at AT&T in 1969; the system was originally *open source* and free to universities, business organisations and the US government; in 1982, AT&T began releasing Unix commercially. As a result, subsequent versions of the program were proprietary. *Linux* is a complete rewrite of Unix which was, and remains, completely *open source*.

Upcoming

A free events *aggregator* and *social network*, launched in 2003.

URL

A web page 'address' that, when, typed into a browser or search engine, will be able to identify the exact location of that web page; stands for 'Uniform Resource Locator'.

Us Now

An hour long documentary film directed by Ivo Gormley for Banyak Films (2009) which poses the question 'In a world in which information is like air, what happens to power?'[16]

Vector graphics

A type of computer graphics based on geometric shapes; these shapes are constructed using mathematical equations so the graphic images don't lose any clarity when enlarged.

Web 2.0

A term popularised by Tim O'Reilly of O'Reilly Media in 2005; the term aimed to describe a new generation of websites which placed social activity, participation and collaboration at their core.

Web feed

A streamed list of web content, e.g. *blog* posts or status updates, frequently updated; also known as a *syndicated feed*.

Widget

A portable chunk of code which can be inserted into any *HTML* document (web page) and will automatically generate live content (e.g. advertising or news updates) from a third party website.

Wikipedia

A free online encyclopedia, built collaboratively by volunteers using *wiki* software; anyone can edit and contribute to Wikipedia, and the pages are monitored and moderated by the community.

Wiki

A collaborative website with an open interface which means it can be easily edited and updated by any user. 'Wiki' means 'fast' in Hawaiian.

Wordpress

A free and easy to use *blog* publishing tool.

WYSIWYG

Stands for 'What you see is what you get' – a system in which the content displayed during creation/editing is very similar to the final published version.

Xing

A free *social network* for business professionals.

Yahoo! Groups

A free, *wiki*-like service on which you can set up and manage your own discussion groups – similar to *Google Groups*.

Yelp

A free *social network* containing user reviews and local search for shops, restaurants, businesses and other amenities in various North American cities.

YouDevise

A private company offering financial software solutions to investment banks, financial brokers and hedge fund and asset managers.

YouTube

A free *social network* and video-sharing website founded by Chad Hurley, Steve Chen and Jawed Karim in 2005; acquired by Google in 2006.

Zvents

A free local search and advertising network which uses event listings to promote local businesses.

Notes

1. 24.2 million unique visitors in May 2009, figures from Techcrunch.
2. '300 Million and On' by Mark Zuckerberg, 15 September 2009: blog.facebook.com/blog.php?post=136782277130
3. en.wikipedia.org/wiki/Friendster
4. 'LinkedIn reaches 50 million users worldwide' by Nathania Johnson, 14 October 2009: blog.searchenginewatch.com/091014-115402
5. H. W. Chesbrough (2003), *Open Innovation: The new imperative for creating and profiting from technology.* Harvard Business School Press, p.xxiv.
6. en.wikipedia.org/wiki/Outliers_(book)
7. en.wikipedia.org/wiki/The_Pirate_Bay
8. www.poptech.org/about
9. www.presencing.com/presencing-theoryu

10. See Chapter 2, 'Passion'.
11. en.wikipedia.org/wiki/Frederick_Winslow_Taylor
12. www.ted.com
13. www.presencing.com/presencing-theoryu
14. en.wikipedia.org/wiki/Troll_(Internet)
15. www.businessinsider.com/chart-of-the-day-twitters-boom-around-the-world-2009-8
16. www.usnowfilm.com

Acknowledgements

First off, I have to thank my long-time friend and collaborator Karen McCarthy, without whom none of this would have been possible. Karen introduced me to Triarchy Press founder, Gerard Fairtlough, and commissioned the book while she was working at Triarchy. If Karen hadn't seen value in this idea, *Monkeys with Typewriters* would not have seen daylight.

A mega thanks to Matthew Fairtlough, my editor, who has offered nothing but encouragement throughout, and has done a great job on filling in my knowledge gaps and pulling me up on any egregious flights of fancy. Thanks also to Andrew Carey, for lending his excellent editor's eye and offering up an exhaustive list of thoughtful comments. Special thanks are due, too, to my friend and *social media* whiz, Joanne Jacobs, whose comprehensive comments and guidance on the first draft were invaluable.

I am particularly grateful to those I interviewed for the book, who kindly gave up their time to talk about the impact of *social media* on leadership: Andy Bell, Stowe Boyd, James Boyle, Lee Bryant, Dominic Campbell, Suw Charman, Tom Coates, Lloyd Davis, Arie de Geus, Benjamin Ellis, Jason Fried, Matt Glotzbach, James Governor, Roland Harwood, John Horniblow, David Jennings, Pat Kane, Ramsey Khoury, Tariq Krim, Steve Lawson, Barry Libert, Adriana Lukas, Stewart Mader, Ross Mayfield, Matthew McGregor, Alistair Mitchell, Scott Monty, Johnnie Moore, Steve Moore, Ziv Navoth, Craig Newmark, Tim O'Reilly, Emma Pace, Christian Payne, Emma Persky, Gina Poole, George Por, Cameron Price, Nic Price, MT Rainey, JP Rangaswami, Arseniy Rastourguev, Kathryn Roberts, Karin Robinson, Mark Rock, Richard Sambrook, Natasha Saxberg, Otto Scharmer, Euan Semple, David Sims, Maria Sipka, Chris Thorpe, David Weinberger, David Wilcox, Duncan Wilson and my foreword writer, Luis Suarez – to all, a major thank you.

Thanks must go to Lobelia Lawson for her fantastic transcripts, and additional editorial suggestions beyond the call of duty. It's been a pleasure working with her and getting to know her, especially during this transformative time in both our lives.

Thanks, too, to Deborah Dignam for her tireless research and fastidious fact checking (not least of everything sourced from *Wikipedia*), and to the delightful Sian Prime for introducing us.

Finally, this book would be nothing without the tireless support and commitment of my partner, Noam, and (less conscious but probably more life-impacting) my three year old daughter Lila, who enabled me to work early in the morning, throughout the day and occasionally through the night to meet deadlines. The space they gave me and have made for me has been nothing short of phenomenal. A very big thanks to you both.

Jemima Gibbons is a management writer, consultant and lecturer. She lives in London with her partner and daughter.

She blogs at:

www.monkeyswithtypewriters.co.uk

About the Publisher

Triarchy Press is an independent publishing house that looks at how organisations work and how to make them work better. We present challenging perspectives on organisations in short and pithy, but rigorously argued, books.

Other titles in the areas of leadership and innovation include *The Innovation Acid Test* by Andrew Jones, *Inside Project Red Stripe* by Andrew Carey, *Ten Things To Do in a Conceptual Emergency* by Graham Leicester and Maureen O'Hara, and *The Search for Leadership* and the *Systemic Leadership Toolkit*, both by William Tate.

Through our books, pamphlets and website we aim to stimulate ideas by encouraging real debate about organisations in partnership with people who work in them, research them or just like to think about them.

Please tell us what you think about the ideas in this book at:

www.triarchypress.com/telluswhatyouthink

If you feel inspired to write – or have already written – an article, a pamphlet or a book on any aspect of organisational theory or practice, we'd like to hear from you. Submit a proposal at:

www.triarchypress.com/writeforus

For more information about Triarchy Press, or to order any of our publications, please visit our website or drop us a line:

www.triarchypress.com

We're now on Twitter:

@TriarchyPress

and Facebook:

www.facebook.com/home.php#/pages/Axminster-United-Kingdom/
Triarchy-Press/156843206813

Lightning Source UK Ltd.
Milton Keynes UK
03 December 2009

147101UK00001B/2/P

9 780956 263148